Logical Relevance in English Evidence Law: Its History and Impact on Keynes and Russell

Logical Relevance in English Evidence Law: Its History and Impact on Keynes and Russell

Jan Dejnožka

© Jan Dejnožka 2019

Publisher: Jan Dejnožka
Ann Arbor, Michigan
United States of America

Imprint: CreateSpace Independent Publishing Platform
Printed in the United States of America
Sold at Amazon.com and elsewhere

ISBN: 13: 978-1729844175
       10: 1729844170

Library of Congress Catalog Card Number:
LCCN: 2018914484

For Chung Hwa, Julie, and Marina

Praise for the Book

Jan Dejnožka's *Logical Relevance in English Evidence Law* innovatively explores the links between the evolution of the Anglo-American law of evidence and the philosophical investigations of Keynes and Russell. He provides a fascinating interdisciplinary examination between two disciplines not ordinarily studied together. Dejnoka's study should be of interest to scholars interested in evidence, regardless of discipline. —Barbara J. Shapiro

Barbara J. Shapiro is professor emerita of rhetoric at the University of California at Berkeley. Her books include *Beyond Reasonable Doubt and Probable Cause: Historical Perspectives on the Anglo-American Law of Evidence* (University of California Press) and *Probability and Certainty in Seventeenth-Century England: A Study of the Relationships Between Science, Religion, History, Law, and Literature* (Princeton University Press).

Dejnožka challenges the reader to open his mind for a new interpretation of Russell's work, in particular that relevance notions have a greater place in his philosophy of logic than has been stressed before. Dejnožka's work is full of material which stimulates one to rethink Russell's philosophy of logic, and it is greatly to the author's credit that he brings to light such a wealth of crucial issues in the history and philosophy of logic. —Shahid Rahman

Shahid Rahman is exceptional professor of logic and epistemology at the Université de Lille 3 (Charles de Gaulle). He was Director (for the French side) of the du ANR-DFG Franco-German project 2012–2015 (Lille (MESHS)/Konstanz, Prof M. Armgardt): Théorie du Droit et Logique / Jurisprudenz und Logik.

I have spent my career researching the role of relevance in logic, and I found this book highly "relevant." It points out the profound role that English evidence law had in influencing two of the founders of probability theory and logic, Keynes and Russell. It is well written and very interesting. —J. Michael Dunn

J. Michael Dunn is professor emeritus of computer science and informatics, Oscar Ewing professor emeritus of philosophy, and founding dean emeritus of the School of Informatics at Indiana University. He was a co-editor of *Entailment: The Logic of Relevance and Necessity*, volume 2 (Princeton University Press).

Table of Contents

Preface

This is the first book on the history of logical relevance in English evidence law and its impact on the probability theories of John Maynard Keynes and Bertrand Russell.

Like my other books, this book upends received thought. Following J. L. Montrose, whom he anthologizes, the legal scholar William Twining denies that some of the great evidence law writers had relevance rules. I quote and discuss their relevance rules. The Keynes scholar Robert Skidelsky holds that Keynes must have discovered the relation between probability and logical relevance himself. I quote and discuss that relation as affirmed throughout the last five centuries of English evidence law. Most of the relevantists were members of the Inner Temple law bar, and Keynes was too.

I argue that Keynes' theory that probability is degree of logical relevance is the most likely origin of Russell's very similar theory of probability from *The Problems of Philosophy* on. I then argue that Keynes' theory in turn most likely originates from the concept and terminology of logical relevance in English evidence law. Since the evidence is strong for both conclusions, I conclude further that it is very likely that Russell's theory of probability indirectly originates from evidence law through Keynes. But I have no evidence that Russell was aware of the legal origin of his theory.

I can offer here no thorough discussion of the probability theories of Keynes or Russell, much less of the history of relevance in English evidence law. I can only hope to have done enough to substantiate my interpretation of Russell's theory of probability as basically the same as and originating from Keynes' theory, and of Keynes' theory as originating in turn from English evidence law.

This book originally appeared as chapter 10 in the second edition of my *Bertrand Russell on Modality and Logical Relevance* (2015). Changes were minimal. I decided that making it a book in its own right could be a service to legal scholars. Legal scholars not interested in probability theory can simply read chapter 2.

I owe special thanks to Richard O. Lempert and Richard D. Friedman, who respectively taught evidence and advanced evidence to me at The University of Michigan School of Law in 1995–96. Professors Lempert and Friedman both kindly commented on my first paper on logical relevance, written for Friedman's seminar on advanced evidence (my 2004). I also studied relevance in their textbooks on evidence law (Lempert 1983; Friedman 1991).

Ann Arbor, Michigan
March 12, 2019

1

Probability as Logical Relevance

In his 1912 *The Problems of Philosophy*, Russell holds that the principle of induction, that the future will resemble the past, can be neither proved nor disproved, nor even rendered probable or improbable in the slightest, by experience. He infers that if it is to be accepted, then it must be on the basis of its "intrinsic evidence" (PP 68, 70, 76). Such evidence must be *a priori*, and therefore must be based on relations among timeless universals (PP 101–10, 149). Since the principle is not formally demonstrable, its self-evidence must be intuitive. And since the principle is not certain, its degree of self-evidence must be less than full certainty (PP 114–18).

This view is not only astonishing in itself, but it appears to imply something even more fantastic: that logical relevance has degrees—which are degrees of probability. That would collapse the distinction between deductive and inductive logic as different kinds of logic. There would only be a distinction of degree.

It would seem that ever since Aristotle invented formal logic over two thousand years ago, logicians have understood logical relevance as being a conclusion's *following from* premises with logical necessity. Thus it would seem that logical relevance has always belonged to deductive logic. The one thing logicians seem to agree on without exception is that logical relevance obtains only within deductive logic, and never for probabilistic arguments. For the premises of a probabilistic argument are not and logically cannot be logically relevant to its conclusion. For if they were, then the conclusion would follow from the premises with logical necessity, not merely with some degree of probability.

Thus the 1912 Russell appears not only confused as to the epistemology of induction, but even as to its logic. He is not only conflating the inductive with the *a priori*, but he is even conflating deductive logic with inductive logic. How is this possible?

Probability in *The Problems of Philosophy*

It may be well to describe the 1912 Russell's theory briefly at the outset. It will be useful to discuss both induction and the causal relation, since they are arguably closely related, and since

Russell treats them in the same way.

Russell states four closely related versions of the inductive principle (PP 66–67). We may ignore the differences for present purposes. He argues that since the inductive principle cannot be either proved or disproved by experience without begging the question by assuming the principle, "we must either accept the inductive principle on the ground of its intrinsic evidence, or forgo all justification of our expectations about the future" (PP 68). He says "the inductive principle itself cannot be proved by induction" (PP 84). He agrees with Hume that the connection of cause and effect is not *formally* deductive, but finds it a *non sequitur* to infer that there is nothing *a priori* about the connection (PP 83). He agrees with Kant that the connection of cause and effect is synthetic as opposed to analytic (PP 83–84). All our empirical generalizations are ultimately based on the inductive principle, since they are "derived from instances, and not an *a priori* connexion of universals" (PP 107). But he holds that the inductive principle itself is a *priori*. He speaks of "some wholly *a priori* principle, such as the principle of induction" (PP 149, Russell's emphasis). As such, it is wholly a matter of relations of universals. For "*All* a priori *knowledge deals exclusively with the relations of universals*" (PP 103, Russell's emphasis). But while it is purely and wholly *a priori* (PP 149), it is by no means as certain as our *a priori* knowledge in logic and mathematics. Russell says, "The inductive principle has less self-evidence than some of the other principles of logic" (PP 117). The term "some of the *other* principles of logic" is confusing, since surely he holds that, like the causal principle, the inductive principle does not belong to formal deductive logic at all. Russell never tells us just how self-evident the inductive principle is. And perhaps its degree of self-evidence is logically indeterminate. In fact, it would seem absurd to assign it a determinate degree of intrinsic probability. Could it be 93% probable? But since it would have the sort of self-evidence that belongs to judgments as opposed to acquaintance with a fact, its degree of self-evidence, determinate or not, might be anywhere on the scale "from the very highest degree down to a bare inclination in favour of the belief" (PP 138). I think that for Russell its likelihood of being true, as opposed to its degree of self-evidence, increases with time, since likelihood is largely a matter of coherence with all our probable views (PP 140), and we are discovering new uniformities all the time. In his review of John Maynard Keynes' *A Treatise on Probability*, Russell quotes Keynes as making this last point (Russell 1922: 157).

In *Problems*, Russell appears to treat causation in the same way he treats induction. He says that "the principle that sense-data are signs of physical objects is itself a connexion of universals" (PP

148–49), and that whenever we go beyond immediate experience, which always requires knowledge by description, "we need some connexion of universals" (PP 148). But then, due to (1) the sheer universality of causal laws and (2) our own finite limitations, it follows that causal laws always range over things we are not directly acquainted with. And from this it follows further that the causal principle that all events are governed by causal laws must be known *a priori* too, if it is known at all. Thus Russell agrees with Kant that causation *is* synthetic *a priori*. But he rejects Kant's view that the *reason* why causation is synthetic *a priori* is that it is *innate* to us and is unconsciously *imposed by our mind* on our experience (PP 73–74, 86–90; see 159). Instead, for Russell, the principle of causation is synthetic *a priori* simply as a relation among timeless universals, though weakly so, like the principle of induction. This raises the question whether either principle might be more strongly self-evident than the other. I see no reason why either would be. And on the face of it, they seem so linked that they would stand or fall together to the same indeterminate degree.

Keynes as Origin of Russell's Theory

I hold that the 1912 Russell's theory of probability is best interpreted as basically being an adoption of, and also as basically being the same as, the probability theory of John Maynard Keynes. Keynes developed a theory of probability which interprets degrees of probability as degrees of logical relevance, and published it in 1921 in his *A Treatise on Probability*. In chapter 1, "The Meaning of Probability," Keynes says on the first page, "The terms *certain* and *probable* describe the various degrees of rational belief about a proposition which different amounts of knowledge authorize us to entertain" (Keynes 1962 / 1921: 3, Keynes' emphasis). Keynes says "describe," not "define." Yet surely his description is intended to be of the essence of probability, of what it is to be probable. Surely Keynes would not think that probability could be anything different in even one possible world other than the actual world. Thus I take Keynes to be really saying that probability essentially *is* degree of rational belief. And degree of rational belief is just what he means by degree of logical relevance. It is not just a theoretical definition. It is a logicist definition intended to belong to logic.

Keynes discussed probability with Russell on and off from 1904, when Keynes read a paper on probability to the Apostles, until 1913. Thus Keynes easily could have inspired Russell to admit degrees of logical relevance. Not only is the historical timing right, but Keynes is famous for pioneering the view. That is how I explain Russell's admission of the principle of induction as a weak (fallible) logical principle in 1912. Keynes' theory that probability is degree of logical relevance, and its undermining of the distinction between deductive and inductive logic, logically and historically underlie and explain the epistemology of Russell's book.

My interpretation is strongly supported by a "smoking gun" text in the preface to *The Problems of Philosophy*: Russell says:

> I have derived valuable assistance from unpublished writings of G. E. Moore and J. M. Keynes: from the former, as regards the relations of sense-data to physical objects, and from the latter as regards probability and induction. (PP vi)

Richard B. Braithwaite notes that Russell thanks Keynes—and *only* Keynes—for "valuable assistance" on "probability and induction" (Braithwaite 1975: 237). And if Russell is not referring to Keynes on degrees of logical relevance, it is hard to see what else he could be referring to. The "unpublished writings" surely include Keynes' *Treatise* manuscript as the main writing.

Robert Skidelsky, the Keynes biographer, agrees:

> Keynes' view of induction as a logical principle influenced Russell, who acknowledged his debt to Keynes in his *Problems of Philosophy* (1912). (Skidelsky 2005: 286)

João Paulo Monteiro speaks not of influence, but of adoption:

> Russell's own despair with what he was able to see in Hume's philosophy led him, as is well known, to adopt Keynes's theory of induction, and to remain faithful to this theory at least from 1912, in *The Problems of Philosophy*, to 1948 in his *Human Knowledge*. (Monteiro 2001: 66)

Thus the view that Russell adopted Keynes' theory of induction and accepted it throughout his philosophical career is not only "well known," but even seems uncontroversial. I agree with Braithwaite, Skidelsky, and Monteiro in everything they say on this, including Monteiro's statement that Russell accepts Keynes' theory of induction from 1912 to 1948.

In his *Treatise*, Keynes says that probability is a relation of *partially* following from:

> Inasmuch as it is always assumed that we can sometimes judge directly that a conclusion *follows from* a premiss, it is no great extension of this assumption to suppose that we can sometimes recognise that a conclusion *partially follows from*, or stands in a relation of probability to, a

premiss. (Keynes 1962 / 1921: 52, Keynes' emphasis)

This sounds as if Keynes views entailment, or following from, as deductive validity, and views probability as partial entailment, or partial following from, in indefinitely many degrees. Per his other views, not all of these degrees would be numerically measurable. Further, it sounds as if he views deductive entailment as a limit to which probability approaches indefinitely closely, on a scale that covers all logical relevance, with deductive relevance at one end and zero relevance at the other.

Donald Gillies concludes from the just-quoted text:

> So a probability is the degree of a partial entailment. Keynes further makes the assumption that if e partially entails h to degree p, then, given e, it is rational to believe h to degree p. (Gillies 2003: 115)

I agree with Gillies's first sentence completely. But because I do, I find that what Gillies calls Keynes' further assumption is not an assumption at all, but part of a threefold theoretical identification of degree of probability with partial entailment, and also with degree of rational belief. This threefold identification implies *six* assumptions. For in general, any triple identification, $A = B = C$, implies if A then B, if B then A, if A then C, if C then A, if B then C, and if C then B. I leave it to the reader to work out the six assumptions from the second sentence of the Gillies quote.

Here Russell and Keynes belong to a major early modern tradition of understanding probability as purely logical and *a priori*. This is the tradition of Leibniz, Bernoulli, Laplace, Lambert, Bolzano, De Morgan, Boole, Peirce, and MacColl (Hailperin 1988). Keynes attributes the origin of the "subject matter" of his book to Leibniz (Keynes 1962 / 1921: xiii). Leibniz says, "I have said more than once that we need a new kind of logic, concerned with degrees of probability..." (Leibniz 1966 / 1765 / 1704: 466). This should remove the impression that the 1912 Russell has a historically isolated, oddball theory of probability. Russell does not discuss Leibniz on probability in his Leibniz book (PL), or anywhere else I know of. It is Keynes' influence that brings Russell into this Leibnizian tradition. But the 1912 Russell qualifies for membership in any case.

Keynes' general idea that a probable inference is a partial logical entailment is also found in Russell's greatest student, Ludwig Wittgenstein (T 5.15). Max Black says:

> Wittgenstein's theory of probability is of the type commonly called 'logical', of which other well-known instances are the theories of Laplace, Keynes, and

> Carnap. Such theories characteristically construe
> probability as a logical relation depending solely on the
> meanings of the propositions involved. (M. Black 1970:
> 247)

I am merely adding Russell to the list.

Georg Henrik von Wright says, "Aristotle says in the *Rhetoric* that the probable is that which usually happens" (Wright 1960: 167). The great Aristotelian tradition of frequency theory of probability makes probability theory empirical in that the naturally occurring frequencies we start from in natural science must be empirically observed. However, the theory is logical insofar as the notions of "many" or "few" members of a class are logical notions. This makes *reasoning* about probabilities *a priori*. And induction, or reasoning from particular instances to universal conclusions, is a purely intellectual activity for Aristotle (Ross 1960: 43) as well. Keynes and the 1912 Russell are not frequency theorists, but their theories appear less unusual in this perspective as well.

To classify probability as part of logic, with probability being purely logical and approaching logical truth as an asymptote, as Leibniz and Keynes do, is a plausible view that, as we have just seen, belongs to a main tradition of probability theory. However, I wonder if it might be more illuminating to speak of probabilistic relevance and logical modality here, than to speak of probability and logical truth. I shall offer three arguments for this.

First, probabilistic relevance approaches logical necessity as its asymptote; therefore it is best classified as belonging to logic. This argument is, of course, inconclusive. We might as well say that yellow and orange approach red as an asymptote; therefore yellow and orange are best classified as belonging to red. It might be that our only possible reply is that we have a simple intuition that logic and color differ in this respect. Of course, different people have different intuitions. Thus our argument could neither be strictly proved nor strictly refuted. For our own intuition might be either the correct one or the incorrect one. But we might also reply that the premiss is really that logical necessity is the *only* asymptote that (increases in) probabilistic relevance logically can approach. (This is why I said "*its* asymptote.") But yellow can and does approach *any* other color as an asymptote. For example, yellow approaches green through degrees of yellowish green, and so on. Therefore color asymptotes are very unlike the asymptote of logical necessity. And the respect of nonresemblance could scarcely be more relevant. All the same, if my argument is ultimately based only on a simple classificatory intuition, then its strength is only the strength of this intuition. My rejoinder is that this is only to be expected, since there is a very ordinary sense in which deductive logic is ultimately based on our logical intuitions. But my rejoinder is somewhat lame, since there are many different deductive logics based on many different logical intuitions.

Things are often clearer in philosophy of mathematics. Consider the series of proper fractions that are regularly diminishing halves: ½, ¼, ⅛,.... The series approaches zero as an asymptote. Zero cannot be a member of the series. The fractions may serve to represent regularly diminishing positive probabilities, and zero may serve to represent zero probability in the sense of deductive logical impossibility. (The number one would represent logical necessity.) Thus such proper probabilities cannot belong to deductive logic. Yet all the fractions in the series and zero are equally numbers; and at least on the logicist program, all equally belong to logic. Therefore the study of probability, or at least of such proper fractional probabilities, belongs to logic. One might object that the term "proper" is ambiguous. A proper fraction is a fraction whose numerator is smaller than its denominator, while a proper probability is a probability lying between logical necessity and logical impossibility. My reply is that in this example, all proper fractions represent proper probabilities, but zero cannot.

Second, it seems necessary that relevance in general shift multivocally across topics exactly as modalities do. I mean that just as we speak of logical, legal, scientific, political, social, aesthetic, ethical, and epistemic necessities, so we also speak of logical, legal, scientific, political, social, aesthetic, ethical, and epistemic relevancies which are more than logically possible but less than necessary. (Philosophers will recall that a moral necessity is the same as a duty, and that being epistemically necessary is the same as being known.) Therefore, in the topic of deductive logic, just as in any other topic, there is a type of relevance that is more than mere logical possibility but less than logical necessity. I rate this second argument as illuminating and plausible. The problem with it is, of course, that logic might be an exception to the general rule that relevance and necessity shift multivocally across topics. For all the other topics concern both *a priori* and contingent matters, and so have conceptual room for a concept of relevance which is more than mere possibility but less than necessity. But deductive logic is only *a priori*, and there seems to be conceptual room only for the deductive sort of logical relevance I discussed in chapter 9 of my Russell book (2015), and for the early Wittgenstein's truth-table probability. My reply is that we commonly *do* speak of probability in the other deductive sciences. In particular, we often use "rough mathematics" involving rounded numbers, other approximations, "short cut" calculations, and even educated guesses based on our mathematical experience. We often estimate, for example, that the number we seek is probably greater than a certain round number, or probably within 100 integers of that number. The problem with my reply is, of course, that this would only equate to our educated guesses that some deductive argument is probably valid, based on, say, an experienced but quick look at its structure. We could accept *that* use of "probable" in deductive logic and still reject the assimilation of *epistemic* probability to logical necessity as an asymptote. My rejoinder would be that *that* use is a form of epistemic probability itself, and it is specifically intended to approach to the correct mathematical answer as an asymptote. My rejoinder does not logically remove the problem, but at least it reveals a strong tension, going beyond the mere ad hominem, in the objector's position. For it is something of an internal conflict to admit the ordinary use of rough arithmetic as giving approximations to the *mathematical* truth, approximations which have increasing degrees of epistemic probability depending on how rough they are, and at the same time to reject the view that epistemic probabilities increasingly approximate to *logical* truths depending on how rough the approximations are. Indeed, for Russell mathematics is but a species of logic.

My third argument is for the premiss that probabilistic relevance approaches logical necessity as an asymptote. It is ultimately intuitive, but relies on the common understanding of deductive logical relevance as some sort of connectedness or relatedness of the premises to the conclusion. Let us grant that probabilistic relevance is some sort of rational objective relatedness, and that so is deductive relevance. But that gives us right away a higher genus of which both of these sorts of relevance are species, namely, rational objective relatedness of premises to conclusion in general. But logic is just primarily the study of rational objective inference. Thus both sorts of relevance belong to logic. I think the objection here would be that this argument begs the question. For the whole question is whether probabilistic relevance is the sort of relevance that belongs to logic in the first place. Also, intuitions can differ.

My three arguments that probability belongs to logic are all inconclusive. Still, they may help illuminate what is conceptually at stake. Indeed, there are those who find it obvious that "the epistemic notion of probability...is nothing but the notion of rational belief" (Butchvarov 1970: 316). And reason is just what logic in the broad sense is.

Russell's Influence on Keynes' Theory

I hold that Keynes developed the theory of probability as degree of logical relevance, and Russell adopted it and modified it slightly over the years. But I shall argue that Keynes' theory is based in turn partly on Russell's 1903 *Principles of Mathematics*.

It seems clear that Keynes was making a brilliant new extension of ideas he found in Russell's *Principles*. That Russell's 1903 *Principles* should thus be an indirect source of his own 1912 *Problems* theory of induction should not be surprising, since both works belong to Russell's early phase of Platonic realism of "abstract logical universals" (PP 109). That *Principles* accepts a jungle realism of nonexistent beings, and *Problems* does not, is simply irrelevant.

Russell published *Problems* in 1912, and Keynes published his *Treatise* in 1921. But they were friends at least as early as 1904, the year after *Principles* was published (Russell 1987: 68). Russell says:

> I first knew Keynes through his father....
> I had no contact with him in his economic and political work, but I was considerably concerned in his *Treatise on Probability*, many parts of which I discussed with him in detail. It was nearly finished in 1914, but had to be put aside for the duration [of the war]. (Russell 1987: 68)

Both Russell and his student, C. D. Broad, wrote reviews of the *Treatise* the year after it was published (Russell 1922; Broad 1922). Their reviews remain excellent discussions of the *Treatise* today, and perhaps there are no better brief introductions to the work. Russell and Broad praise the work highly; and while they offer criticisms, they give the impression that they agree with most of it. Broad "well remembers going over the proofs of the earlier parts of it in the long vacation of 1914 with Mr. Keynes and Mr. Russell," and says he is "substantially in agreement with" Keynes (Broad 1922: 72). Indeed, Broad joined Keynes and Russell in taking the logicist approach to solving the problem of induction, and took it at the same time they did (Wallenmaier 1967). Russell says, "The book as a whole is one which it is impossible to praise too highly" (Russell 1922: 159).

That Keynes was "much influenced by Bertrand Russell" is clear (Keynes 1962 / 1921: xiii).

Skidelsky says:

> Moore, Russell and Keynes were all philosophic realists: they insisted on the *reality* of the intuitive knowledge which was the foundation of all knowledge. They believed that to *perceive* qualities or logical relations was to perceive *something*; that the indefinable objects of thought had a 'real' existence, and that this reality was

> ...necessary to guarantee the truth of the intuition
> ....Russell confessed that when he wrote *The Principles
> of Mathematics* he shared with Frege a belief in the
> Platonic reality of numbers, which people a timeless
> realm 'of Being'. Keynes, too, wrote that probability is a
> 'real objective relation' which we 'cognise'. (Skidelsky
> 1994: 68, Skidelsky's emphasis)

Skidelsky continues:

> Keynes worked on his thesis on probability in 1906
> "under the joint influence of Moore's *Principia Ethica*
> and Russell's *Principia Mathematica*" [quoting Keynes]
> What he got equally from Moore and Russell (but
> perhaps also from his father) was the idea that logic was
> the foundation of philosophy, and that the foundational
> truths of ethics, mathematics and science were self-
> evident logical propositions, incapable of proof or
> disproof. A crucial debt was to Russell's extension of
> logic from its traditional subject-predicate form,
> exemplified by the syllogism, to include 'real' or
> 'external' relations....The recognition of such relations
> was fundamental to any principle of ordering or ranking.
> Equally important was Russell's distinction between
> magnitude and quantity....It makes sense to call A
> happier than B, not to say he is 50 per cent more happy.
> Russell's emphasis on the relational aspect of logic was
> fundamental to Keynes' theory of probability, though
> Keynes extended the scope of logical relations to include
> non-demonstrative inference. (Skidelsky 1994: 74; see
> Keynes 1962 / 1921: 6, 8, 90 on probability as a
> relation)

Skidelsky is right about all of this. And Skidelsky corrects Keynes
for citing *Principia* as an influence in 1906 (Skidelsky 1994: 658
n.56). In 1906 Keynes could not have been influenced even by the
unpublished manuscript of *Principia*, since Russell and Whitehead
wrote it from "1907 to 1910" (Russell 1987: 155). Surely this was a
slip on Keynes' part, and Keynes meant to say *Principles*. Instead it
is Keynes' final *Treatise on Probability* that discusses *Principia*
and not *Principles*, as Piero V. Mini observes (Mini 1994: 41;
Keynes 1962 / 1921: 19n, 115).

One key element of the *Treatise*, the thesis that it is false
that "two magnitudes of the same kind must be numerically
comparable," and specifically, the observation that "thirty per cent.
healthier or happier," is "destitute of meaning," is in *Principles*
(POM 176). The distinction between quantity and magnitude is
there as well (POM 157–83). The admission of relations (POM
95–100), and their use to define ordered series (POM 199–226), are

in *Principles* too. And so is the foundational logicist approach. And Keynes was surely aware of *Principles* as early as 1904, the year he presented his first paper on probability. This was, after all, the year he first met Russell. They must have become good friends quickly, since it was also the year of Keynes' famous attempt to escape from his admirers by staying with Bertrand and Alys Russell in their cottage—a secret visit interrupted by twenty-six unexpected guests (Skidelsky 1986: 124, 152–53, 183–84; Russell 1987: 68).

Annabella Carabelli adds:

> In his discussion of the measurement of probability in the first version of the *Principles of Probability* (1907), Keynes considered the contemporary status of the philosophy of measurement and, in particular, of the measurement of relations. His main interest is in the 'philosophy of magnitude', not in the mathematics of magnitude....He devotes particular attention to Russell's *Principles of Mathematics* (1903). (Carabelli 1992: 6; see 5–10)

Later on, *Principia* was a major influence on Keynes too. R. F. Harrod cites *Principia* as the source of Keynes' views that probabilities are features of propositions as opposed to events in the world, and that the task of a science of probability is to derive theorems from as few axioms as possible (Harrod 1951: 653–54). Harrod notes that this would make Keynes as indebted to Whitehead as to Russell (Harrod 1951: 653–54, 654n); both Whitehead and Russell praised the *Treatise* (Harrod 1951: 135).

However, Skidelsky, Harrod, and Carabelli find nothing in Russell to explain Keynes' specific theory that probability is degree of logical relevance. That is not in either *Principles* or *Principia*. Russell does briefly discuss what he calls empirical "induction" in *Principles* (POM 441–42), but he is really sketching an analysis of abduction, which we now call "inference to the best explanation." Russell's only purpose in writing about "induction" there is to sketch what is logically needed to tell which kind of geometry applies to the actual world, given our empirical observations. Granted, Keynes might have simply applied Russell's *general* view in *Principles* that logic is the foundation of mathematics to mathematical probability theory in particular. But that only gets us a logicization of mathematical probability theory, not a theory that epistemic probability is degree of logical relevance.

Russell, of course, does not use the terms "relevance" or "logical relevance" in *Problems* to describe his probability theory or his theory of induction. But this is only to say that my thesis is not handed to us on the platter of express terminology.

Other Influences on Keynes

It is easy to place Keynes on the Russellian conceptual map of logical relevance as discussed in chapter 9 of my (2015) book. For Keynes says in his *Treatise*,

> We have still, however, to make precise what we mean by...one proposition *following from* or being *logically involved in* the truth of another. We seem to intend by these expressions some kind of transition by means of a *logical principle*. A logical principle cannot be better defined, I think, than in terms of what in Mr. Russell's *Logic of Implication* is termed a formal implication. (Keynes 1962 / 1921: 124, Keynes' emphasis)

We may charitably say this puts Keynes on the level of *always true* formal implication in Russell's theory of logical relevance, and squarely on the level of implicit FG–MDL in Russell's views on modality. It appears, then, that Keynes never made the jump with Russell to implicit FG–MDL*, and is thus relying on a theory of logical truth which Russell rejected three years before Keynes' *Treatise* was published. See my (2015) on these modal logics.

Nor is there in Keynes any concept of modality as based on truth-tables, of relevance as truth-ground containment, or of purely logical probability as based on truth-tables in the *Tractatus*. For Tractarian probability admits of limited degrees indeed. Every probability is a proper fraction whose numerator is the number of rows on which a statement is true and whose denominator is the total number of rows in its truth-table. A or $\neg A$ is 100% probable, $A \lor B$ is 75%, A is 50%, $A \& B$ is 25%, $A \& B \& C$ is 12.5%, and so on. Nothing can be 76% or 49% probable. In the *Tractatus*, nothing can fail to have a numerically determinate probability. Among logical theories of probability, it is hard to conceive of anything more deeply inimical to Keynes, even though Keynes speaks of "*partial*" following from, and even though both Wittgenstein and Keynes make logical necessity the asymptote of logical probability.

There were many influences on Keynes' *Treatise*. The young Keynes often heard his father, John Neville Keynes, and his father's closest friend, William Ernest Johnson, discuss logic; both made well-known contributions to logic (Skidelsky 1986: 69; Harrod 1951: 6–8).[1] The impact of Moore on the 1904 Keynes was tremendous (Skidelsky 1996: 36–37; 1994: 68, 74; 1986: 133–34; Bateman 1991: 56–59; Davis 1991: 89–92; Fitzgibbons 1991: 127–30; Braithwaite 1975: 242–45). Keynes' view that probability is indefinable seems inspired by Moore's view that goodness is indefinable (Harrod 1951: 652). Keynes' first paper on probability, read at the January 23, 1904 meeting of the Apostles (Cambridge

Conversazione Society), and entitled "Ethics in Relation to Conduct," was a critical discussion of Moore's *Principia Ethica* (see Skidelsky 1986: 152–53). For Keynes, Moore's open question test, "This has property *F*, but is it good?" arguably applies to probability too: "This stands in relation *R* to body of evidence *e*, but is it probable?"

In his *Treatise*, Keynes cites Johnson, Moore, and Russell as chief influences (Keynes 1962 / 1921: xiii). Broad is very good at describing Johnson's contributions (Broad 1922), but does not mention degrees of logical relevance as one of them. And surely Moore did not develop a theory of inductive degrees of logical relevance, but had only the theory of deductive "degrees" of implicative logical necessity which Russell adopted in *Principles* (POM 454n). In fact, Keynes says that Moore's ethical theory of the future consequences of our acts "must be derived from the empirical or *frequency* theory" (Keynes 1962 / 1921: 310, my emphasis). This implies that Keynes believes that Moore has a theory of probability incompatible with his own, and does not believe that Moore is the source of his own.

Keynes completed the first draft of the *Treatise* on September 29, 1910 (Skidelsky 1986: 255). In 1914 his father Neville Keynes, Johnson, Russell, Moore, and Broad read the proofs and presumably offered suggestions (Skidelsky 1986: 285). However, it seems unlikely that any of those proofreaders is the origin of the theory that probability is degree of logical relevance. At any rate, I found nothing in their works to suggest that.

Mini notes that Keynes distances himself from his father's traditional logic (Mini 1994: 33). And Carabelli argues that Keynes tries to distance himself from Moore and Russell (Carabelli 1991: 120n). Keynes' 1904 paper criticizes Moore. And if Keynes is really the source of Russell's theory that the principle of induction is a weakly (fallibly) self-evident *a priori*, as Russell appears to say in *Problems*, then the reverse would not be true. Broad says he follows Keynes on probability, so the reverse would not be true.

Finally, there is the extensive list of works Keynes cites in his bibliography (Keynes 1962 / 1921: 431–58). Keynes confesses he did not read them all (Keynes 1962 / 1921: 432), but he did read a great deal. Harrod speaks of Keynes' "immense erudition" on probability and says, "It may well be that Keynes had a wider knowledge of the literature of probability than he ever acquired in his chosen subject of economics" (Harrod 1951: 136). Thus there are hundreds of potential sources of the theory of degrees of logical relevance.

Keynes was primarily an economist; but no economist seems to be the origin of his theory that probability is degree of logical relevance. I shall discuss the economists Keynes knew best,

Francis Ysidro Edgeworth and Alfred Marshall, later in this book. I found nothing on logical relevance in *German Social Democracy*, Russell's 1896 book on economics and political science, either.

Keynes already spoke of "irrelevancy" in his 1904 paper (quoted in Skidelsky 1986: 184), and that seems to eliminate any origins of the theory later than 1904.

Thus from everything that has been said so far, it seems that we should be looking for a pre-1904 source which is outside of Keynes' readings in logic, philosophy, and economics.

The main object of this book is to argue it is more likely than not that the origin of Keynes' theory of logical relevance is not to be found in logic, philosophy, or economics, but in evidence law. I have, of course, already given my negative case that it is not likely to be found in any logician or philosopher. Perhaps I should restrict that claim to logicians and philosophers Keynes would have been likely to read. For as we shall see, many lawyers studied logic and philosophy in the centuries before Keynes, and studied them on theory of evidence. Thus logicians and philosophers might still have influenced Keynes indirectly, through their influence on the history of evidence law.

I shall begin with a brief review of probability theory because that is our main topic, and also because knowing what the main probability theories are will help us tell whether and when Anglo-American evidence law is concerned with these theories. But since we are concerned with origins of any kind, we will be looking for anything *like* Keynes' theory in evidence law, regardless of whether the old evidence law treatise writers took it from a theory of probability, or even considered it to be a theory of probability.

Probability Theory: Introduction

Probability theory divides into (i) mathematical statistics, also known as the probability calculus, dating to the seventeenth century, and (ii) its several interpretations. The calculus itself is as unobjectionable as arithmetic or algebra. But people have never agreed on how to interpret its key undefined notion, the notion of probability, or if you like, h/e, the probability of hypothesis h given evidence e. Arguably, there is no single best interpretation.

My (2015: ch. 9; 2012; 2010) were all about diagramming logically relevant entailment in deductive logic. And whether or not we logicize mathematics, we all know that mathematics can be diagrammed. Thus, insofar as the probability calculus is part of mathematics, it should come as no surprise that it too can be diagrammed, and that there can be diagrammable containments of probabilities within probabilities in probability arguments.

If probabilities can be assigned numbers at all, then they can be graphed. John Neville Keynes says, "In the use of statistics, considerable assistance may often be derived from the employment of diagrams" (N. Keynes 1986 / 1917: 339). More fully, Neville Keynes says:

> In the use of statistics, considerable assistance may often be derived from the employment of diagrams. The graphic method is not only useful for the popular exposition of statistics...; but it also has a genuine scientific value. Thus by means of graphic representation we may employ the special method of quantitative induction called by Whewell the method of curves. (N. Keynes 1986 / 1917: 339–40)

And just as there can be logics of "many" and "few," there can be diagrams of relations of merely greater or lesser probabilities. Such diagrams can be made numerical too, but they would use ordinal numbers instead of cardinal numbers. Just as the hardness scale for minerals allows a Venn diagram of the hypothetical syllogism, "Diamond is harder than carborundum, carborundum is harder than shale, therefore diamond is harder than shale," so too we can diagram the hypothetical syllogism, "It is more likely that the sun will rise tomorrow than that there will be a solar eclipse, it is more likely that there will be a solar eclipse tomorrow than that the sun will cease to exist, therefore it is more likely that the sun will rise tomorrow than that it will cease to exist."

Besides cardinal probabilities and ordinal probabilities, Maynard Keynes admits incommensurable probabilities. These are the only probabilities that cannot be diagrammed, since they cannot even be ranked or classified ordinally.

The great legal scholar John Henry Wigmore is famous for his argument charts. These directly concern the stages of a legal argument, but their purpose is to help assess the likelihood of the argument's success. "Wigmore's...Chart Method of analysing mixed masses of evidence...., Bayes' Theorem and other axioms of probability, are extraordinarily flexible and powerful tools which, if used with sensitive awareness of their nature, make clear the operation of 'subjective' values, biases, and choices at almost every stage of complex intellectual procedures" (Twining 1994: 6–7). Thus Wigmore admits diagrams of probability arguments.

There are three main rival interpretations of the probability calculus: frequency theory (Aristotle); logical theory (Keynes); and subjectivist theory (Ramsey).

Aristotle's Frequency Theory of Probability

The frequency interpretation of probability starts with Aristotle, who defines probability as what is usually the case: "A probability is a thing that usually happens" (*Rhetoric* 1357*b*35 / Aristotle 1968c: 1332). John Venn was its champion in the nineteenth century; Richard von Mises and Hans Reichenbach were its main champions in the twentieth. Again, the frequency theory is a logical interpretation of probability, insofar as the notions of "many" or "few" members of a class are logical notions. But actual frequencies are empirical, so we need empirical interpretations of this logical interpretation of probability. There is nothing wrong with having interpretations of interpretations. For example, Russell interprets ordinary things in terms of molecules, molecules in terms of atoms, and atoms in terms of quantum events (see AMA 2–9). Indeed, empirical interpretations of frequency theory are just *applications* of frequency theory.

The frequency theory is naturally popular with scientists, statisticians, and epidemiologists. In fact, it is basic for anyone who works with huge populations of repetitive items. But it is hard to apply to unusual or nonrecurrent events. It is also hard to apply if the events in question belong to two equally huge opposing classes of events, and occur more frequently in the less relevant class.

Keynes' Logical Theory of Probability

Keynes developed his theory of probability as logical relevance to replace frequency theory, at least as Keynes found it in Moore. Keynes gives a purely logical interpretation of probability as degree of logical relevance, where relevance is a logically intuited relationship among propositions. Besides Russell and perhaps Russell's student Broad, Keynes is the only major thinker in 1912 who interprets probability as degree of logical relevance.

Keynes says of "the term *probability*": "In its most fundamental sense, I think, it refers to the logical relation between two sets of propositions" (Keynes 1962 / 1921: 11, Keynes' emphasis). The first set describes the body of evidence, and the second the "object of...rational belief" (Keynes 1962 / 1921: 12). Keynes also allows two derivative senses. (1) The term can mean the degree of rational belief which we are entitled to have based on our evidence; and (2) it can even be elliptically used to mean the probability of the statement believed (Keynes 1962 / 1921: 11–12). Derivative sense (1) is the sense with which we are most directly concerned. Derivative sense (2) is casual and strictly incorrect, since the probability of the statement believed is essentially related to, and therefore must be tacitly understood as related to, the body of evidence the probability is based on.

Keynes finds that being probable is just as *"relational"* as being equal to, being greater than, or being three miles distant from (Keynes 1962 / 1921: 6–7), Keynes' emphasis. This does not mean that probability is relative. Keynes' example illustrates this well. The fact that I was three miles from home yesterday remains objectively true even if I am home today. Likewise, the fact that a view was improbable based on the evidence I had yesterday remains objectively true even if the view is probable based on the evidence I have today. We may say Keynes' view is that probability statements are logically indeterminate (logically incomplete) unless they have two logical subject-terms, one about a body of evidence, and the other about the object which the evidence is ostensibly evidence for. That is, probability statements essentially assert that a relation of probability obtains between those two relata. Keynes cites Ludovicus Martinus Kahle, Boole, and Laplace as his predecessors in holding "[t]hat "probability is a *relation*" (Keynes 1962 / 1921: 90–91, Keynes' emphasis).

Keynes means by "degree of logical relevance," degree of objective rational credibility. This concept is not at all the same as the concept of degree of probability or likelihood, and that makes Keynes' definition significantly informative and, on the face of it, based on a synthetic *a priori* insight. I plan to show later that this is Russell's view as well.

Keynes says:

> [I]n the sense important to logic, probability is not subjective. It is not, that is to say, subject to human caprice. A proposition is not probable because we think it so. When once the facts are given which determine our knowledge, what is probable or improbable in these circumstances has been fixed objectively, and is independent of our opinion. The Theory of Probability is logical, therefore, because it is concerned with the degree of belief which it is *rational* to entertain in given conditions, and not merely with the actual beliefs of particular individuals, which may or may not be rational. (Keynes 1962 / 1921: 4, his emphasis)

He repeats this view: "[I]f our grounds are reasonable, are they not in an important sense logical?" (Keynes 1962 / 1921: 98). Besides *it's a priori* character, this is all he means by calling his theory a logical theory. And here I would like to make a major classificatory point. Merely to be *a priori* is not yet to be analytic *a priori*, or logical in the formal sense. For there is also the synthetic *a priori*. But there is also a second, broader sense of "logical" in which even the synthetic *a priori* is logical. And that is precisely Keynes' sense of being rational and objective. For if Kant and Frege are right that geometry is synthetic *a priori*, for all that it would still be just as rational and objective as logic or arithmetic. And in point of fact, I think Keynes' intuitions of degrees of relevance are synthetic *a priori*. My tests are simply Russell's: the statements describing relevance relations between bodies of evidence and our hypotheses are not fully generalized, nor are they truth-preservingly fully generalizable. Still less are they true in virtue of their logical form. Therefore, if such statements are true *a priori*, then they can only be synthetic *a priori* truths. Even if we speak generally of bodies of evidence 1, 2,...*n*, and similarly of hypotheses 1, 2,...*n*, as well as of relations 1, 2,...*n* between bodies of evidence and hypotheses, this is still not full generality. For terms like "hypothesis" and "body of evidence" are descriptive terms, not logical terms. Nor are they variables. If they were, we should be able to substitute "apple" and "cat" for them, or any other terms we like, and preserve the truth of our original statements of relevance relations. The truth is quite the opposite. Judgments of degree of relevance for Keynes are nothing without their particularity; and the only fully general theory here is the uninterpreted probability calculus.

Keynes says that "probability is, in the strict sense, indefinable" (Skidelsky 1986: 183; 2003: 109 quoting Keynes 1908). Skidelsky is right to note Keynes' qualification, "in the strict sense." Many simply hold that probability is indefinable for Keynes, such as Harrod (1951: 652) and even Russell (OP 286; HK 373; MPD 142). But Russell says more cautiously in his review of Keynes only that "Mr Keynes holds that a *formal* definition of probability is impossible" (Russell 1922: 152, my emphasis). Keynes actually says:

> A *definition* of probability is not possible, **unless** it contents us to **define** degrees of the probability-relation by reference to degrees of rational belief. We cannot analyze the probability-relation in terms of **simpler** ideas. (Keynes 1962 / 1921: 8, Keynes' italic emphasis, my boldface emphasis)

Keynes is saying that we cannot define probability in the sense of analyzing it into simpler ideas. He is saying that we cannot give a *compositional* definition of probability. Now, if we define degree of probability as degree of rational belief, the term "degree of" occurs on both sides of the definition, and that term is therefore not a logical part of what is actually being defined. Clearly, in "degree of probability =Df degree of rational belief, we are really defining "probability" as 'rational belief'. If we treat 'rational belief' as a simple term that does not break down into two simpler ideas, 'rational' and 'belief', then we are defining probability without analyzing it into simpler ideas. Instead, we are defining probability as being something equally simple, namely, rational belief. This is a *theoretical definition*. To give a theoretical definition of a thing is to state what the thing is, typically in terms of a scientific or other theory (Copi 1978: 140–41). From Aristotle on, this has been widely regarded as the most important kind of definition. And Keynes' theory is a theoretical definition. For whether he calls it a definition or not, he is saying that *this is what probability is*: degree of rationality of believing. The definition is not only theoretical, but is also an *informative identification*, since the terms "probable" and rational belief" express very different intensional senses.

A second view, better than the first, is that defining degree of probability as degree of rationality believing is compositional because "rational" and "belief" are two different concepts. In fact, this looks for all the world like a definition by genus and difference, with belief as the genus and rational as the difference. Even if we held that all belief is intrinsically rational—which is decidedly not Keynes' view, since he says "the actual beliefs of particular individuals...may or may not be rational" (Keynes 1962 / 1921: 4)—the concepts of rationality and of belief would be different, though distinct only in reason, so that the definition of probability as rationality of believing would still be compositional.

A holder of the first view might reply that the definition is really of degree of probability as degree of *rationality* of belief. For that is what counts, and not the degree of *strength* of belief, i.e., degree of *psychological* certainty or conviction, to which it is chiefly opposed. And I am sure that is what Keynes has in mind. For he says it is "the degree of belief which it is *rational* to entertain" Keynes 1962 / 1921: 4, Keynes' emphasis).

But a holder of the second view the objector might rejoin, "But rationality *of* what? Of a theory? Of a course of action? Here for Keynes it must be rationality *of belief*, and so belief must be a logical element in the definition after all."

A subtle holder of the first view might reply that if every belief were essentially minimally rational, then rationality and belief would be not *wholly* distinct, and thus not *really* distinct, but only *formally* distinct *á la* Scotus, or distinct only in reason.

A subtle holder of the second view might reply, "Yes, but rationality and belief are still not the same. Even on the view that all beliefs are minimally rational, belief and rationality are different *because* they are formally distinct, or distinct in reason." And it is in this sense that I think Keynes' definition of (degree of) probability as (degree of) rational belief logically must be compositional after all. And we might arguably even consider it a definition by genus and difference. However, if all beliefs were essentially minimally rational, then belief could not be the genus, since rationality could not function as a difference. Instead, rationality would have to be the genus, and the differences would be things like theory, course of action, or belief. But if we take that approach, we must be sure that "reason" is said univocally, and not ambiguously, nor *pros hen* in Aristotle's sense of *pros hen*, in which living bodies are primarily or literally healthy, and climates and foods are said to be healthy in a derivative sense if they tend to produce healthy living bodies, and urine is said to be healthy in another derivative sense if it is the sort of urine produced by healthy living bodies. But for present purposes, we need not reach such questions. It is enough to note that belief and rationality are distinct in reason, and are therefore different, and that therefore the one definition of probability which Keynes says he *would* accept *is* logically compositional, *pace* Keynes—and that therefore probability is not indefinable for Keynes after all. Of course, he may still *take* it as a primitive term in his theory, even though I think we must say it *is* not in fact genuinely primitive. Since I agree with Keynes that beliefs logically need not be rational, I can take the definition as defining probability by the genus belief and the difference rational. Thus I criticize Keynes for not noticing that if "it contents us to define degrees of the probability-relation by reference to degrees of rational belief," then we *do* in fact "analyze the probability-relation in terms of simpler ideas" (Keynes 1962 / 1921: 8), namely, the two simpler ideas of belief and rationality. Obviously he distinguishes these two ideas, since he says "beliefs may or may not be rational."

I proceed to compare Keynes' theory of probability with the definition of relevance in the American *Federal Rules of Evidence* (*FRE*) Rule 401, and also with Bayes' Theorem.

Keynes offers an initial simple definition of "irrelevance" as follows: if $h/e1,e2 = h/e1$, then $e2$ is irrelevant to $h/e1$ (Keynes 1962 / 1921: 54–56; I alter his notation). This means that if the probability of hypothesis h given bodies of evidence $e1$ and $e2$ is the same as the probability of h given $e1$ alone, then $e2$ is irrelevant to establishing h. This conception of irrelevance is basic to discussions of logical relevance in today's evidence law casebooks, such as the one by Richard O. Lempert and Stephen A. Saltzburg (Lempert 2011: ch. 3).[2]

Keynes' initial simple definition of irrelevance seems to be a negative version of the definition of relevance in *FRE* Rule 401:

Rule 401. Definition of "Relevant Evidence"
"Relevant evidence" means evidence having any tendency to make the existence of any fact that is of

> any consequence to the determination of the [judicial]
> action more probable or less probable than it would be
> without the evidence (West Publishing Company 1995:
> 24).[3]

Unless Keynes allows *e1* to be nothing, Rule 401 improves on him by not requiring a prior body of evidence *e1*. Thus Rule 401 avoids the vicious infinite regress of prior bodies of evidence which Keynes faces. (This is an old criticism of Keynes; I am merely noting that Rule 401 avoids it.) But Rule 401 appears to be worse than Keynes in that it does not admit of degrees of relevance. Lempert says of Rule 401:

> There are no degrees of relevance; evidence is either
> relevant or it is not. Strictly speaking, it is a mistake to
> say that one item of evidence is *"more relevant"* than
> another. What differentiates items of different
> evidentiary weight is *probative value*, i.e. their power to
> persuade a reasonable person about a fact in issue
> Admissible evidence varies widely in probative value.
> (Lempert 2011: 213, Lempert's emphasis)

Lempert is correctly reporting current legal usage, but this seems to be a mere difference in terminology. The nineteenth century legal scholars often write as if having relevance and having probative value are the same. Indeed, one might define relevance as having any degree of probative value greater than zero. Of course, "any" is a logical term, but "zero" is not, unless we are logicists. To make the definition more purely logical, we may say that to be relevant is to have *some* probative value. In any case, if we define relevance as having at least *some* minimal (or non-zero) probative value, then we reject degrees of relevance, and admit only degrees of probative value. That may make relevance a useful threshold requirement for the admissibility of evidence in a courtroom. But it is just as silly as saying that to be probable is to have at least minimal (or non-zero) logical relevance, and on that basis denying that there are any degrees of probability, and admitting only degrees of logical relevance.

If we are to admit a definition here at all, I think the only one that makes any theoretical sense, as opposed to practical or courtroom sense, is to define degree of probability as degree of logical relevance. This is what Keynes has in mind. And we would not wish to reverse the definition, since probability is the more obscure term, and is the term we wish to illuminate. Lempert does not discuss Keynes here (Lempert 2011: 213). But surely Lempert would agree that any conflict between Rule 401 and Keynes is merely verbal. In *court*, Rule 401 is useful, since there we wish to have a threshold requirement for the admissibility of evidence. But in *theory of probability*, we wish to state what probability is. And here, we wish to preserve and illuminate its essential feature of having various sorts of degrees, which intuitively include cardinal, ordinal, and incommensurable degrees. Degrees of logical relevance seem to do this perfectly.

Bayes' Theorem is used as "a method for using assumed probabilities to derive other probabilities" (Friedman 1991: 66n.) It is an equation for multiplying or dividing probabilities. Ephraim Nissan says:

> **Bayes' theorem** When dealing with a hypothesis H, and some evidence E, Bayes' Theorem states:
>
> $$P(H\backslash E) = P(E\backslash H)P(H)/P(E)$$
>
> this can be read as follows: The *posterior probability* $P(H\backslash E)$, i.e. the probability that H is true given E, is equal to the product of the likelihood $P(E\backslash H)$, i.e., the probability that E given the truth of H, and the *prior probability* $P(H)$ of H, divided by the *prior probability* $P(E)$ of E. (Nissan 2012: 1029–30, Nissan's emphasis)

Nissan's "this can be read" is already an interpretation of the theorem, in terms of probability, evidence, and hypothesis. It is the *further* interpretation of the term "probability," in terms of a theory of probability, such as Aristotle's, Keynes', or Ramsey's, that would concern us here. Nissan's prior probabilities are Friedman's assumed probabilities. Bayes' Theorem itself, of course, belongs to the uninterpreted probability calculus.

Keynes calls Bayes' Theorem the "first...appearance" of "the Principle of Inverse Probability, a theorem of great importance in the history of the subject" of probability (Keynes 1962 / 1921: 174). Keynes discusses the principle's history, proof, and formulation (Keynes 1962 / 1921: 174–81, 379–80), and discusses "various arguments which have been based upon it...in Chapter XXX" (Keynes 1962 / 1921: 174). Keynes, of course, has no real choice about accepting Bayes' Theorem, since it is part of the probability calculus, and his theory must interpret that calculus, if his theory is to be considered an adequate theory of probability.

Bayes' Theorem is not the same as Keynes' definitions of irrelevance. Keynes says:

> The simplest definition of Irrelevance is as follows: h_1 is irrelevant to [conclusion] x on evidence h, if the probability of x on evidence hh_1 is the same as its probability on evidence h.[1] But for a reason which will

appear in Chapter VI., a stricter and more complicated definition, as follows, is theoretically preferable: h_1 is irrelevant to x on evidence h, if there is no such proposition, inferrible from $h_1 h$ but not from h, such that its addition to evidence h affects the probability of x.[2] Any proposition which is irrelevant in the strict sense is, of course, also irrelevant in the simpler sense; but if we were to adopt the simpler definition, it would sometimes occur that a part of evidence would be relevant, which taken as a whole was irrelevant. The more elaborate definition by avoiding this proves in the sequel more convenient. If the condition $x/h_1 h = h/h$ alone is satisfied, we may say that the evidence h_1 is 'irrelevant as a whole'.[3]

It will be convenient to define also two other phrases. h_1 and h_2 are independent and complementary part of the evidence, if between them they make up h and neither can be inferred from the other. **If x is the conclusion, and h_1 and h_2 are independent and complementary parts of the evidence, then h_1 is relevant if the addition of it to h_2 affects the probability of x.**[4]

1. That is to say, h_1 is irrelevant to x/h if $x/h_1 h = x/h$.
2. That is to say, h_1 is irrelevant to x/h, if there is no proposition $h'_1/h_1 h = 1$, $h'_1/h \neq 1$, and $x/h'_1/h \neq x/h$.
3. Where no misunderstanding can arise, the qualification 'as a whole' will be sometimes omitted.
4. I.e[.] (in symbolism) h_1 and h_2 are independent and complementary parts of h if $h_1 h_2 = h$, $h_1/h_2 \neq 1$, and $h_2/h_1 \neq 1$. **Also, h_1 is relevant if $x/h \neq x/h_2$.** (Keynes 1962: 55, Keynes' italic emphasis, my boldface emphasis)

It should be clear that Keynes' two definitions of irrelevance are negative versions of Rule 401, and are logically more precise than Rule 401, the second even more so than the first. It should also be clear that the two boldfaced sentences are positive versions of Rule 401, and are logically more precise than Rule 401, the second even more so than the first. The two boldfaced sentences appear to be statements, not definitions; but they could be considered as definitions, or as helping further logically clarify the two negative definitions Keynes gives. Except for the greater degree(s) of precision, and except for the fact that the two boldfaced sentences appear to be statements of a principle, and not definitions, all of four of these appear to be logically equivalent to Rule 401. Certainly they all discuss relevance in terms of probability, just as Rule 401 does.

But this is true only on the surface of Keynes' theory. At bottom, Keynes reverses Rule 401. For at bottom, he understands probability as degree of logical relevance.

Four closely related comments follow.

First, Rule 401 defines relevance in terms of probability, and that is what Keynes does in his various versions of the Principle of Inverse Probability. But for Keynes, the whole question is what probability is in the first place. The fundamental task of probability theory is to answer that question. Aristotle, Venn, Keynes, Ramsey, Mises, and Reichenbach all agree that probability is the obscure and basic notion needing explanation.

It may seem that all this makes Keynes' theory circular. For Keynes holds that probability is degree of logical relevance, and then defines irrelevance (twice) in terms of probability. This might also seem to mean that Keynes has two notions of relevance, one which he takes to be primitive and to define probability, and one which he takes to be defined in terms of probability. But this is not so. His use of the word "relevance" is univocal. His definition of probability as degree of logical relevance (or rational belief) is fundamental. It is his metaphysical theory of the nature of probability as timeless, intuited logical relevance. The definition of irrelevance in terms of probability is his formalization. It is his formally defined *test* of when irrelevance occurs, and conversely, of when relevance occurs. The test succeeds precisely because probability *is* degree of logical relevance. For essential identity implies logical equivalence.

Second, to distinguish Bayes' Theorem from Rule 401 and from Keynes' definition of probability as degree of logical relevance, we need only note that they are definitions, while Bayes' Theorem is an uninterpreted theorem of the probability calculus. As such, Bayes' Theorem ought to be adequately interpretable by any serious theory of probability, including Aristotle's frequency theory, Keynes' logical theory, and Ramsey's subjectivist theory. Clearly, neither Rule 401 nor Keynes' definition of probability as degree of logical relevance is an uninterpreted theorem of the probability calculus. They are not theorems at all, but definitions. Far from being uninterpreted, they are definitional interpretations. Granted, definitions do imply axioms. In general, definition $F = $ Df G implies the axiom that F is logically equivalent to G. However, they interpret the axioms they imply, as well as any theorems the axioms imply.

Third, Rule 401 does not even attempt to interpret the probability calculus. For it defines relevance in terms of probability, and leaves probability undefined. Rule 401 does not tell us how to understand probability in turn. Is probability a matter of frequency? Is it a matter of logical intuition? Is it a matter of willingness to bet? As far as Rule 401 is concerned, probability could be any of these things. Ramsey criticizes Keynes for making this mistake. Ramsey says "it is as if everyone knew the laws of geometry but no one could tell whether any given object were round or square" (Ramsey 1931: 162; compare Frege 1974: 35–36; Russell 1956 / 1897: 40, 72–74, 80, 93, 101, 104–5). Ramsey is wrong about Keynes, since Keynes does tell us what he thinks probability is. But Ramsey's point does apply to Rule 401.

Fourth, if Rule 401 is an endorsement of Keynes, then it is a rejection of all of Keynes' rivals. And the chief rival to Keynes, the frequency theory, is the one used by scientists dealing with mass repetitive phenomena, as in mass toxic injury cases. We would be treated to the spectacle of Rule 401's using Keynes' interpretation of probability to evaluate scientific theories which are based on the chief rival to Keynes, or for that matter, to evaluate the frequency theory itself, as well as all other rivals to Keynes' theory. Those who favor Keynes might not find that a bad idea, and it certainly is an interesting one. But it would make Rule 401 beg the question of what probability is by simply assuming that Keynes' theory is correct, since Rule 401 certainly does not argue for that.

I discuss Rule 401 further in the section "Anglo-American Relevance Law Today." For more on Bayes' Theorem, see Bayes (1963) and Swinburne (2002), both of which contain Bayes' paper. There are large literatures on Bayes in both philosophy and law.

I shall now discuss Locke, Leibniz, and Jakob (also called James) Bernoulli as major antecedents of Keynes.

In his *An Essay Concerning Human Understanding*, book 4, chapter 16, "Of the Degrees of Assent," Locke discusses witnesses and testimony in an ordinary general sense. For Locke, degrees of assent are or correspond to degrees of probability. He says, "The grounds of probability...as they are the foundations on which are *assent* is built, so are they also the measure whereby its several degrees are, or ought to be regulated" (Locke 1959 / 1690: vol. 2, 368, Locke's emphasis). Like Keynes, Locke makes probability relative to a body of evidence. Locke says:

> Probability is likeliness to be true, the very notation of the word signifying such a proposition, for which there be arguments or proofs to make it pass, or be received for true. The entertainment the mind gives this sort of propositions is called *belief, assent*, or *opinion*, which is the admitting or receiving any proposition for true, upon arguments or proofs that are found to persuade us to receive it as true, without certain knowledge that it is so. (Locke 1959 / 1690: vol. 2, 365, Locke's emphasis)

The context makes it clear that such "arguments or proofs" are less than logically certain. His general distinction is between uncertain probability and certain demonstration. This is basically the same as

Keynes on probability as relational, if we replace Locke's term "arguments or proofs" with Keynes' term "body of evidence."

Leibniz was an encyclopedic thinker one of whose many fields of study was jurisprudence. His *New Essays*, book 4, chapter 16, "Of the Degrees of Assent," corresponds to and comments on Locke's *Essay*, book 4, chapter 16, "Of the Degrees of Assent," which I discussed in the previous paragraph. (*New Essays* is a dialogue: Theophilus represents Leibniz, and Philalethes represents Locke.) In his book, Leibniz finds examples of Lockean degrees of assent in the law, including evidence law. He says, "When jurists discuss proofs, presumptions, conjectures, and evidence, they have a great many good things to say on the subject and go into considerable detail....The entire form of judicial procedures is, in fact, nothing but a kind of logic, applied to legal questions" (Leibniz 1966 / 1765 / 1704: 464). He also cites physicians as recognizing "many differences of degree among their signs and symptoms," and adds, "Mathematicians have begun, in our own day, to calculate the chances in games" (Leibniz 1966 / 1765 / 1704: 465).

Leibniz says, "I have said more than once [on pages 206, 373] that we need a new kind of logic, concerned with degrees of probability, since Aristotle in his *Topics* could not have been further from it: he was content to set out certain familiar rules..." (Leibniz 1966 / 1765 / 1704: 466, editor's bracketed page cites).

Russell wrote his first philosophy book on Leibniz. Probability is not a topic, but empirical knowledge is. Russell discusses *New Essays* on the thesis that all necessary truth, including mathematical truth, is analytic. At least by implication, that would include the probability calculus. See Russell (1937 / 1900: ch. 14).

I turn now to Bernoulli. In his book, *History of Probability and Statistics and Their Applications before 1750*, Anders Hald distinguishes "[o]bjective, statistical, or aleatory probabilities" and "[s]ubjective, personal, or epistemic probabilities" (Hald 2003: 28, Hald's emphasis deleted). Hald says of the latter:

> Such probabilities refer to our imperfect knowledge and thus only indirectly to the things or events about which a statement is made. Some philosophers consider epistemic probability, which they call logical probability[,] as a measure of the strength of a logical relation between two propositions, i.e., a weaker relation than that of logical consequence. (Hald 2003: 28)

Hald's notion of indirect reference ("refer...indirectly") in this text is an instance of Russell's notion of propositional attitude, and of Quine's notion of referential opacity. Hald says, "A clear distinction between the two kinds of probability is due to James Bernoulli (1713)" (Hald 2003: 28). Hald says, "According to Hacking (1971), similar ideas had been previously expressed by Leibniz; however, Bernoulli gave the first systematic exposition of these fundamental concepts, and his formulations and viewpoints have been influential ever since" (Hald 2003: 247, cites omitted; see 247–54). Hald says that for Bernoulli, "probability is a degree of certainty and as such a measure of our imperfect knowledge; probability is personal in the sense that it varies from person to person according to his knowledge, and for the same person it may vary with time as his knowledge changes" (Hald 2003: 249). This is basically the same as Keynes on the variability of probability across persons and times, if we replace Bernoulli's term "knowledge" with Keynes' term "body of evidence." Hald adds, "The distinction between objective and subjective probability was [also] formulated clearly by Cournot (1843...)" (Hald 2003: 246).

Finally, I shall make a distinction between the mathematics and the philosophy of Keynes' theory of probability, only to set it aside. Vincent Barnett says, "...Keynes' book was soon made almost completely obsolete as a mathematical theory of probability by the publication of A. N. Kolmogorov's groundbreaking *Foundations of the Theory of Probability* in 1933, which pioneered a comprehensive set-theoretic approach to the subject" (Barnett 2013: 121). Barnett concludes that "it would not be too far from the truth to suggest that" Keynes' *Treatise* is now "mainly valuable for" what it has to offer "outside of mathematics" (Barnett 2013: 121, Barnett's emphasis). This is a mathematical criticism and does not concern Keynes' philosophical theory. In fact, even Barnett finds the philosophical theory "valuable" (Barnett 2013: 121).

Ramsey's Subjectivist Theory of Probability

Keynes' theory was criticized in turn by the brilliant young Cambridge mathematician Frank Plumpton Ramsey, whom Keynes and Russell knew well (Harrod 1951: 320–21). Ramsey champions the subjectivist theory of probability, which may be found in his *The Foundations of Mathematics*, posthumously edited and published in 1931 (see Skidelsky 1994: 67–73). Ramsey criticizes Keynes for relying on logical intuitions which nobody could intuit. Ramsey cannot discover such intuitions in himself, and finds that other people's supposed logical intuitions conflict with each other (Ramsey 1931: 161–63). Ramsey abandons objectivism concerning the probabilities of specific events' occurring, and cashes out the rationality of our probabilistic beliefs about specific events in terms of their pragmatic success (Ramsey 1931: 171ff). Specifically, he cashes out subjective belief in terms of observable willingness to make bets (Ramsey 1931: 172, 183).

Ramsey admits two basic requirements: (i) not allowing Dutch book, that is, not allowing betting against your own bet; and (ii) general overall "consistency" in the learning process of making successful bets (Ramsey 1931: 176–83; see Skidelsky 1994: 70–71; Bateman 1991: 59–61; Davis 1991: 99–100; Braithwaite 1975: 240–41). As to requirement (ii), Ramsey holds that in the long run, such a program would *approximate* objective probabilities (Ramsey 1931: 182–83).

Subjectivism dates back at least to Venn, if not also to Augustus De Morgan (Venn 1964; Mares 1997). I think that Jeremy Bentham, whom Ramsey cites, anticipates subjectivism by construing probability in terms of tendencies of facts to produce convictions in the mind, and by construing probability ultimately in terms of its utility (see e.g. Bentham 1827: 1, *pace* Ramsey 1931: 173). As a utilitarian, Bentham's basic approach "is the utilitarian one of allowing all rationally helpful evidence to be considered by the tribunal of fact, subject to guidance as to its weight," notably in his major work *Rationale of Judicial Evidence* (Murphy 2008: 8). This too is subjective in the sense that utilitarianism cashes out values in terms of pleasures and pains. I shall not attempt to determine the ultimate origins of subjectivist probability here; the first utilitarians in any case were the ancient Epicureans.

Ramsey's theory avoids some major difficulties with the other theories. As long as people are willing to bet, it does not matter whether the events are uniform or unique, nor whether they are more frequent in less relevant classes and less frequent in more relevant classes. Those were the main difficulties with the frequency theory. And Ramsey obviously does away with logical intuitions, the mysterious and often conflicting relations basic to Keynes' theory.

I shall offer five criticisms of Ramsey.

First, there cannot be a learning process for unique events. This kills Ramsey's second basic requirement.

Second, on his own admission, Ramsey's program is only a theory of mathematical *approximations* to probability. But how could we know whether his program approximates objective probabilities in the long run, unless we already know what the objective probabilities *are*? And if we already know them, then why should we be satisfied with mere approximations, when we already have the thing itself? It would be like returning to the shadows in Plato's cave after being out in the sunlight. Like the imitative poets Plato criticizes, Ramsey is a mere imitator of, or approximator to, the real thing.

Third, if my first criticism is correct, then the question is, What *is* the true theory of probability? That is, which theory of probability best describes the objective probabilities to which Ramsey's subjective probabilities merely approximate? It cannot be, of course, Ramsey's own theory, since we need an objective theory, not a subjective approximation. Even worse, we do not want Ramsey to be approximating to himself. Curiously enough, Ramsey himself appears to answer this question. He says, "And the answer is that it will in general be best for his degree of belief that a yellow toadstool is unwholesome to be equal to the proportion of yellow toadstools which are in fact unwholesome" (Ramsey 1931: 195). Thus Ramsey appears to admit the frequency theory as the true theory of objective probabilities, to which his subjectivist theory approximates. But even if that is not the case, my criticism remains.

Fourth, Ramsey is right that our ostensibly logical intuitions about probabilities often conflict, and that this casts doubt on their reliability. But it is a *non sequitur* to infer from this that such logical intuitions do not *exist*. Evidence is often conflicting and doubtful no matter what our theory of probability is. In particular, I see no reason why our probability intuitions would be either more or less conflicting or doubtful than our sense-perceptions. Eyewitnesses are notoriously conflicting and unreliable. Does it follow that sense-perceptions do not exist? Does it follow that there are no sense-perceptible objects such as trees? Ramsey's criticism even applies to his own theory. Our bets are often conflicting and doubtful, and at least as much as our logical intuitions. This includes bets across persons, bets across time for the same person, and cases where one person at one time is internally conflicted on how to bet. In fact, if we all always bet the same way, there would be no games of chance, and far less conflict in human affairs. Life would be very different from what it is. Thus Ramsey's theory is no better than the others in this regard. Namely, on his own criticism, we *ought* to conclude that bets do not exist any more than logical intuitions do. That bets obviously *do* exist is intended by Ramsey to avoid the problems he raises with logical intuitions. But ironically, it is a counterexample to his criticism that what is conflicting and doubtful does not exist. is This may be called Ramsey's gambling problem. Of course, it is not a counterexample to his criticism that he is unable to apprehend any such logical intuitions; my next criticism will address that issue.

Fifth, it has been long noted that we cannot apprehend *any* relations as if they were objects, but only as they occur in relational situations. Whether the relations are specifically logical intuitions or other relations of apprehension does not matter in the least to the general problem. On this general level of our being unable to apprehend any relations at all, Ramsey's criticism of Keynes is not on the appropriate level of depth. For on this level, his criticism would apply not just to Keynes' theory in particular, but to all theories across the board which admit relations, including any other probability theories. Indeed, Ramsey's criticism applies to his own admission of deductive logical relations. It seems that on his own view, he can apprehend deductive logical relations such as modus ponens, but cannot apprehend inductive logical relations such as probability relations. Of course, he can consistently admit the intuition (what else could it be?) of deductive logical relations which are abstract entities, and reject both the intuition of and thereby the abstract entityhood of nondeductive logical relations, since the two sets of relations are mutually exclusive. But that is very awkward. indeed. For all logical relations belong to the same metaphysical and cognitive category. I do not see how he is entitled to admit that we can intuit deductive logical relations, but not nondeductive logical relations.

That deductive logical intuitions are often exact and agreed upon, while nondeductive logical intuitions are often inexact and conflicting, is a fig leaf. The leaf is the word "often." Nondeductive logical intuitions are often neither inexact nor conflicting. And there are plenty of deductive logical intuitions which are both conflicting and doubtful. Just look at any subtle logic paper. My own (2015: ch. 9) is all about the conflict between two entire families of logical intuitions about which deductive logics to count as reliable logics at all. On his own arguments, is Ramsey going to reject deductive logical intuitions and approximate to deductive logical relations by betting on them in a learning process?

All the criticisms given so far have nothing to do with the question whether probabilities are logical, or are to be assimilated to deductive logic, or approach to logical necessity as an asymptote. For even if we reject the view that probability relations belong to the specific category of logical relations, all the problems would remain. For all these relations are intellectual and abstract in general, and that is enough for my criticisms to succeed.

Sixth, making Dutch book logically can be and often is just as objective and rational as making non-Dutch book. Some Dutch oddsmakers can be and often are rationally better than others. For example, suppose five horses are in a race, and ten oddsmakers, who are the only oddsmakers available, all offer different odds. Each horse is favored to win by exactly two of the oddsmakers. Smith makes Dutch book by placing bets on each horse to win with the first set of five oddsmakers, each of whom has picked a different horse to win; and Jones does likewise with the second set. Clearly Smith could consistently make a better profit, or at least avoid a greater loss, over time than Jones. If it aids the imagination, we may suppose that Smith places bets with amateur oddsmakers who are just starting on their own learning curve, and Jones with seasoned experts. That is to say, if we flip around from Ramsey's negative requirement *not* to allow Dutch book to be made *against* yourself, to cases where you *must* allow Dutch book to be made against you by *someone*, it would be objectively far better to be a Smith betting against inept oddsmakers than a Jones betting against good ones, because you would probably make more money, or at least lose less.

I have been describing an example which applies directly and reflexively to the Dutch book aspect of Dutch book bets. But it is easy to see that how good the horses are is the other main factor.

So, why does Ramsey insist on his requirement (i)? That is, why is he so against Dutch book? Why does he think it would not have just the same sort of objective learning curve as non-Dutch book? Why would he not think a theory of probability ought to apply to Dutch probabilities just as much as to non-Dutch ones?

I suggest that it is just as basic to objective probability theory to explain how to minimize your guaranteed losses, as it is to explain how to maximize your non-guaranteed gains. That is to say, Dutch and non-Dutch bookmakers alike ought to have the objective rationality of their bets grounded in the same general theory of objective probability. And while such a general theory logically could be a "mixed" theory, using, say, frequency theory to explain Dutch objective probabilities and using Keynes to explain non-Dutch objective probabilities, that would be very odd if all the bets were on the same thing, say, if they were all on the very same horse race. It is easy to see why we might consistently use Keynes for *horse races* and frequency theory for *roulette*, since these are mutually exclusive categories, and since racing odds (not: bets) are typically conflicting and doubtful, while roulette odds are typically uniform and clear. But if all the betting is on horse races, then there simply *is* no difference between Dutch and non-Dutch objective probabilities, except for the mere fact that the Dutch ones are Dutch and the non-Dutch ones are not. Of course, it could sometimes be that some particular horse race is very predictable and some roulette wheel is not. But the whole idea of a mixed theory of probability is to use appropriate theories for appropriate situations, typically frequency theory for uniform events and some other theory for anomalous or unique events. For unique events, Keynes seems best. By definition, unique events are not what is usually the case. That all events might be unique does not detract from this point. And per my first criticism, there is no learning curve for unique events. That all events might be unique does not detract from this point either.

Of course, there can be a huge area between strictly unique events and strictly uniform events. Perhaps we could have a three level theory with frequency theory for uniform events, Ramsey's theory for fairly anomalous events for which there is a learning curve, and Keynes' theory for unique events, or at any rate for events sufficiently anomalous that there can be no learning curve. Intuitively, that seems rather satisfying. For it appeals to all of the reasonable, ordinary intuitions that each of the three theories appeals to, and always in the situations appropriate to each theory. But if Keynes is good enough for unique events, why not also for anomalous events, or even for all events?

It emerges that there are at least three senses of objectively "coherent" or "consistent" betting on a learning curve over time. First, there is Ramsey's sense, in which making Dutch book is prohibited. Second, there is the opposite sense. in which making Dutch book is the only type of bet available. Here the learning curve can involve not only the odds of a horse winning, but the odds of the oddsmakers' competency. But that could also be a factor where Dutch book is prohibited. Third, there is the most general and in that sense deepest sense, in which it is coherent or consistent to pick a strategy that maximizes profit and minimizes loss for all bets in general, regardless of whether they are Dutch.

More deeply, this means that there are three different senses or kinds of objective, rational betting probabilities. Ramsey's is one of the two shallow and limited ones, and the third is the deepest and most general one, since it is the genus of which the first two kinds are species. And surely we ought to pursue the deepest and most general theory. This leaves out Ramsey practically by definition. But Keynes' theory should apply to Dutch book just as well as to non-Dutch book, and so should frequency theory. And perhaps that is why those two theories make no prohibitions against Dutch book. In any case, those two theories' not making Dutch book a factor makes them in that sense more general than Ramsey's, and in that sense deeper. Here we seem to have an argument for a general level mixed theory consisting of Keynes' theory and frequency theory. Theoretically we could add Ramsey at the lower level of non-Dutch book bets; but why should we?

We can see now that by prohibiting Dutch book, Ramsey is picking one conception of consistency or coherence, and one conception of objective rationality, over others, and is picking an essentially limited conception: it is limited by that very prohibition.

Perhaps the most general level can be Ramseyan, even if it cannot be Ramsey's theory. That is, perhaps we can make Ramsey's theory fully general by (a) dropping the Dutch book requirement, (b) keeping only the general consistency requirement, and (c) interpreting that requirement in terms of the third and most general sense of consistent rational betting strategy. On such a fully general Ramseyan theory, making Dutch book on yellow toadstools would approximate exactly as well to the actual frequency of healthy toadstools in the long run as making non-Dutch book. If it aids the imagination, we may suppose that our Dutch bookmaker gradually moves in a Ramseyan rational learning process from novice to veteran in choosing which sets of toadstool oddsmakers to place bets with. But even this fully general Ramseyan theory would still face my first four objections. (This sense of "fully general" probability theory must not be confused with Russell's sense of "fully general" statement, which means that the statement consists only of variables and logical constants.)

Economic theory is largely based on probability, as Keynes and Ramsey well know. And people face win-win and lose-lose life choices perhaps at least as much as win-lose. I am tempted to suggest that most of the people in this world face more choices of the least among evils than brilliant young academicians protected from the world in their Cambridge ivory tower, and that perhaps this is why it never occurred to Ramsey that exactly the same probability theory can and must apply to the choices of the masses, as to the choices of the more fortunate few who can often actually *win* or lose, or even choose the best among good outcomes. There might even be some truth in that, but I decline to make such a judgment, because we are all human and we all have problems, even those who are in the so-called ivory tower. Ramsey in particular died young, and I am sure there were some lose-lose choices there. Not only that, but he was sympathetic to the unfortunate. My suggestion is simply that the general sort of probability theory that covers *all* of our life choices, be they win-lose, win-win, or lose-lose, is best. Please note that of these three sorts of choices, two are of the Dutch book *sort*; we might call win-win "*converse* Dutch book." Of course, there are also "break even" choices where all the odds are even; but we cannot have a rational theory of them precisely because there is no reason to prefer one choice over another. This is the problem of Buridan's ass, who is equidistant from two equally good piles of hay, and who dies of starvation because it has no reason to prefer one pile to the other. This is Buridan's counterexample to the principle of sufficient reason, which states that everything has a reason. Hegel goes so far as to say that where a rational parliament cannot find a reason to prefer one policy over another, meaning a reason good enough to prevail by rational vote, it is perfectly fine to have a constitutional monarch whose sole function is break tie votes, even by arbitrary whim, precisely because it does not rationally matter. Of course,

Hegel is one of the most ironic of thinkers. I am sure he is well aware that one might just as well flip a "monarch coin."

Another way to put my sixth criticism is this. Just like the probability calculus, a probability theory must apply in all possible worlds. For probability theories interpret the probability calculus, which is a branch of mathematics; and mathematics is true in all possible worlds. Now, in some possible worlds there are only lose-lose choices, in others only win-win, in still others, only win-lose, and in still others, some mix of these choices; and the rest have no probability choices at all. We may respectively call these five sorts of worlds: Dutch book worlds, converse Dutch book worlds, non-Dutch book worlds, mixed worlds, and non-probability worlds in which all events are either known to be determined or known to be capricious. Ramsey's theory fails the possible worlds test because it fails to apply to the first two of these five sorts of possible worlds. But it can be fully generalized so as to pass the test, simply by doing away with any reference to Dutch book. At least, it will then pass the test with respect to my sixth criticism; but I also offered five other criticisms. Please note that a mixed probability theory must apply in all possible worlds, but its disjuncts need not do so. Within a mixed theory, worlds of uniform events would be best for frequency theory, and Keynes' theory would be best for worlds of unique events.

My criticisms of Ramsey are not intended to be conclusive. I think they are right as far as they go; but there is more to Ramsey that is beyond the scope of this book. See Zabell (2005: 126–34).

Much like Keynes', Ramsey's mathematics is out of date (Zabell 2005: 131–34 discussing Bruno de Finetti). And just as with Keynes, Ramsey's philosophical interest is unaffected by this.

This concludes my survey of the main probability theories. There are many different technical probability theories, and as far as I can see, there logically can be indefinitely many.[4]

The Ontological Locus of Probability

Each of the three main probability theories just discussed assigns probability to a radically different ontological *locus*. This in itself is food for thought.

Aristotle's frequency theory locates natural or empirical probabilities in the natural world, or in classes of natural things.

Keynes' logical theory places all probabilities in a timeless Platonic realm. They are timeless relations among what can only be timeless propositions.

Ramsey's subjectivist theory locates probabilities within ourselves. They are our dispositions (our willingness) to bet, as modified over time into a learning curve based on our rewards (bets won) and punishments (bets lost). This is classic psychology of reinforcement theory with positive and negative reinforcements.

We may add that Hume's skepticism locates probability as being nowhere. But Hume's theory of causation assigns a mixed location to causation, partly in nature (constant conjunction) and partly in ourselves (habitual expectations). Perhaps then Hume could have assigned probability the same mixed location, partly in nature (frequent conjunction) and partly in ourselves (less habitual expectations).

The main food for thought on this level is this. Shakespeare may be right that our faults lie "not in the stars, but in ourselves." But can we seriously think that the likelihood that the sun will rise tomorrow lies in ourselves, and not in the star and its planet?

2

History of Relevance in English Evidence Law

I shall argue that Keynes' theory that probability is degree of logical relevance most likely originates from evidence law, and that therefore Russell's theory most likely does too, indirectly through Keynes.

The main argument of the present book may be stated as a syllogism. (1) From 1912 *Problems of Philosophy* on, Russell's theory of probability originates from Keynes and is fundamentally that of Keynes. This is both accepted in the literature (Skidelsky 2005: 286; Monteiro 2001: 66) and fairly obvious from a "smoking gun" acknowledgment by Russell in the book's preface (PP vi), not to mention from the nature and timing of Russell's theory. (2) The circumstantial case is overwhelming that Keynes' theory of probability originates in turn from Anglo-American evidence law and is fundamentally that of Anglo-American evidence law. This is except for Keynes' Platonic realism, which originates from and is basically the same as that in Russell's *Principles*. (3) Therefore, the circumstantial case is overwhelming that except for its Platonic realism, Russell's theory of probability indirectly originates from Anglo-American evidence law through Keynes, and is basically that of Anglo-American evidence law. Premiss (2) and conclusion (3) are new to the study of Russell on probability, and bring it to a new level of depth and understanding.

Keynes admired English evidence law. He praised judges for understanding that probabilities can rarely be assigned exact numerical values. He clearly wished to conform his theory of probability to the law in this regard (Keynes 1962 / 1921: 24–27). Perhaps then Keynes developed his theory of logical relevance from evidence law as well. But how? And from what sources?

Leading scholars on the legal origins of probability, such as Barbara Shapiro and Ian Hacking, have nothing to say about the legal origins of logical relevance. Shapiro's *Probability and Certainty in Seventeenth-Century England: A Study of the Relationships between Natural Science, Religion, History, Law, and Literature* has nothing on point (Shapiro 1983). Shapiro's second book, *"Beyond Reasonable Doubt" and "Probable Cause": Historical Perspectives on the Anglo-American Law of Evidence*, and Hacking's book, *The Emergence of Probability: A*

Philosophical Study of Early Ideas about Probability, Induction and Statistical Inference trace the legal origins of probability theory back to Roman law and canon law (Shapiro 1991: 235–55; Hacking 1978: 85–91). But these excellent books do not even attempt to trace the origins of Keynes' theory of probability as degree of logical relevance, or to trace the origins of logical relevance as it is understood in *Federal Rules of Evidence* Rule 401 and similar rules today. To his credit, Peter Murphy, in *Murphy on Evidence*, sect. 1.4.1, "Nature of probability in judicial reasoning," says, "Among the more important older contributions [is] J. M. Keynes, *A Treatise on Probability*" (Murphy 2008: 6 n.17). But even Murphy mentions Keynes only on probability, not on logical relevance.

Perhaps the leading scholars have nothing to say because there simply *is* no theory of probability in the old legal treatises, except for some remarks about the "common course of events" which suggest the frequency theory offered by Aristotle and Venn. The frequency theory is the chief historical rival to Keynes' theory, as Keynes was well aware (Keynes 1962 / 1921: 92ff.). In contrast, Keynes interprets degrees of probability as degrees of intuited logical relevance—as Platonically real logical relations among propositions describing evidence and propositions describing what the evidence is evidence for. I very much doubt that in general, Anglo-American evidence law can be saddled with an extreme metaphysical realism of this sort. Only evidence law's superficial, syllogistic deductive format for probability arguments might appear to be Platonically real, and even then only for any metaphysical realists in the crowd. But in any case, since the leading scholars do have nothing to say on our topic, we are left to investigate on our own.

My primary aim is to document the extent, substantially and in detail, but not comprehensively or exhaustively, of the Anglo-American evidence law literature on probabilistic logical relevance before Keynes wrote on the topic. To this end, it is more important what was published when, and how available it was to Keynes, than who wrote it. Thus I shall not care whether a text is a plagiarism, or written "with" someone, or even posthumously published, so long as Keynes could have read it before he develop-ed his theory.

I shall focus mainly on law treatise writers in the modern period. For our purposes, this period starts with John Locke, since Descartes is not an origin of logical relevance in evidence law. I shall only briefly mention or discuss ancient and medieval legal sources, so as to give a minimal sense of historical perspective.

I mainly want to show the development of the concept of probabilistic relevance in the evidence law, so as to show that historically speaking, this is probably where Keynes got the idea. I also want to give something of the flavor of the concerns the law had with relevance, so as to see *why* relevance developed as a major topic in the law, and eventually as the most fundamental concept of evidence in law today. But for the most part, I shall omit explaining minor technical points in the texts to follow, and let the legal literature speak for itself on the main points in which we will be interested. I hope the few comments I do make will help philosophers identify and understand the main legal issues. I hope at least that they will learn more about the modern history of evidence law than they knew before. But they will not learn as much as they would from legal scholars who devote their careers to that subject.

Two legal scholars, J. L. Montrose and William Twining, give fine introductions to evidence law in this period (Montrose 1992 / 1954; Twining 1994: ch. 3; and much more briefly, Twining 1985: ch. 1). Their introductions basically agree on the main points. In fact, Montrose's 1954 paper is reprinted in Twining's and Alex Stein's 1992 anthology, *Evidence and Proof*. In what follows, I follow Montrose and Twining closely. I disagree only with their interpretation of Geoffrey Gilbert and William Best. For I find that Gilbert and Best have a relevant evidence rule, and they deny that.

I also recommend a fine introduction to modern evidence law that was written at the end of the period itself by an active participant. This is Courtenay Peregrine Ilbert's article on evidence law in the 1902 *Encyclopedia Britannica* (Ilbert 1902). And perhaps the best introduction specifically to logical relevance in evidence law is still George F. James, "Relevancy, Probability and the Law" (James 1941). This too is reprinted in Twining and Stein, eds. (1992). James wrote well after the period I discuss, but his championship of logical relevance was instrumental in America's adopting that concept as fundamental in *Federal Rules of Evidence* Rule 401.

My aim is not to provide a full history of modern evidence law, nor even of the topic of logical relevance within modern evidence law. My aim is only to provide sufficient evidence for my claim that it is more probable than not that Keynes' concept and terminology of logical relevance came from the legal tradition. To this end, I will err on the side of abundance. Certainly, I would not like to understate my case! But my task is only to prepare a review of this area good enough for its purpose, which is to show how much more likely it is that Keynes acquired his conception of probability as relevance from the legal community than from anywhere else, including from his own inventive mind. This last alternative is the main account accepted today, and the main rival to my own. Its chief proponent is Robert Skidelsky, who is in my opinion the world's best Keynes historian.

Moore is the point of departure proposed by this main rival account. It appears to be Skidelsky's view that Keynes read Moore's book *Principia Ethica*, was horrified by Moore's account of probability, though praising and accepting almost everything else, and basically went on to develop his own theory of probability all by himself. Thus Skidelsky's view is not at all that Moore was the origin of Keynes' theory, in the positive sense that Moore held that probability is degree of relevance, and Keynes came to agree with him. Skidelsky's view is that Moore is the origin only in the negative sense that Keynes felt that Moore's work was inadequate, and that this inspired Keynes to work out his own original theory.

Skidelsky is well aware of the many sources Keynes cites in his *Treatise* for many of his views about probability. But Skidelsky has nothing to say about the origin of Keynes' theory that probability is degree of logical relevance, except that it sprang out of Keynes himself, like Athena from the head of Zeus. In contrast, my view is that the origin is like the actor's phony deus ex machina on the stage, where it merely looks like a god is rising up onto the stage all by himself, and the real work is done by someone else hidden under the stage, whose machine is lifting the actor up.

Skidelsky is a wonderful scholar, and the learning has been almost entirely on my side. I greatly appreciate all his books on Keynes. However, I disagree with Skidelsky on this one point of origin. For I think that the legal literature is the probable origin of Keynes' theory that probability is degree of relevance. Naturally, most people outside the legal profession would not know anything about this. And this includes most, if not all, Keynes and Russell scholars. And such a legal origin is far from clear from Keynes' *Treatise* itself, even if you know where to look. So, much research will be involved. The case for my view will take time to present.

There is a sharp divide in professional training on "logical relevance" between philosophers and attorneys. The studies appear to be completely different, and the term appears to have completely different meanings. Philosophers study deductive logical relevance as it is discussed in my 2015: ch. 9; 2012; 2010). They study systems of formal logic, and try to paraphrase the inferences found in ordinary talk, science, or elsewhere, into those formal systems. But lawyers study logical relevance as the most basic concept of probabilistic evidence. Evidence law would be the first thing even a mere law student would think of as a possible origin of Keynes' term "logical relevance." For Keynes is concerned with probabilistic evidence, and the evidence law concept is basically the same as Keynes'. Keynes, of course, reconciles the two studies by making deductive relevance the asymptote of probabilistic relevance. And I further reconcile them by noting that both are mere species of the genus of objective rational relation or connection. But the argument needs developing. How could it be likely, or even possible, that Keynes knew anything about evidence law? He is famous for philosophy and economics, and not in the least for law. Where is the connection between Keynes and evidence law?

I shall discuss only the general concepts of probabilistic relevance and of admissibility of evidence. I shall not discuss more limited and specific concepts of relevance, such as doubtful relevance or conditional relevance, or more limited and specific concepts of admissibility, such as limited admissibility or weight of the evidence as a factor in determining admissibility. See Murphy (2008: 31–33) for a description of those more limited concepts.

I shall present my sources basically in a historical time line of authors by date of publication. The time line is accurate for the sources I use. I omit many works, and many editions of the works I discuss. I believe further research is not needed, and would only strengthen my case. Just as with fossils, so any earlier finds would only push my time line further back in time, and any other finds would only show the widespread flourishing of logical relevance in evidence law even more.

For these reasons, I would be the first to admit that my presentation of the modern history of evidence law is incomplete. I am only pointing out that a complete presentation is not my aim.

I shall start with the earliest works we will consider. Since they are the most remote from our own time, they can be the most difficult and obscure. I hope they may at least become clearer in retrospect when we come to the nineteenth century materials.

I shall discuss all or nearly all the great names of modern evidence law: Edward Coke, Geoffrey Gilbert, William Blackstone, John Morgan, Samuel March Phillipps, Thomas Starkie, William Mawdesley Best, Jeremy Bentham, Simon Greenleaf, John Pitt Taylor, James Fitzjames Stephen, James Bradley Thayer, and John Henry Wigmore, plus a few more to round out the picture.

I shall often specify which bar an author belongs to. This may help to give some geographic sense of the spread of the talk of relevance across the Anglo-American world. But that is not my main reason for doing so. In fact, far from giving a good sense of the spread, the bars are mostly just English or American. And I am really interested only in the four English bars, or as I may as well say, the four London bars: The Inner Temple, The Middle Temple, Gray's Inn, and Lincoln's Inn. I am interested most of all in the Inner Temple. For Keynes was a member of the Inner Temple, dined there a few times, and presumably had access to the law library. And most of the law treatise writers I discuss were also members of the Inner Temple. I think this significantly increases the likelihood that Keynes acquired the concept of logical relevance from evidence law. Indeed, he may well have learned of it directly from fellow members of the Inner Temple. If he even mentioned at lunch that he was interested in probability, by way of introducing himself and his chief interests to the lawyers dining with him, surely it would have been the first thing they told him. Certainly it would have been the most relevant.

The History of Logical Relevance in Evidence Law

I turn now to the history of evidence law, and mainly to modern Anglo-American evidence law, on the topic of relevance. I shall present an extremely brief sketch of this history. Even this single topic is a huge area that would take several books to cover. I shall mainly concentrate on the nineteenth century, that is, on the legal literature that was flourishing just before Keynes came along.
Twining says:

> The study of...[the logical aspects of] evidence and proof in forensic contexts....can be traced back all the way to classical rhetoric,....from Corax of Syracuse in the 5th century BC. [The intellectual history of] inductive logic [is] inextricably bound up with the long and complex story of rhetoric as an academic subject[, and] part of the trivium of logic, grammar and rhetoric. (Twining 1994: 4)

Douglas Walton says:

> The notion of relevance in argumentation has ancient roots, both in the classical *stasis* theory of Greek rhetoric, and in the Aristotelian theory of fallacies (Walton 2005: 116, Walton's emphasis, cites omitted)

Socratic dialectics or eristic might be called higher forensics. Indeed, law schools today often pride themselves on using what they call the Socratic method.
I turn now to England. For the most part, I shall omit the influence of ancient Roman or medieval canon (church) law on English law. Historically, one would expect canon law in England to flourish in the Middle Ages, and Roman law to be studied in England in the Renaissance as part of the general influx of Greek and Roman texts.
Frederick Pollock and Frederic William Maitland say of the old Anglo-Saxon law, "Trial of questions of fact, in anything

like the modern sense, was unknown. Archaic rules of evidence make no attempt to apply any measure of probability to unknown cases" (Pollock 2010 / 1898: 43 citing Brunner 1887). "Oath was the primary method of proof, an oath not going to the truth of specific fact, but to the justice of the claim or defense as a whole" (Pollock 2010 / 1898: 43).

The first English evidence law treatise, in effect, was by a highly respected medieval judge, Lord Justice Henry (or Henrici) de Bracton (originally Bratton or Bretton) ca. 1210–c. 1268). I say "in effect" because it was not a separate work, but part of his master work, *De Legibus et Consuetudinibus Anglaie* (*On the Laws and Customs of England*). Bracton wrote *De Legibus* no later than 1256, less than two centuries after the Norman Conquest. The evidence law part of it shows no signs of using probable or relevant evidence rules. Bracton was satisfied if twelve lords swore an oath on the justice of a claim or defense. I read once that this was probably a more reasonable approach for the times than one might think, since if you could get twelve lords to agree on anything, it was probably true. He does admit *types* of proof. Probatio duplex is by witnesses viva voce, and probatio mortua is by documents (Eure 1666: 138; Duncombe 1702: 158; 1739: 308; Shapiro 1991: 208). Apparently the lords decide on the proof too. Bracton is widely regarded as the best English legal scholar of the Middle Ages. *De Legibus*, or the four volumes he was able to finish, is regarded as by far the best contemporary account of medieval English law.

There were other early authors besides Bracton. Thomas Blount (1618–1679) posthumously says, in the third edition of his *Law-Dictionary and Glossary*:

> He who peruseth all the *Saxon, Danish*, and *Norman* laws published by *Brompton, Lambard*, and others; and all the antient Books treating of the Common-Law, as *Bracton, Fleta, Glanvill,* &c. will find them very difficult to be understood without the help of this *Dictionary*; for the *Jus Anglorum* of the *Saxons*, the *Danelaga* of the *Danes*, and our *Common Law*, which from thence was collected by the *Normans*, are all delivered in very abstruse and uncommon Words....; and where the *Latin* is plain, the Sense is obscure.... (Blount 1717, To the Reader, Blount's emphasis)

The first two authors Blount lists are John Brompton and William Lambard. "Fleta" is not actually the name of a person, but came to be the nom de plume of the anonymous English author who wrote a law treatise in Fleet Prison (Gaola / gaol / jail de Fleta / Fleet Jail) ca. 1290. It is thought that Fleta was one of several judges imprisoned by King Edward I. Lord Chief Justice Ranulf de Glanvill ca. 1112–1190) is also called Ralph Glanville.

We now come to early modern times. I will not take much time with Locke and the other philosophers. (I already discussed Locke and Leibniz.) Suffice it to say that they studied evidence, and the evidence law writers studied them. Locke in particular was admired by the early evidence law writers. All this is still a little remote for our purposes, and is more in the nature of setting the stage for the legal talk of relevance to come.

Edward Coke

I begin with Sir Edward Coke (1552–1634). I shall discuss him somewhat indirectly. Blount says in his *Law-Dictionary*:

> EVIDENCE (*Evidentia*) is used generally for any proof, be it Testimony of Men, Records or Writings....**It is called Evidence, because thereby the point in Issue is to be made Evident** to the Jury; *Probationes debent esse Evidentes, i.e. perspicuæ & faciles.* See *Coke on Litt., fol.* 283. Blount 1717: pdf file pages 134–35, Blount's italic emphasis, my boldface emphasis)

Coke upon Littleton dates to 1628 (Macnair 1999: 21), or 276 years before Keynes read Moore's book. Blount is not citing Thomas Littleton (de Littleton / de Lyttleton) here (ca. 1415–1481), but Coke's comment on Littleton. Coke's work is not really about Littleton that much; brief quotes are followed by long comments on the laws of England. I take the last sentence to say, "See Sir Edward Coke on Sir Thomas Littleton, folio 283" of *Institutes of the Laws of England.* Per the Inner Temple online site, both Coke and Littleton were members of the Inner Temple. Coke was also a student at Trinity College, Cambridge University, just like Russell; Keynes went to King's College, also at Cambridge University.

Blount's definition may seem little more than a circular definition of evidence as that which makes something evident to someone. But I think that more than this going on here. First, there is a complex relation. Item *A* is evidence just in case there exists an item *B* and a person (or jury) *C* such that *A* makes *B* evident to *C*. The "thereby" indicates that evidence is that *by which* something is shown or made evident to someone. Second and more important for our purposes, evidence is positively characterized as being relevant. It is evidence for the point in issue, as opposed to some extraneous or irrelevant point. Third and also very important to us, the phrase "It is called *Evidence*, because" implies that this is a definition of evidence. It is a statement of what evidence is. It states that to be evidence is to be relevant, that is, to make the point in issue evident (to someone). This definition is a positive characterization. But I think that an exclusionary aspect is implied by the fact that the characterization is definitional. Namely, it is implied that if evidence is not relevant, then it is not evidence.

Even if the definition is circular, that is the least important thing to note. Dictionary definitions are often circular, yet that does not prevent their being useful and illuminating in various ways. The only important thing for us is that the definition defines evidence in terms of relevance, thereby making evidence essentially relevant.

The "Probationes" maxim appears to be relevantist as well. For it appears to be offered as the ground of, or at least as a comment on, the thesis that the word "evidence" means 'that which makes the point in issue evident'.

Per Seymour S. Peloubet (1844–1914), the full and correct maxim is *Probationes debent esse Evidentes, id est perspicuæ et faciles intelligi*, and may be translated, "Proofs ought to be evident, that is, clear and easily understood" (Peloubet 1880: 231 citing "Coke, Litt. 283.a"). As before, "Litt." is Littleton. This maxim might be considered to state the *mode*, or *ideal mode*, of relevance. That is, "Proofs ought to be so related to, or connected to, or so probative of, the point in issue that the relationship, connection, or relevance is evident, that is, clear and easily understood." I take it that clarity and ease of being understood are two very different but related things. For a long and complex proof may be very clear step by step, but still hard to understand because it is complicated. Of course, both clarity and ease of being understood are mere modes of relevance, and not relevance itself, which is a third thing. However, there is a negative limit. If evidence is totally unclear, or impossible to understand, then it is not relevant.

Many things are both clear and easily understood without being relevant. The main relationships of the Eiffel Tower to the pen on my desk are obvious: the Tower is far larger, far heavier, at a certain distance from my pen, and so on. But it is not evidence for anything about my pen. Conversely, a gun thrown into a river after a murder may be very relevant indeed. It may be the murder weapon. But if it is found by chance by a swimmer years later, its relevance might not be clear or easy to understand at all. The swimmer might not even have heard of the murder.

Thus perspicuity ("perspicuous" is sometimes used to translate *perspicuae* in the maxim) and relevance are very different relations. But just as someone who is not swimming well enough is not swimming at all, evidence which is not clear enough is not evidence at all, just as an unintelligible proof is no proof. Thus some minimal clarity, or better, intelligibility, is essential to being evidence. Perhaps that is what Coke, whom Peloubet was citing, has in mind when Coke says posthumously in 1703:

> Evidence, *evidentia*. This word in legal understanding doth not only contain matters of record,...which are called evidences, Instruments [probatio mortua]; but in a larger sense it containeth also Testimonia, the Testimony of witnesses [probatio duplex], and other proofes to be produced and given to a jury, for the finding of any issue joyned between the parties. And **it is called evidence, because thereby the point in Issue is to be made evident** to the Jury. *Probationes debent esse evidentes, (id est) perspicuæ et faciles intelligi.* But let us now return to *Littleton.* (Coke 1703: folio page 283, sect. 485, Coke's italic emphasis, my boldface emphasis)

Again, that seems both relevantist ("thereby the point in issue is to be made evident") and definitional ("it is called evidence, because"). And for Coke, the "Probationes" maxim appears to be relevantist. For he appears to be offering the maxim as the ground of, or at least as a comment on, his view that the word "evidence" means 'that which makes the point in issue evident'. We may now see that the "thereby" also appears to indicate that the mode, or ideal mode, of evidence is evidentness, or obviousness. If I am right, then at least for Coke, that mode, or at least its being the ideal mode, would seem essential to the nature of evidence as well.

One might question whether someone encountering this maxim, and no more, might be led to think of the concept of relevant evidence. I am not sure that is so. First, the term "relevant" is not used. Second, the ordinary understanding of evidentness and evidence, or if you please, obviousness and relevance, are different concepts. I think that very few people, other than those familiar with the history of evidence law, would see any relationship between evidentness and relevant evidence. You would have to know that 'evidence for the point in issue' is legalese for relevant evidence, and you would have to notice that the probationes maxim is being cited in support of the legalese. The size and weight of the Eiffel Tower are evident and obvious, without the Tower's evidently or obviously being evidence for the existence of my pen. But that only shows the difference between a mode as it applies to a thing (the Eiffel Tower) considered in itself, and the same mode as it applies to any evidentiary relation between that thing and another thing (my pen).

I briefly return to Blount, our point of departure for the *probationes* maxim. There is no entry for "relevancy" in Blount's *Law-Dictionary*. Nor would I expect there to be, since the main use of that term comes later in the legal literature. But here we must distinguish between a term and what it means. This is just like deductive relevance in Wittgenstein's *Tractatus*. Wittgenstein does not use the current term "relevant," but surely he is talking about we now call deductive relevance when he speaks of truth-ground *containment* and of *following from*. See my (2015: ch. 9).

The title page says that Blount is "of the *Inner-Temple*."

William Nelson, Samson Eure, and Giles Duncombe

Michael Richard Trench Macnair says:

The first free-standing book on evidence is William Nelson's *The Law of Evidence*, published 1717.[27] Slightly earlier is Sir Jeffrey Gilbert's "Treatise" on *Evidence*[, which] was published [posthumously] as a free-standing book in 1754. There are earlier instances of the general usage. The trial lawyers' manual *Tryalls per Pais*, first published in 1665, had a short chapter on *Evidence* in this sense, elaborated in subsequent editions[29];....

The law of evidence stated in Gilbert and Nelson, and in earlier treatments, and which appears in the cases (which I will call for convenience the 'old law of evidence') had two fundamental elements,

The first, though usually treated second in the sources, is a body of rules about **what evidence will maintain an issue; that is, the substantive relevance of evidence**....To give a couple of examples from the first edition of *Tryalls per Pais*:

> But if a feoffment be pleaded in fee, upon issue non feoffavit modo et forma, a feoffment upon condition **is no evidence, because it does not answer the issue; and wheresoever Evidence is contrary to the issue, and does not maintain it, the evidence is not good.** 11 Hen 3 Feoffments 41....[34]

27. The book is anonymous, and the *National Union Catalogue* offers an attribution to Gilbert. The traditional attribution in England is to Nelson, and the style is most unlike Gilbert's style.

29. The first edition is by S. E. of the Inner Temple; chapter 11 on evidence occupies 18 pages. The second edition by G. D. of the Inner Temple is attributed to Giles Duncombe.....

34. Page 141. (Macnair 1999: 20–23, cites omitted, Macnair's italic emphasis, my boldface emphasis)

Thus Macnair finds a relevance rule in 1665 *Tryalls / Tryals / Trials per Pais / Country / Countrymen / jurymen of one's own country*. That is because Macnair rightly finds it obvious that to "answer" or "maintain" the point in issue is just to be relevant evidence. This is the typical terminology for relevance during the modern period of English law. We saw it in Coke, we see it here in 1665 *Tryalls*, and we will see it repeatedly in the sections to come.

Macnair says the 1665 first edition of *Tryalls* is by "S. E.," or posthumous Samson Eure (d. 1659). Montrose and Twining omit Eure. Macnair attributes the second edition to Giles Duncombe. Thus I think it safe to say that Macnair would find a relevance rule in both editions, since basically the same text Macnair quotes is in both. Macnair says he also finds a relevance rule in Nelson and in Gilbert. I shall not discuss Nelson, but I discuss Gilbert's relevance rule in the sections on Gilbert and Burke.

It seems that for Eure, just as it was for Coke, relevance is necessary to, not to say essential to, or definitional of, evidence. That seems evident from the phrase Macnair quotes from Eure: "is no evidence, because it does not answer the issue." That is, if proposed evidence does not "answer the issue," then it is by that very fact not evidence at all. No doubt "is contrary to the issue," which sounds confusing to modern ears, simply means "does not answer the issue," or as we might say today, "does not concern the issue."

The 1665 *Tryalls* was published 239 years before 1904, the year Keynes read Moore's book and read his first paper on probability to the Apostles. No doubt the fief (land or property) case that Nelson cites is earlier than that, looking to the cite, 11 Hen 3 Feoffments 41.

There is also a 1666 version called *Tryals*. I do not say the 1666 version is a second edition, since the 1666 version does not say it is a second edition. Yet it is not a mere reprint, since the wording is not exactly the same, as the reader will see.

In 1666, the posthumous Eure says in *Tryals per Pais*, Cap. 11, "Evidence," citing Coke:

> Evidence, *evidentia*. This word in legall understanding (saith Coke I. Inst. 283) doth not only contain matters of record,...which are called evidences Instrumenta. But in a larger sense, it containeth also Testimonia, the Testimony of Witnesses, and other proofs, to be produced and given to a Jury for the finding of any Issue, joyned betweene the parties; And **it is called Evidence, because thereby the point in Issue is to be made**

evident to the jury. *Probationes debent esse evidentes (id est) perspicuæ & facile intelligitur.* But let us now returne to *Littleton.* (Eure 1666: 137–38), Eure's roman emphasis given here as italic (the main text is in gothic), my boldface emphasis)

I have already discussed this text in the section on Coke, where it is worded only slightly differently.

Later in this chapter (or "Cap."), Eure says:

But if a Feoffment be pleaded in fee, upon Issue non feoffavit modo et forma, a Feoffment upon Condition *is no Evidence, because it does not answer the Issue; and wheresoever Evidence is contrary to the Issue, and does not maintain it, the Evidence is not good.* 11 H. 3 Feoffments 41. (Eure 1666: 141, my emphasis)

This is on the page that Macnair cites, but is not exactly as Macnair quotes it from 1665 *Tryalls*; I do not mean the use of capital letters, which no doubt Macnair removed editorially. I mean the use of "H." for "Hen". Thus the 1666 version is not a mere reprint. I shall return to the term "contrary to the issue" when I come to Duncombe.

Eure says in the same chapter:

Upon the general Issue, the Defendant may give any-thing in Evidence, which proves the Plaintiff hath no cause of Action, or which doth intitle the Defendant to the thing in question. (Eure 1666: 142)

This is a positive rule that relevant evidence is always admissible on the general issue. Along these lines, Eure also says:

Upon Issue, payment at the day [or] payment before or after the day [is] no Evidence. More 47. but upon Nil debet, *it is good Evidence, because it proves the Issue.* (Eure 1666: 148, my emphasis)

This too is clearly a relevance rule.

Eure also says:

Where the Evidence proves the effect and substance of the Issue, it is good. (Eure 1666: 140)

I call this the substance rule. In the section on Buller, I argue that it is a rule that limits relevant evidence to the substantive merits of the issue. In chapter 13 on verdicts, Eure goes so far as to say:

> If the matter and substance of the Issue be found, it is
> sufficient, though it be against the Letter of the Issue.
> (Eure 1666: 196)

In the margin to the left of the just-quoted text, Eure repeats:

> The Verdict may be against the Letter of the Issue, so
> [long as] the substance is found. (Eure 1666: 196, left
> margin)

The title page of the 1666 *Tryals* says "By S. E. of the *Inner
Temple*,..." The Preface is initialed "S. E." as well.

Macnair says that Duncombe (or Duncomb) was the second
editor of *Tryalls*. Duncombe says:

> The Plaintiff in Bar, that *W.* was seized in Fee of an
> House and Land, *&c.* whereunto he had in Common,...
> on 30th of *March*,...., and the Jury found that *W.* made
> the Lease to Plaintiff on 25 *March*...; and held Plaintiff
> should recover, for tho' this not be the same Lease [with
> respect to its date], yet the **Substance of the Issue is**,
> whether Plaintiff has such a Lease as would entitle him
> to Common, and that he had, and the *Modo & forma* as
> to the rest **is not material**. *Hob.* 72. *Pope* v. *Skinner*.
> (Duncombe 1739: 363–64, Duncombe's italic emphasis,
> my boldface emphasis)

This looks like a substance rule. Duncombe says that in general:

> If the Matter and **Substance of the Issue** be found, it is
> sufficient, though it be against the Letter of the Issue....
>   And generally where *modo & forma* are not of
> the **Substance of the Issue**, there it sufficeth, though the
> Verdict doth not find the precise Issue. (Duncombe
> 1739: 269–70, Duncombe's italic emphasis, my bold-
> face emphasis; see 262 and 271 for other statements of
> this rule)

This is basically the same as Eure.
Another important text for us is:

> ***Evidence which is contrary to that in Issue, or which is
> not agreeable to the Matter in Issue, is not good.***
>   As appears by several cases which you may find
> in the Chapter of Evidence. **As upon the Issue**, Nothing
> passes by the Deed, **you cannot give in Evidence**, that it
> is not your Deed, for this is **contrary to the Issue**, and
> to that which is acknowledged in the Plea by Implica-
> tion. 5 *H.* 4. f. 2.

And so upon Not guilty in Assault and Battery, and Evidence that it was done in his own Defence, is not good.

And so in Debt upon a Bail-Bond, you must plead, That there is not the name of Sheriff in it, & *issint nient son fait*, and **cannot give it in Evidence** upon *Non est factum*, **for it is contrariant**. 3 *E*. 4. 5.

So upon issue of Common appendant, Common *pur Cause de vicinage* is **not agreeable to the Issue**, and **therefore cannot be given in Evidence**. 13 *H*. 7. 13.

Where the Evidence proves the Effect and Substance of the Issue, it is good.

As to prove a Grant or Lease pleaded *simplement*, a Grant or Lease upon Condition, and the Condition executed, **is good; for this proves the Effect and Substance of the Issue**, 14 *H*. 8. 20. So a Promise to the Wife, and the Husband's Agreement proves a Promise to the Husband; and this you may see in many Cases in the Chapter of Evidence. (Duncombe 1739: 469–70, Duncombe's italic emphasis, my boldface emphasis; see 1702: 382)

This is confusingly written. Is Duncombe saying that any evidence against the plaintiff's claim is not good, and that only evidence that proves the plaintiff's claim is good? How then could a plaintiff ever lose? But I am sure he is not saying this, for three reasons.

First, sheer charity in interpretation supposes that even back in the 1600s and 1700s, not only could there be good evidence against a plaintiff's claim, but a plaintiff could lose.

Second, plaintiffs are not even mentioned in the two rules which Duncombe italicizes. Only issues, or matters in issue, are.

Third and decisively, Duncombe equates being *contrary* to the issue with not being *agreeable* to the issue; and agreeing with the *issue* does not mean *proving* as opposed to disproving the issue, but only being *relevan*t to the issue. Likewise, "the evidence is good" can only be read, "the evidence qua evidence is good," or in modern terms, "the evidence is admissible" because it is relevant, i.e., goes to the substance of the issue.

Thus the first rule means, "Evidence which does not agree in content with proving or disproving the issue is inadmissible."

And, just as did Eure, Duncombe says in his editions:

Evidence, Evidentia:....and it is called Evidence, because thereby the point in Issue is to be made evident to the Jury: Probationes debent esse evidentes (id est) perspicue & facile intellegi. (Duncombe 1702: 158; see 1739: 308)

We have now seen this text several times, and evidently as early as Coke in 1628. But what it reports (it is a report) can only be older.

We also find language of "Matter collateral" (Duncombe 1739: 206), "Matter of Surplusage" (Duncombe 1739: 474), and "the Variance" (Duncombe 1739: 472). This is implicitly negative or irrelevantist terminology best discussed later. The basic idea is that if proposed evidence is collateral to the issue, or is surplusage, or is a variance from the substance of the issue, then it is irrelevant. The terms "variance," "surplusage" and "collateral" matters do have different technical legal meanings. Phillipps explains "variance," and Greenleaf explains "surplusage" and "collateral facts," in different ways. But all of these terms concern relevance in one way or another. Phillipps discusses variance as a form of irrelevance, and Greenleaf discusses both surplusage and collateral facts in a chapter entitled "Of the Relevancy of Evidence." The differences among these terms should be duly noted. But for our purposes, the main point is that they all concern relevance in one way or another.

I omit more than I mention on relevance in Duncombe, but I doubt that readers will be interested on pleadings on the general issue or on special matters. Duncombe praises earlier writers such as Mascardus (*De Probationibus*), Fortescue (*De Laudibus*), and Faranacius (*De Testibus*) (Duncombe 1739: To the Practicers of the Law). On the title page of the 1702 gothic print edition of *Tryals Per Pais*, Duncombe is said to be "G. D. of the *Inner-Temple*" (Duncombe 1702). By 1739, he is "Giles Duncombe late of the *Inner-Temple*" (Duncombe 1739).

Geoffrey Gilbert

We come next to Lord Chief Justice of England Geoffrey Gilbert (1674–1726). Many see Gilbert's book as the first English evidence law treatise. It may well have been written before Nelson's, but it was published posthumously some decades later. We may say it was the first major evidence law treatise, both in scope of presentation and in impact on the history of evidence law.

Gilbert was "Lord Chief Baron of the Court of Exchequer from 1722 until his death in 1726" (Twining 1994: 35). Montrose says, "The first substantial exposition of the [modern] law of [English] evidence was by Gilbert" (Montrose 1992 / 1954: 348 / 528). According to Montrose, Gilbert's 1756 *The Law of Evidence* is "largely a digest of case law" whose sole principle of evidence is the best evidence rule (Montrose 1992 / 1954: 348 / 528). Montrose says the 1756 published first edition "was written before 1726" (Montrose 1992 / 1954: 348 / 529 citing E. M. Morgan). Thus, according to Montrose, the theoretical interest of the work is that it attempts to subsume all evidence law under a single rule, the best evidence rule. And that is the received view today.

Gilbert states the best evidence rule as follows:

> The first therefore, and most signal Rule, in Relation to Evidence, is this, That a Man must have the utmost Evidence the Nature of the Fact is capable of; for the Design of the Law is to come to rigid Demonstration in Matters of Right, and there can be no Demonstration of a Fact without the *best evidence* that the Nature of the Thing is capable of. (Gilbert 1754: 4, my emphasis)

I do not think it follows from this text that for Gilbert, the best evidence rule subsumes all evidence law under a single rule. I think it follows at most only that he thinks, perhaps mistakenly, that the rule is the primary and most important rule of evidence law, or at least in his own exposition of evidence law. Even if he intends the rule to apply to all *evidence*, it does not follow that he thinks it subsumes all *rules* of evidence. For there logically might be other rules which, though perhaps less important, also apply to all evidence, and which are logically independent of the best evidence rule. We might then look for any such other rules in evidence law, or even in Gilbert's own exposition. But back to our story.

John H. Langbein quotes and agrees with Twining's view that "'Gilbert tried to subsume all the rules of evidence under a single principle, the "best evidence rule"'" (Langbein 1996: 1173 quoting Twining and citing Twining 1990: 178, 188; this is our Twining 1994). Langbein adds, "The later eighteenth-century writers on evidence, Bathurst and Buller, followed Gilbert's emphasis on the best evidence rule as the organizing principle of the law of evidence" (Langbein 1996: 1173). Langbein says the reason for this is simply that they were primarily concerned with documentary evidence, and primarily with the original document. The quest for evidence was, first and "foremost, a search for the determinative piece of written evidence" (Langbein 1996: 1173 n.21 quoting and citing Landsman 1990: 1149, 1154). Langbein adds, "The preference for written evidence extended back to the Middle Ages, and was particularly apparent in contract and [land] conveyancing" (Langbein 1996: 1183).

Thus it is curious that Langbein says, "The rest of Gilbert's book concerns the sufficiency of evidence" (Langbein 1996: 1174), which sounds like the sufficient weight or probative value, not to say sufficient relevancy, of evidence. Langbein specifies "Gilbert, Evidence [Dublin 1754] at 113–99" as what he means by "the rest of Gilbert's book" (Langbein 1996: 1174 n.25, 27; see 1172, 1172 n.16 for the Dublin 1754 original publication cite). Thus there may be some doubt whether Gilbert is really subsuming all evidence law under the best evidence rule, or whether he finds "sufficient evidence" to be a second basic topic.

Let us abstract for a moment from the law's historical concern with original documents as being the best. In every field, we always want the best *and* the most relevant evidence. And these are not the same, if we mean 'best in intrinsic quality' and 'most relevant to the point in issue'. Yet if we were to speak in ordinary language today of the "best" evidence, I think we would say that the best evidence is the most relevant evidence. If I am right, then I think that for us today, "If anything is evidence, then it is the best evidence if and only if it is the most relevant evidence" would be a synthetic *a priori* truth.

But as Langbein says, this is not at all what Gilbert means. He technically means evidence of the best quality, and he mainly has documents about property in mind. Thus he mainly means that we should admit an original document over a mere copy, or a good copy over a damaged copy. We today might think that there is nothing wrong with that, as far as it goes; but we would scarcely think that all evidence law could be subsumed under such a limited rule. Today, the best evidence rule is just one rule among many: Rule 1002 in the *Federal Rules of Evidence*. (To be fair, *FRE* article 10, entitled "Contents of Writings, Recordings, and Photographs," includes seven other rules as part of this.) The rule "largely withered away in the face of mechanical production" (Macnair 1999: 23). This started with Gutenberg's printing press, and greatly accelerated with cameras, photocopiers, scanners, and emails.

Even on the technical understanding of the best evidence as the original document, or the closest to the original document that we can find, one might still argue for a connection between best evidence and relevant evidence. Namely, the original document is causally the most directly connected, and in that sense the most relevant, document to the matter at hand; and an excellent copy is more clearly, not to say more visibly, causally connected than a poor copy, or possibly even than a very badly damaged original. We may say that a good copy better or more intelligibly "preserves" the causal link of the original document to the matter at hand than a poor copy or a very badly damaged original. But this sort of causal "quality of preservation" relevance logically can be, and often is, overwhelmed by relevance per se. For millions of original documents around the world will be totally irrelevant to a certain local matter, and copies of copies of copies will be far more relevant. For example, the original Declaration of Independence in Philadelphia totally lacks the relevance of even a poor photocopy of my car title to the issue of whether I own the car in my driveway.

Thus the best evidence rule is dimly related at best to the concept of relevance. At most, it relates to relevance only within its own limited sphere of originals, copies, and records and testimonies about documents. We can only say that, *other things being equal*, an original document is causally more directly related to a matter in issue than a copy of that very same document. We can only say that the original, as such, is more relevant with respect to time and with respect to causal proximity.

Twining notes that Gilbert's philosophical hero is John Locke, and quotes Gilbert's quotation of Locke on the admission of degrees of probability which fall short of demonstration (Twining 1994: 36). Montrose, Twining, and Langbein may not know it, but Locke discusses the best evidence rule in his *Essay Concerning Human Understanding*. Locke says:

> ...I think, it may not be amiss to take notice of a rule observed in the law of England; which is, That though the attested copy of a record be good proof, yet the copy of a copy, ever so well attested and by ever so credible witnesses, will not be admitted as a proof in judicature. This is so generally approved as reasonable, and suited to the wisdom and caution to be used in our inquiry after material truths, that I never yet heard of any one that blamed it. This practice...carries this observation along with it, viz. *That any testimony, the further off it is from being the original truth, the less force and proof it has.* The being and existence of the thing itself, is what I call the original truth. A credible man vouching his knowledge of it is a good proof; but if another equally credible do witness it from his report, the testimony is weaker: and a third that attests the hearsay of an hearsay is yet less credible. So that in traditional truths, each remove weakens the force of the proof.... (Locke 1959 / 1690: vol. 2, 377–78, Locke's emphasis)

Locke generalizes the best evidence rule to include all testimony, as well as written records. But Locke does not even appear to reduce all rules of evidence to the best evidence rule. He simply calls it "a rule."

Keynes is well aware of Locke's endorsement of the best evidence rule, quotes Locke, and substantially agrees with Locke, though finding Locke's view "excessive." Keynes says:

> 20. One of the most ancient problems in probability is concerned with the gradual diminution of the probability of a past event, as the length of the tradition increases by which it is established....Locke raised the matter in chap. xvi. bk. iv. of the *Essay Concerning Human Under-*

standing: "Traditional testimonies the farther removed the less their proof....No probability can rise higher than its first original."...." This is certain," says Locke, "that what in one age was affirmed upon slight grounds, can never after come to be more valid in future ages, by being often repeated." In this connection he calls attention to "a rule observed in the law of England, which is, that though the attested copy of a record be good proof, yet the copy of a copy never so well attested, and by never so credible witnesses, will not be admitted in a proof in Judicature." If this is still a good rule of law, it seems to indicate an excessive subservience to the principle of the decay of evidence.

But, although Locke affirms sound maxims, he gives no theory that can afford a basis for calculation. (Keynes 1962 / 1921: 184–85 quoting Locke 1959 / 1690: vol. 2, 377–79)

In his chapter 16 on "fundamental theorems," Keynes discusses Bayes' Theorem and the Principle of Inverse Probability in sections 11–14, and discusses the principle of the decay of evidence in section 20. There is no indication that he regards the principle of the decay of evidence as less fundamental than, much less as a special case of, the principle of inverse probability. And no wonder, since Bayes' Theorem is a same-time analysis, while decay is calculated as a rate over time. Keynes does not give a mathematical analysis of the principle of the decay of evidence, but he says that Arthur "Cayley's [algebraic solution] is correct" (Keynes 1962 / 1921: 185). No doubt, of course, he considers the two principles to be logically consistent. Thus there is no doubt that he can *apply* his analysis of irrelevance, as mathematically formalized in terms of probability, to any given moment in the decay of evidence over time. The mathematical principle of decay can be used to calculate the rate of decay. Strictly speaking, it can be used to calculate not the decay of the evidence itself, but of its probative value. Keynes' definitions of irrelevance can then identify the end point at which the probative value is so diminished that the evidence is no longer relevant, and is thus no longer evidence.

Both Locke and Keynes are well aware of the importance of the principle of the decay of evidence to religious traditions. Keynes dryly says, "'Craig', says Todhunter, 'concluded that faith in the Gospel so far as it depended on oral tradition expired about the year 880, and that so far as it depended on written tradition it would expire in the year 3150'...." (Keynes 1962 / 1921: 184).

For us, the most important thing is that Montrose, Twining, and Langbein claim that Gilbert subsumes or tries to subsume all evidence law under a single evidence rule, the best evidence rule. Gilbert does call the best evidence rule "[t]he first...and most signal rule." (Gilbert 1754: 4). But Macnair, Burke, and I hold that Gilbert also has a relevance rule, and that Gilbert does not even appear to subsume the relevance rule under the best evidence rule. Nor do I think that any such subsumption is conceptually possible.

In 1754, Gilbert says in the posthumous first edition of *The Law of Evidence*, concerning the admission of a prior verdict as evidence in another case:

> If a Verdict be had *on the same Point*, and between the same Parties, *it may be given in Evidence*, tho' the Trial was not had for the same Lands; for the Verdict in such Cases, is a very persuading Evidence, because what twelve Men have already thought of the Fact, may be supposed fit to direct the Determination of the present Jury.... (Gilbert 1754: 22, my emphasis)

Thus, in order to be admissible, evidence must be on point. Gilbert continues:

> But it is not necessary that the Verdict shou'd be in Relation to the same Land, for the Verdict is only set up **to prove the Point in Question,** and if the Verdict arise upon the same question, then 'tis, no Doubt, **a good Evidence,** for *every Matter is Evidence, that amounts to Proof of the Point in Question.* (Gilbert 1754: 23, Gilbert's italic emphasis, my boldface emphasis; see 1805: 25)

Here Gilbert italicizes his relevance rule. However, Gilbert says that the following sort of objection can be made:

> [W]hen a Verdict is produced in Evidence, it may be answer'd, that it *did not arise from the Merits of the Cause,* but from some formal Defect of the Proof, *and that makes it no Evidence, toward gaining the Point in Question....* (Gilbert 1754: 24, my emphasis)

This is Gilbert's substance rule, or merits rule. It is a modification or clarification of his relevance rule. Note that the rule appears to be of the essence of evidence. For a verdict is "no Evidence" at all if it does not concern the "merits" of "the point in question."

Gilbert says more extensively:

> But a private Act of Parliament or any other private Record **may be brought in before the Jury if it relate to the Issue in Question,** tho' it be not pleaded, for **the**

> **Jury are to find the Truth of the Fact in Question,
> according to the Evidence brought before them**, and
> therefore **if** the private Act brought before them, **doth
> evince the Truth of the Matter in Question, it is as
> proper Evidence to the Purpose as any Record or
> Evidence whatsoever.**
>
> [T]he Allegata to the Jury, says *Hobart*, is
> **every thing that may be offered in evidence so
> relating to the Issue....**
>
> ....for tho' this be a private Statute, yet **since it
> relates to the Issue, it may like all other Matters be
> given in Evidence**.... (Gilbert 1754: 32, Gilbert's italic
> emphasis, my boldface emphasis)

Here Gilbert states his relevance rule over and over again. It seems
clear that his term for relevance is "relate" and its cognates.
Gilbert also says:

> [I]f the Wi[t]nesses prove Delivery at another Place than
> where it bears Date, it *doth not warrant the Issue;...and
> therefore no Proof of the Deed in question*....for the
> Place where the Deed was made *is no material Part of
> the Deed*. (Gilbert 1754: 114, my emphasis)

Once again, if the ostensible evidence does not "warrant the issue,"
then it is "no proof" at all. Once again, relevance is the essence of
evidence.
Gilbert also says:

> [W]here the *Issue* [of Infancy, i.e., of not being of legal
> age to make a contract] *relates to* a solemn Contract
> executed with the necessary Solemnities,...that is a *full
> Proof of the Issue* [of whether the contract is to be
> discharged, i.e., voided];.... (Gilbert 1754: 130, my
> emphasis)

Thus Montrose, Twining, and Langbein overlook six passages in
the first edition of Gilbert in which Gilbert states a relevance rule
in various ways. And I see nothing that even appears to suggest that
Gilbert subsumes his relevance rule under his best evidence rule.

This relevance rule was published in the first major English
evidence law treatise 150 years before the 1904 Keynes.

I proceed now to the 1791 edition of Gilbert. In volume 2,
we actually see the word "relevant":

> On an Action of *Slander*, the Defendant may either
> justify, or if he think proper, give in ***Evidence*, under
> the general Issue**, that the Words were spoken by him
> as Counsel, and are **relevant to the Cause**;.... (Gilbert

1791: 617, Gilbert's italic emphasis, my boldface emphasis)

Here we see the word "relevant" as relevance to the point in issue:

> With regard to personal or private Libels, a Bill or Declaration in a legal suit is not to be considered as libellous, though it may import the severest Censure on the Character of the Party, if it be *relevant* **to the Point under judicial Inquiry**. (Gilbert 1791: 640, Gilbert's italic emphasis, my boldface emphasis)

See also:

> ....material to the Point in question. (Gilbert 1791: 640)

Here is the word "relevant" a third time:

> The Perjury must be **in a point** *material*, that is, *relevant* **to the Point in issue**; it is by no means necessary it should be on a point sufficient to decide the Cause [of action]; if it is to any *circumstance* material, as the colour of a coat, in case of an highway robbery, the party thus wilfully swearing false is equally liable as if it were directly decisive on **the point in issue**. (Gilbert 1791: 660, Gilbert's italic emphasis, my boldface emphasis)

Here Gilbert cites Cicero:

> If the Words of the Defendant are false in the only sense in which they **relate to the subject in dispute**,* this is sufficient to convict him of Perjury, though in another sense, **foreign to the issue**, they might be true.
> * *Fraus enim adstringit, non dissolvit, Perjurium.*—Cic. de OFF. III. 32. (Gilbert 1791: 661, Gilbert's italic emphasis, my boldface emphasis)

Gilbert also cites Lord Mansfield:

> Lord Mansfield, in delivering the Opinion of the Court, recognized the Doctrine already stated, that Perjury must be a wilful false swearing on an Oath taken in a judicial Proceeding before a competent Jurisdiction, and **on a Point material** to the question depending. (Gilbert 1791: 662, Mansfield's italic emphasis, my boldface emphasis)

In these texts too, I see nothing that even appears to suggest that Gilbert subsumes his relevance rule under his best evidence rule. If Montrose, Twining, and Langbein do, they owe us an explanation. They provide no evidence for their claim that Gilbert even attempts to subsume all his evidence rules under his best evidence rule, where all his evidence rules include his relevance rule. In fact, I see nothing indicating that they even know he *has* a relevance rule.

The word "relevant" appears to be posthumously added to Gilbert. At least, I did not see it in the (also posthumous) 1754 edition. This is not much of a defense for Montrose, Twining, and Langbein, since there are plenty of other passages that do not use the word, but mean the same thing, and that presumably *are* from Gilbert, in the 1754 edition. But the word "relevant" in the 1791 edition is a major anticipation of Keynes. For the word occurs three times in an edition of the first major English evidence law treatise 113 years before the 1904 Keynes. Note the casual editorial equation of being relevant to / relating to / material to / the point in issue / the subject in dispute. This is typical of the times.

Consider now the 1805 edition of Gilbert. The "smoking gun" text where Gilbert states his relevance rule is in volume 1:

> [E]very matter is evidence, that amounts to the proof of the point in question. (Gilbert 1805: 25)

Also:

> And upon *non est factum*, if the witnesses prove delivery at another place than where it bears date, it does not **warrant the issue**; for this is a testimony contrary to the plain words of the deed, and therefore **no proof of the deed in question**. (Gilbert 1805: 144, Gilbert's italic emphasis, my boldface emphasis; 1760: 162)

See also:

> ....that is a full *proof of the issue*.... (Gilbert 1805: 164, my emphasis; 1760: 186)

And:

> ....nothing can come in proof but the truth of the matter alleged. (Gilbert 1805: 244)

Mercifully, I will cut the quotations short.

The only possible way that I can see for there to be such a subsumption is to say that the best evidence is the most relevant. Then greatest relevance would be a consequence of best evidence.

But this way is not open to us if "best evidence" simply means the original document or the closest thing we can get to the original document. For as we have seen, that is a *non sequitur*. For there are indefinitely many counterexamples in either direction. There are millions of original documents in the world that are irrelevant to any given point in issue, and there are millions of cases where there are far-from-original items of evidence that are far more relevant to the point in issue than most of the original documents in the world. Even worse, on this way out, the implication would be mutual. For the most relevant evidence would be the best. Thus we could equally well subsume the best evidence rule under the relevance rule. And then, if Gilbert really subsumes all his *other* evidence rules under his best evidence rule, then he would also be subsuming all his other rules, *including* his best evidence rule, under his relevance rule! He would be subsuming all evidence law under the relevance rule. And that would be the more rational and illuminating way to go. For what is the use or point in requiring the most original document if it is not the most relevant evidence? But here I depart from scholarship and enter into criticism, not of Gilbert, but of his main interpreters.

For a "smoking gun" citation to Gilbert's relevance rule, see the Burke section below. Macnair does not provide a cite, but is quite correct in saying Gilbert has a relevance rule.

.   Similarly for Best. Much the same scholars claim that Best, too, has only a best evidence rule. But there is a "smoking gun" text for a relevance rule in Best as well, as we shall see.

William Blackstone

Twining omits William Blackstone (1723–1780) from his review of modern English evidence law (Twining 1994: ch. 3, "The Rationalist Tradition of Evidence Scholarship"). Yet Blackstone's *Commentaries on the Laws of England* is widely considered to be the best book ever written on English law. It influenced American common law to remain basically English, and influenced attorneys from the first Chief Justice of the United States Supreme Court, John Marshall, down to the sixteenth President, Abraham Lincoln.

In the 1783 posthumous ninth edition of his *Commentaries*, "with the last corrections of the author," Blackstone says:

> The nature of my present design will not permit me to enter into the numberless niceties and distinctions of what is, or is not, legal *evidence* to a jury.[n] I shall only therefore select a few of the general heads and leading

maxims, relative to this point, together with some observations on the manner of giving evidence.

AND, first, evidence signifies that which demonstrates, makes clear, or ascertains the truth of the very fact or point in issue, either on the one side or on the other; and no evidence ought to be admitted to any other point....

...And the one general rule which runs through all the doctrine of trials is this, that the best evidence the nature of the case will admit of shall always be required, if possible to be had; but if not possible, then the best evidence that can be had shall be allowed. For if it be found that there is any better evidence existing than is produced, the very not producing it is a presumption that it would have detected some falsehood that at present is concealed.

n[.] This is admirably well performed in lord chief baron Gilbert's excellent treatise of evidence: a work which it is impossible to abstract or abridge, without losing some beauty and destroying the chain of the whole.... (Blackstone 1783: 367–68, 367 note n, Blackstone's italic emphasis, my boldface emphasis)

Since Blackstone is discussing existing law, these rules clearly go back earlier than 1783.

In the boldface text, the terms "signifies" and "general rule" suggest that Blackstone is *defining* evidence as being (at least in part) that which is relevant to the point in issue. Thus it is once again *definitional* that evidence must be relevant. The text also suggests that he would find it a *non*definitional, though perhaps also a trivial, obvious, or even self-evident truth, that one ought always to require the best evidence that can be had. (Perhaps he might consider it synthetic *a priori*.) Thus the best evidence rule takes the back seat in Blackstone. This is why he discusses evidence as ascertainment of the point in issue *first* ("AND, first,") and the best evidence rule *second*. Note also that in effect he rejects evidence that does not (help) ascertain the point in issue as inadmissible.

Blackstone was a member of the Middle Temple.

Francis Buller

Francis Buller (1746–1800) says in the 1772 first edition of his *Introduction to the Law Relative to Trials at Nisi Prius*:

The Ninth general Rule is, That if the Substance of the Issue be proved, it is sufficient. (Buller 1772: 294)

Buller repeats this rule in the corrected fourth edition of 1785 (Buller 1785: 299). The title page of each edition says that Buller is "of the Middle Temple."

This rule, which we may call the substance rule, is stated by many authors in many treatises. But is it a relevance rule? This also brings up a more general question: How do we recognize talk of relevance in the legal literature? Or at least, what is the usual terminology used? "Relating to the point in issue" may be easy enough. But these questions might be very controversial concerning the substance rule. However, the substance rule is typically used in conjunction with another rule that *is* clearly concerned with relevance. This other rule is that evidence is to be *confined* to the point in issue. We may call it the confinement rule. The substance rule modifies the confinement rule by saying that you do not have to establish the point in issue exactly and in every last detail, but only substantively. This does impact on relevance in the case. It means you do not have to provide relevant evidence, in the sense of evidence confined to the point in issue, for every detail of the point in issue. Thus it is a sort of scope-limiting rule. But its scope-limiting role is not enough to show that the substance rule itself is a relevance rule. I would say further that in fact the substance rule is not itself a relevance rule, but what we might call a "significant content" rule that concerns the content of the *point in issue* as opposed to the content of the *evidence for* the point in issue. The policy reason for the substance rule is to ensure that people will not lose important cases merely because they fail to provide sufficient evidence to establish some insignificant *part* of the point in issue, e.g., an unimportant mere formality in a contract. Thus the substance rule necessarily, but only indirectly, impacts on relevance as set forth in the confinement rule. The impact is that since you only have to show the substance of a point, you do not need to provide evidence for any insignificant minor aspects, i.e., evidence confined to establishing such minor aspects.

We may say that the substance rule is a relevance rule, but not a relevant *evidence* rule. For when the rule says that we need not provide evidence for insignificant, unimportant, or minor parts of the point in issue, it is really saying that insignificant *parts* of the point in issue are not relevant to the *substance* of the point in issue. Thus, the substance rule is a *sub-issue* or *sub-pleadings* relevance rule.

However, even if the substance rule is not itself a relevant evidence rule, and is only a relevant sub-pleadings rule, it is tightly connected to the confinement rule in the seventh edition.

Buller's posthumous seventh edition was edited by Richard Whalley Bridgman. The following note is now appended to the rule:

> The Ninth general Rule is, That if the Substance of the Issue be proved, it is sufficient. (*a*)
>
> (*a*) As the evidence must be applied to **the particular fact in dispute**, evidence which does not **relate** to the issue, or is [not] in some manner **connected** with it, **cannot be received**. Nor can character be called in question in a *civil* cause, unless **put in issue** by the very proceeding itself, for **every case is to be decided on its own circumstances**, and not to be prejudiced by any matter **foreign** to it. (Buller / Bridgman 1817: 298c; 298c n.(a), Buller / Bridgman's italic emphasis, my boldface emphasis)

I inserted the word "not" in square brackets, since otherwise the point opposite from the obviously intended point would be stated. The language in boldface seems very clearly about relevance. The key terms are "relate to," "connected with," and "foreign to." The language is negative or exclusionary. The note says that unrelated evidence cannot be "received" in the case or be used to "decide" the case. And "particular fact in dispute" is the same as "point in issue." Thus there seems no doubt that Bridgman's Buller not only admits a relevant evidence rule in this note, but takes it to be connected (literally, as a note) in some way to the substance rule.

The relevance rule itself is stated in positive terms: "Every case is to be decided on its own circumstances." As a philosopher, I for one find interesting overtones of relevance in the phrase "its own circumstances," e.g., its "proper" or "appropriate" circumstances. That is, relevant evidence is evidence that is proper or appropriate to the case.

Questions arise. First, why is this note appended to this rule? Is the relevant evidence rule intended to clarify or explain the substance rule as itself being a relevant evidence rule? Or does Bridgman's Buller merely take the relevant evidence rule to be a useful additional point worthy of being included as a note? But if the relevant evidence rule is a mere additional point, and if the substance rule is not to be understood as being itself a relevant evidence rule, then is the relevant evidence rule in the note at least intended to be *related* in some way to the substance rule? Is it, so to speak, intended to be *relevant* in some way to understanding the substance rule? And if so, then is this intent correct or mistaken? My best guess is that Bridgman's Buller merely wishes to remind us that even though it suffices merely to prove the substance of the issue, the evidence we provide must be *relevant* to the substance of the issue.

For our purposes, it does not really matter whether the substance rule is related to the relevance rule in this way. The main thing is the note, not the substance rule it is appended to. That is because it is the note that shows that Bridgman's Buller requires that evidence must be relevant. For it states his relevance rule.

William Murray Mansfield

William Murray Mansfield (1705–1793) was Lord Chief Justice of England and the first Earl of Mansfield. His Bristow v Wright was the leading English case on variances well into the nineteenth century. Mansfield, of course, was far more famous for other decisions, especially in Somersett's Case, where he freed any slave of any country who set foot on English soil. He also did much to make English law less medieval, and more rational and pragmatic.

In 1781, Mansfield says in *Bristow*:

> The distinction is that between that which may be rejected as *surplusage*, and what cannot. When the declaration contains *impertinent* matter, *foreign* to the cause, and which the master on a reference to him would strike out (*irrelevant* covenants for instance), that will be rejected by the court, and need not be proved. But if the very ground of the action is misstated, as where you undertake to recite that part of a deed on which the action is founded, that will be fatal. (Powell 1859: 188 quoting Mansfield in Bristow v. Wright, Dougl. 665, 1 Sm. L. C. 223, my emphasis)

Thus surplusage is matter that is impertinent, foreign, or irrelevant in the *pleadings*. More precisely, surplusage is matter irrelevant to the *intended* pleadings, but unfortunately written in the pleadings themselves. Thus it is a bad part of how the pleadings are written, as opposed to bad evidence for the truth or falsehood of the pleadings. Powell gives two examples of this. "If words which are [1] without meaning, or which [2] have been introduced by mistake, be inserted in pleadings, they will be struck out as surplusage at common law" (Powell 1859: 187). I especially wish to note the use of the term "irrelevant" by a Lord Chief Justice of England in 1781. Compare the section below on Powell on the substance rule.

John Morgan

In 1789, John Morgan, "of the Inner Temple, barrister at law," in his *Essays*, praises John Locke and William Paley for their views on the subject of human testimony:

> ....Lawyers are not the persons who have made observations upon human testimony....The subject hath not escaped the notice of Mr. *Locke*, Mr. *Paley*, and others. The observations of Mr. *Locke* are to the following purport: viz. that there are **several degrees from** perfect *certainty* and *demonstration*, down to *improbability* and *unlikeness,* **even to** the confines of *impossibility*; that there are several acts of the mind proportioned to these **degrees of evidence**, which may be called the degrees of *assent*, from full *assurance* and *confidence*, to *conjecture, doubt,* and *disbelief.*
>
> Human testimony, *i.e.* evidence given by one man to another, can [as such] never produce *certainty....*
>
> In the trial of causes, therefore, those to whom evidence is given, and who are to determine upon that evidence, must judge upon *probability*; *viz.* the highest **degree of probability** must govern their judgment; and it necessarily follows, that they ought to have before them *the best evidence of which the nature of the case will admit:* less is productive of *opinion* and *surmise* only, and does not give the mind entire satisfaction; for if, from the nature of the transaction, it appears that there is further [i.e. better] evidence, which hath not been produced, the non-production affords a presumption that it would have contradicted something which hath already appeared, and perhaps have varied the case essentially; therefore the mind does not acquiesce in less than the utmost evidence whereof the fact is capable.
>
> The preceding RULE must, consequently, be considered as *fundamental* in the law of evidence. (Morgan 1789: marginal p. 3, Morgan's italic and small caps emphasis, my boldface emphasis)

This text shows that Locke is the philosophical source for degrees of probability for Morgan as well as for Gilbert. Morgan expressly states that such talk, at least on the subject of testimony, did not come from lawyers. Morgan says that degrees of probability have *two* asymptotes: perfect certainty at the top, and impossibility at the bottom. Morgan then gives two arguments for the best evidence rule. First he argues that in court, "the highest degree of probability must govern their judgment;" therefore "it necessarily follows that they ought to" use "the best evidence" available. Second, he argues that if the best evidence is not produced, then we have a right to be suspicious why not. This second argument is the usual justification given during these times. However, it is stated on a very general level, and does not mention written documents in particular, though perhaps that is implied by the term "transaction," or is even simply assumed to be understood. Perhaps a transaction implies a contract, and a significant transaction would have a written contract.

Morgan says that the best evidence is "fundamental," but does not say that it is the *only* fundamental rule. (Compare logics or geometries which have several axioms.) This is very curious, since in his first argument he derives it from a more fundamental rule that courts are to be governed by the highest degree of probability. This more fundamental rule might be called an extreme relevance rule. That is in keeping with the times; courts across Europe often set the bar very high for evidence and proof.

Morgan says two pages later:

> According to Mr. J. *Blackstone, L.* III. *c.* 23. **evidence signifies** that which demonstrates, makes clear, or ascertains the truth of the **very act or point in issue**, either on the one side or the other, and **no evidence ought to be admitted to any other point**. (Morgan 1789: marginal p. 5, Morgan's italic emphasis, my bold-face emphasis)

Morgan is referring to Mr. Justice William Blackstone, book ("L." means liber) 3, chapter 23 of the *Commentaries*, which I quoted above. Thus it seems that Morgan expressly follows Blackstone in making the relevancy of evidence definitional. The term "ascertain" might be taken to imply that the evidence must be of the highest probability. In any case, it seems that Morgan finds that evidence is relevant by definition, that it is axiomatic that courts must be governed by evidence of the highest degree of probability, and that it is merely a consequent theorem, derived from this axiom, that courts ought to admit the best evidence possible.

Edmund Burke

Edmund Burke (1729–1797) is famous for his political writings, especially his *Reflections on the Revolution in France*. It is less well-known that he also wrote about evidence law, and was "entered at the Middle Temple" (Mahoney 1955: viii). This is of interest because Keynes wrote "an unpublished hundred-page essay on 'The Political Doctrines of Edmund Burke' which was submitted for the University Members Prize for English Essay in November 1904, duly winning it" (Skidelsky 2005: 96). That is to say, we know that Keynes studied Burke in 1904, the same year that he read his first probability paper to the Apostles.

Twining quotes the 1794 Burke as saying that the rules of evidence law fit "'in so small a compass that a parrot... might...repeat them in five minutes'" (Twining 1994: 34 quoting Burke). Twining admits that we must make "due allowance for... rhetorical exaggeration" here, but does not tarry to describe Burke's views on evidence (Twining 1994: 34).

Edward Coke's Latin maxim is in the 1794 Burke. Burke's version of the maxim, posthumously published in 1852, is:

> *In re criminali*, said the rigourists, *probationes debent esse evidentes et luce meridianâ clariores*; and so undoubtedly it is in matters which admit such proof. (Burke 1852 / 1794: 81–82, Burke's emphasis)

This is in Burke's written "Report, made on the 30th April, 1794, from the Committee of the House of Commons, appointed to inspect the Lords' Journals, in relation to their proceeding on the trial of Warren Hastings, Esquire," under the section heading "Debates on Evidence" (Burke 1852 / 1794: 39; see 38).

The *probationes* maxim, as I noted earlier, might not imply relevance in any obvious way. But Burke has more to say about evidence. He even uses the word "relevant":

> Your committee conceives that the trial of a cause is not in the arguments or disputations of the prosecutors and the counsel, but in the *evidence*; and that **to refuse evidence is to refuse the cause**: nothing, therefore, but the most clear and weighty reasons, ought to preclude its production. Your committee conceives that, when evidence on the face of it **relevant, that is, connected with the party and the charge**, was denied to be competent, *the burden lay upon those who opposed it*, to set for the authorities...wherein the courts have rejected evidence of that nature. (Burke 1852: 76–77, Burke's italic emphasis, my boldface emphasis)

Thus relevant evidence, or evidence "connected with the party and the charge," i.e., the pleadings or cause, is always to be admitted unless "the most clear and weighty reasons" prohibit it. He says:

> Your committee....find that the term evidence, *evidentia*, from whence ours is taken, has a sense different in the Roman law, from what it is understood to bear in the English jurisprudence. The term most nearly answering to it in the Roman, being ***probatio***, proof; which, like the term *evidence*, is a generic term, including **every thing**

> **by which a doubtful matter may be rendered more
> certain** to the judge; or, **as Gilbert expresses it, every
> matter is evidence which amounts to proof of the
> point in question.** (Burke 1853: 78–79 citing "Gilbert's
> Law of Evidence, p. 43," Burke's italic emphasis, my
> boldface emphasis)

This is not only relevantist, but close to Keynes. First, Burke says
that the Roman legal term "most nearly answering to" the English
term "evidence" is "probatio," which connotes probativeness. In
the legal literature, that is just another term for relevance. Second,
Burke anticipates Keynes, *Federal Rules of Evidence* Rule 401, and
even Bayes' Theorem, when he says that proof, or evidence,
includes everything that would make a claim more (or less) certain
than it would otherwise be. This anticipation is so clear and so
strong that I wonder if Keynes, who wrote a long paper on Burke in
1904, based his own probability theory on this very text, together
with the earlier block-indented text where Burke uses the word
"relevant."

Note that Burke attributes his relevance rule to Gilbert.
This is in contrast to the scholars of our own time, who know
Gilbert only as a champion of the best evidence rule.

Hadrian was one of the five so-called "good emperors" of
the Roman Empire. Hadrian ruled that empire at its greatest extent,
as marked in part by Hadrian's Wall in Britain. Burke quotes the
Emperor Hadrian on the indefinability of the concept of evidence:

> And there remains a rescript from the same prince ["his
> sacred majesty, Hadrian"] to Valerius Varus, on the
> bringing out the credit of witnesses. This appears to go
> more to the *general* principles of evidence. It is in these
> words: "what evidence, and in what **measure or degree**,
> shall amount to proof in each case, **can be defined in no
> manner whatsoever that is sufficiently certain**....In
> some cases, the number of the witnesses, in others their
> dignity and authority, is to be **weighed**; in others,
> concurring public fame [i.e. public opinion] tends to
> confirm the credit of the evidence in question. This alone
> I am able, and in a few words, to give you as my
> determination, that you ought not too readily to bind
> yourself to try the cause upon **any one description of
> evidence**; but you are to **estimate** by your own
> discretion what you ought to credit, or what appears to
> you not to be established by proof sufficient. (Burke
> 1852: 80 citing "Digest. 1. xxii. part 5, " Burke's italic
> emphasis, my boldface emphasis)

Hadrian and Burke anticipate Keynes' view that evidence is, in a certain basic sense, indefinable. They even anticipate Butchvarov's more radical argument in *The Concept of Knowledge* that we have no concept of evidence at all, not even an indefinable one, since there is no one thing which all the things we call evidence have in common (Butchvarov 1970: part 4). At least they anticipate the premiss of Butchvarov's argument; they do not draw Butchvarov's conclusion. Hadrian and Burke anticipate Keynes' view that there are degrees of evidence, and also Keynes' view that these degrees cannot always be assigned cardinal numbers, since they are to be "weighed," and we "are to estimate" their weight. Burke goes on to argue that the jurists of his own time have not been able to be more precise than Hadrian on the nature or definition of evidence (Burke 1852: 80ff.). I am tempted to recall Aristotle's view that it is a mark of lack of education to demand more precision than a subject matter allows. But per Russell, you never know when you might be able to provide a more precise definition or a further logical analysis in the future. On whether logical analysis logically can be endless, see my (2015: ch. 9).

Might Keynes have read these texts when he was studying Burke? That Keynes does not discuss these topics in his Burke paper does not detract from this possibility.

Thomas Peake

Thomas Peake was a well regarded evidence law treatise writer of his time. In 1801, he says in the first edition of his *Compendium of the Law of Evidence*, chapter 1, "Of the General Rules of Evidence:

> Another rule is, that the evidence must be *applied to the particular fact in dispute*, and *therefore no evidence not relating to the issue, or in some manner connected with it can be received....* (Peake 1801: 3, my emphasis)

Three pages later, he says, "The subject of proof being ascertained by the preceding rules, the next thing which must be attended to is that the best evidence that the nature of the case will admit of, be produced...." (Peake 1801: 6–7). Thus the relevance rule is prior to the best evidence rule. Not only that, but the relevance rule is one of the rules that 'ascertain' 'the subject of proof'; and the best evidence rule is not. This seems to imply that the relevance rule is one of the rules that define what evidence is, and that the best evidence rule is not.

In the 1804 "second edition, with considerable additions," Peake says:

> Another rule is, that the evidence must be applied to the particular fact in dispute, and therefore no evidence not *relating* to the issue, or *in some manner connected* with it can be received; (a) nor can the character of either party to a civil cause be called in question, unless put in issue by the very proceeding itself, for every cause is to be *decided by its own circumstances*, and not to be prejudiced by any matter *foreign* to it. (Peake 1804: 6, my emphasis)

This is in chapter 1, "Of the General Rules of Evidence." Here the rule is only "Another rule" among others. Clearly the rule has an exclusionary or gate-keeping function, as shown by the exclusion of "any matter foreign to it." The title page says Peake is "of Lincoln's-Inn."

Peake says in the 1824 edition:

> Another rule is that the evidence must be applied to the particular fact in dispute; and therefore no evidence not relating to the issue, or in some matter connected with it, can be received. (Peak 1824: 40)

This repeats the relevance rule of 1804 word for word. As before, the terms "relating" and "connected with" connote relevancy.

Samuel March Phillipps

Samuel March Phillipps (1780–1862) was a major evidence law treatise writer of his time. He says in the 1816 edition of his *Treatise on the Law of Evidence*, chapter 7, section 3:

> As the sole object and end of evidence is to ascertain the truth of the several disputed facts or points in issue on the one side or the other, no evidence ought to be admitted to any other point. (Phillipps 1820: 126)

He is saying in effect that evidence is to be confined to the point in issue. He seems to be saying it in a way that implies a relativity of evidence to points in issue, such that evidence for one point need not be evidence for another point. This certainly seems to be a relevance rule. The title page says that Phillipps is "of the Inner Temple."

Phillipps expressly says that evidence is to be confined to the points in issue in the 1820 edition of his *Treatise*. Chapter 7, section 3 is entitled, "Evidence is to be confined to the Points in Issue." There Phillipps says:

> As the sole object and end of evidence is to ascertain the truth of the several disputed facts or points in issue on the one side or on the other, no evidence ought to be admitted to any other point. (Phillipps 1820: 126, prior pagination *126)

Phillipps repeats the point a few pages later: "As evidence is to be confined to the points in issue,...." (Phillipps 1820: 138, prior pagination *139).

But the main thing of interest to us does not show on these pages. If we look at the table of contents, we see that there, and only there, section 3 has a subheading, "Relevancy of Evidence—Examples." (Phillipps 1820: xiv). This subheading is indicated for page 138, the page we were just quoting. The implication seems clear that for Phillipps, relevancy of evidence and confinement of evidence to the points in issue are one and the same thing. The terms "relevant to the point" and "confined to the point" would be logically equivalent and even synonymous for him. For according to the table of contents, he is placing his statement of the confinement rule under the already mentioned subheading, "Relevancy of Evidence."

In the 1822 edition of the *Treatise*, talk of "relevancy" now moves into the main text. Phillipps says:

> The sole object and evidence is, to ascertain the truth of the several disputed facts or points in issue on the one side or on the other; and no evidence ought to be admitted on any other point.
>
> Evidence must always be considered *with reference to* the subject-matter, to which it is applied....And it is material, therefore, to consider the view, with which particular evidence is offered, in order to determine whether it *bears upon* the point in issue. Evidence may be admissible in one *point of view*, though not in another. A question, for instance, which would have been *irrelevant* and improper on the examination in chief, may be rendered necessary by the course of a cross-examination....
>
> Such evidence alone ought to be admitted, as in some manner *bears upon* the *question at issue*. An inquiry into other transactions, besides those immediately contested, may in some cases be entirely *irrelevant*. The *relevancy* of evidence must depend upon

the nature and circumstances of the particular case; for all evidence is to be considered *with reference to* the subject-matter, to which it is applied....

As evidence is to be *confined to the points in issue*, the character of either party cannot be inquired into, in a civil proceeding, unless it is put in issue by the nature of the proceeding itself....

The rule, that all manner of evidence ought to be rejected which is *foreign to the points in issue,* applies more strongly, if possible, to criminal prosecutions than to civil cases. This rule is to be founded in common justice; for no person can be expected to answer, unprepared and at once, for every action of his life. In treason, therefore, no evidence is to be admitted of any overt act that is not expressly laid in the indictment. (Phillipps 1822: 167–79, my emphasis)

He says this in chapter 7, "Of Certain General Rules of Evidence," section 3, "Evidence is to be Confined to the Points in Issue." If we look at the table of contents, we see that once again, section 3 has a subheading, "Relevancy of Proof" (Phillipps 1822: xii). This sub-heading is indicated for page 168, right in the middle of the pages we were just quoting. Thus Phillipps continues to equate relevance with confinement to the points in issue, and now in the main text.

The quotation above commingles materiality, admissibility, and relevancy—terms to which we assign different meanings today. But it clearly indicates that relevant evidence is relative to some things, in some sense or senses. It seems to be relative to (1) the subject matter, meaning the points in issue, (2) one's "point of view," which I gloss as one's theory of the case, and (3) possibly even to newly discovered material, such as might be uncovered "by the course of a cross-examination." If so, this would be yet another remarkable anticipation of *FRE* Rule 401 and of Keynes. We see the exclusionary function in terms like "irrelevant," "confined to the points in issue," and especially in the rule that "evidence ought to be rejected which is foreign to the points in issue."

The 1838 eighth edition of Phillipps' *Treatise on the Law of Evidence* was written with the assistance of Andrew Amos and with help from a Mr. Gale (Phillipps 1838: Advertisement to the Eighth Edition; see title page). Amos was Professor of Laws at Cambridge University, and Charles James Gale was a member of the Middle Temple. Several texts are of interest. Phillipps and Amos begin by saying, in part 1, chapter 1:

The parties to a suit are not permitted to adduce every description of evidence which, according to their own notions, may be supposed to elucidate the matter in dispute; if such a latitude were permitted, evidence might

> often be brought forward, which would lead to error
> rather than to truth, the attention of the jury might be
> diverted by the introduction of *irrelevant or immaterial*
> *evidence,* and the investigation might be extended to a
> most inconvenient length. In order to guard against these
> evils, the law interferes, *in the first instance*, by limiting
> and regulating the admissibility of evidence.
>
>   It is the province of the Judge...to decide all
> questions on the admissibility of evidence...Upon this
> subject, it has been said by Mr. J[ustice] Buller, that
> whether there is any evidence is a question for the Judge,
> but whether the evidence is sufficient is a question for
> the jury. (Phillipps 1838: 2, my emphasis, cite omitted)

The term "according to their own notions" implies that relevance is
an objective matter not to be decided by the parties' own personal
notions of what is relevant. The term "in the first instance" seems
to imply that, concerning the admissibility of evidence, relevance is
the first thing to consider. The second paragraph distinguishes the
admissibility of evidence from its weight. Admissibility concerns
whether the evidence is relevant at all. Weight concerns the degree
of relevance. The distinction is clearly stated, and is still used
today.

Phillipps presents the best evidence rule as an exclusionary
rule which excludes anything less than the best evidence available
(Phillipps 1813: 437). Phillipps says:

> The law excludes such evidence of facts as from the
> nature of the thing supposes still better evidence behind
> in the party's possession or power. The rule has been
> expressed in terms, that the best evidence must always
> be given. Other writers have stated it to be, that the law
> requires the best proof of which the nature of the thing is
> capable. But the precise import of the rule cannot,
> perhaps, be adequately comprehended without reference
> to it's [sic] application in various instances.
>
>   The [rule] is founded on the presumption, that
> there is something in the better evidence which is
> withheld, which would make against the party resorting
> to inferior evidence.... (Phillipps 1838: 437–38)

Thus the best evidence rule is there, and it is important. But it is not
the only rule, nor does it subsume or encompass the relevance rule
in any way that I can see. Quite the opposite. For Phillipps tellingly
says, "the rule in question relates only to the quality, and not to the
quantity or strength of the evidence" (Phillipps 1838: 440). We
may say that the best evidence rule pertains to the quality of the
evidence, and the relevance rule to its strength, and even to its

quantity, in the sense that if there is no relevant evidence, then there is no evidence. If that is correct, then we may say that the best evidence rule and the relevance rule are equally essential. For if our evidence has no quality, then in this sense we have no evidence worthy of the name; and if our evidence has no relevance, then in that sense we have no evidence worthy of the name. In fact, the idea that any thing must have both quantity and quality is very old, and recalls Aristotle. If all this is correct, then neither the best evidence rule nor the relevance rule can subsume the other.

Concerning the substance rule, Phillipps says:

> SECTION 3.
> *The substance of the Issue to be proved.*
> With reference to the question, what will be **sufficient** proof of an issue....it will be convenient to consider, in the first place, what are the rules which determine whether the allegations involved in the issue have been properly **supported by** evidence, or whether there is such a difference between the allegations and the evidence as will constitute a **variance**,—and secondly, what are the cases in which there is a **sufficient approximation** of the evidence to the allegations, to enable the judge to amend the statement in the pleadings, so as to make it **conformable** with the evidence. In treating of these subjects, **the term, *variance*, is to be understood to mean a fatal difference between the evidence and the pleadings, unless the latter can be amended**.
>
> A general rule, **governing the application of evidence to the points in dispute** on any issue, is, that it must be **sufficient to prove the substance** of the issue.
>
> It is a general principle of evidence, that all the **material** facts in the declaration, which are **put in issue**, must be established by legal proof. Another principle is, that the nature and extent of the proof will depend upon the manner in which the alleged facts are introduced.... **Evidence**, as Lord Mansfield used frequently to observe, **is always to be taken with reference to the subject-matter to which it is applied, and to the person against whom it is used**. (Phillipps 1838: 845–46, Phillipps' italic emphasis, my boldface emphasis)

It seems from the boldface words that the substance rule, and also the concept of variance, have *something* to do with the relevance or relatedness of the evidence to the point in issue. We also see that Phillipps adopts Lord Mansfield's version of the relevance rule.

The substance rule "governs" the relevance rule in the sense that it requires that the relevant evidence "be sufficient to prove the substance of the issue." Thus the substance rule goes, so to speak, to the quantity or degree of relevant evidence needed, as opposed to its quality.

The interesting thing about the concept of variance is that if the evidence does not conform to the pleadings, then, at least to some extent, the pleadings can be amended so as to make the *pleadings* conform to the *evidence*, provided that the substance of the pleadings remains. This basically seems to mean omitting insignificant details from the pleadings. Thus relevance is a two-way street. If our evidence is not relevant to the point in issue, we would normally wish to find and present new evidence that is relevant to the point in issue. But here it emerges that conversely, we can amend the pleading, so that the existing evidence is now relevant to the point in issue. The threshold requirement for doing so is that the point in issue remain *substantially* the same. I suppose that we could even take both approaches at once. That is, we could both remove insignificant parts of the pleadings from the pleadings, and find new evidence that is more relevant to the substance of the pleadings. But I also suppose that the writers of the time may have found there was no practical point in doing so, since they do not discuss this dual possibility. I imagine that this is because if the pleadings are changed so as to make the evidence suffice, then the existing evidence need not be changed, since it has just been *made* to suffice. And that seems a trivial, if not tautological, point.

My conclusion is that the substance rule is a sort of reverse relevance rule. It reverses the approach of the relevance rule in that it does not require our evidence to be relevant to the pleadings as they are stated, but permits us to change our pleadings so as to plead only the substance of the issue, so that if our existing evidence is relevant to the substance of the issue, then we need not seek further evidence to help establish the now-eliminated irrelevant pleadings. That is, within the pleadings themselves, some pleaded issues may be irrelevant to the substantive pleaded issues.

By parity of reason, talk of variance is a sort of reverse talk of relevance, that is, a sort of talk of irrelevance. See also the index on "RELEVANCY, of proof. See *Substance, variance*" (Phillipps 1838: 1050, Phillipps' emphasis). It seems that the substance rule may be also called the variance rule.

Phillipps also says:

SECTION 2.
On the Relevancy of Presumptions.
With respect to presumptions which are too remote to admit of any reasonable direction to the jury in regard to the issue which they have to try, a very nice exercise of discretion often devolves upon the Judge. It is his duty to **confine the evidence to the points in issue**, lest the attention of juries be distracted, and the public time

needlessly consumed.... (Phillipps 1838: 481, Phillipps'
italic emphasis, my boldface emphasis)

Again, we see an express equation of relevancy with confinement
to the point in issue. Phillipps seems to make it a judge's duty in
general to confine evidence to the points in issue, and thereby to
require relevance. This becomes even clearer when Phillipps later
refers back to this text as follows:

> The power of cross-examination is generally acknow-
> ledged to afford one of the best securities against
> incomplete, garbled, or false evidence. Great latitude,
> therefore, is allowed in the mode of putting questions.
> The rule, however, is subject to certain limitations; the
> questions put must be *relevant* to the investigation, in
> which they are offered. The *relevancy* of a question, as
> directly bearing upon the *matter in issue*, has already
> been considered.(1)
> (1) *Ante*, p. 481. (Phillipps 1838: 907–8, 908 n.(1), my
> emphasis)

Here, to be relevant is to bear directly on the point in issue. But I
am sure Phillipps would agree that this does not mean that every
single item of evidence, taken by itself, must be relevant in the
sense of bearing directly on the point. For it is generally understood
that items of evidence must often work together in order for their
relevance as a whole to be understood.

Phillipps does not limit the relevance rule to presumptions
and cross-examination. On the next page, he writes generally of
"The rules of evidence, excluding irrelevant matter" (Phillipps
1838: 909).

An irrelevant issue may also be called a "collateral issue"
(Phillipps 1838: 909–10). Phillipps says, "It is settled, that a
witness cannot be cross-examined as to any fact,— which, if
admitted, would be collateral, and wholly irrelevant to the matter in
issue" (Phillipps 1838: 910).

In 1849, Phillipps says, in the sixth American edition from
the ninth London edition of his *Treatise*:

> It is [the judge's] duty to *confine the evidence to the
> points in issue,* that the attention of jurors might not be
> distracted, nor the public time needlessly consumed....
> (Phillipps 1849: 460, my emphasis)

This is in chapter 9, section 2, "Of the Relevancy of Presumptive
Proofs; and of the Rule which Confines Evidence to the Points in
Issue," The section title makes it clear that Phillipps considers

confinement to the point in issue to be the same as relevancy. The best evidence rule is independently discussed in chapter 8.

In 1859, Phillipps and Thomas James Arnold say, in the 10th English / 4th American edition of Phillipps' *Treatise*, chapter 10, section 3, "Of the Relevancy of Presumptive Proofs; and of the Rule which Confines Evidence to the Points in Issue":

> With respect to presumptions which are too remote to admit of any reasonable direction to a jury in regard to the issue which they have to try, a very nice exercise of discretion devolves upon the judge(1.) It is his duty to *confine the evidence to the points in issue*, that the attention of juries may not be distracted, nor the public time needlessly consumed....
>
> (1) NOTE 195.— The court always protect the jury from *irrelevant* testimony....
>
> If evidence be *irrelevant* at the time it is offered, it is not error to reject it because other evidence may be afterwards given, in connection with which it would become *relevant*. If it would be *relevant,* in conjunction with other facts, it should be proposed in connection with those facts, and an offer to follow the evidence proposed, with proof of those facts at a proper time. (Phillipps 1859: 732, my emphasis)

We see once again the equation of relevance with confinement to the points in issue, and once again that the relevance of a piece of evidence may be relative to the relevance of other items of evidence.

In 1868, Phillipps, now posthumous, and Arnold repeat this quotation word for word, under the same section 3 title, in the 10th English / 5th American edition (Phillipps: 614–15 / prior pagination *732). In both editions, we also see clearly how talk of variance is the logical contrapositive of talk of confinement to the issue. Phillipps says, in the very next note to the very same paragraph, "NOTE 196.—That proof must not vary from the issue, will be more clearly seen in the notes to the twelfth chapter" (Phillipps 1859: 733; Phillipps 1868: 615 / prior pagination *733). Clearly, "Proof must be confined to the issue" and "Proof must not vary from the issue" are logically equivalent to each other, and also to "Proof must relate to the issue." Recall that we are using the word "proof" not in the formal logical sense, but to mean sufficient probable evidence. The standard of sufficiency can vary depending on the type of case, from "beyond a reasonable doubt" in criminal law, through "clear and convincing" in some statutory law, to mere "preponderance of the evidence," meaning more likely than not, in civil law. All these standards are in effect rough degrees of probability.

Jeremy Bentham

Jeremy Bentham (1748–1822) was not just a great philosopher. He was also a bencher of Lincoln's Inn, and produced a huge amount of writing on evidence law and the philosophy of evidence. This writing was edited twice. First, there was a French edition that was soon translated back into English. Second, there was the monumental edition edited by John Stuart Mill, Russell's godfather. Bentham's influence was monumental in the nineteenth century. He was praised by some, criticized by others, and sometimes both at once.

In 1825, *A Treatise on Judicial Evidence*, the English translation of (Pierre) Étienne Louis Dumont's French edition of Bentham's writings, appeared. Dumont had met Bentham in person and was a great admirer. In book 7, "Of the Exclusion of Evidence," chapter 5, "Causes which Render Exclusion Always Proper," Bentham says:

> [Even when] the witnesses ought not to be excluded, there are cases in which the testimony ought to be thrown out of doors;
>
> 1. When it is not *pertinent*; 2. When it is **superfluous**.
>
> To say that testimony is not **pertinent**, is to say that it is **foreign** to the case, has no **connection** with it, and does **not serve to prove the fact in question**; in a word, **it is to say, that it is not evidence**.
>
> To say that testimony is **superfluous**, is to say, that, though it were admitted, it would **add nothing** to the effect of the other evidence, and would in no way **contribute** to the discovery of the truth.
>
> Evidence, which is not **pertinent**, is more injurious than **superfluous** evidence. The latter occasions loss of time to the judge, and, to the parties, a proportional quantity of expense, delay, and vexation; but the former, in addition to these inconveniences, covers the case with clouds, creates incidental inquiries which only mislead, and infuses doubt and hesitation into the minds of the judges. This evil is still greater with a jury; because the men who compose it, having less experience than the judges, know not how to find their way out of the labyrinth. The case is in a proper condition to develope its true character, only after **all the evidence, which is not pertinent, has been set aside**.

(Bentham 1825: 230, Bentham's italic emphasis, my boldface emphasis)

Pertinence would seem to be the same as relevance. It also seems that Bentham is *defining* evidence as that which is pertinent. Note the phrase, "in a word, it is to say, that it is not evidence." He is saying that pertinence is essential to evidence at the very least. For if it is not pertinent, then it is not evidence.

"Superfluous" is ordinarily taken to mean 'redundant'. But "superfluous" is defined differently here. Here, to be superfluous is to "add nothing to the effect of the other evidence," and to "in no way contribute to the discovery of the truth." That is, an item can be superfluous in either of two ways. First, it can be pertinent but redundant. Second, it can be nonpertinent. The first quoted phrase anticipates *FRE* Rule 401, or more precisely the exclusionary aspect of that rule. The second phrase implies that superfluity is the logical contrary, not to say contradictory, of use-relevance. This is due to the word "contribute." Indeed, I would say that for Bentham, the use or function of evidence is what defines evidence ("serve to prove"). Evidence is as evidence does. Compare deductive use-relevance in my (2018, ch. 9; 2012).

In 1827, *Rationale of Judicial Evidence*, John Stuart Mill's edition of Bentham, appeared. Mill was said to have edited it extensively. Indeed, the prose reads much like Mill's prose, at least to me. Mill's Bentham, says in volume 1:

> Evidence is a word of relation; it is of the number of those which, in their signification, involve, each of them, a necessary reference to the import expressed by some other; which other must be brought to view at the same time with it, or the import cannot be understood.
>
> By the term evidence, considered according to the most extended application that is ever given to it, may be, and seems in general to be, understood,—any matter of fact, the effect, tendency, or design of which, when presented to the mind, is to produce a persuasion concerning the existence of some other matter of fact: a persuasion either affirmative or disaffirmative of its existence. (Bentham 1827: vol. 1: 17)

In the first paragraph, Bentham says that evidence is relational to other evidence. He is saying that the relevance of items of evidence (often) cannot be understood except in relation to other items of evidence. This anticipates the later Russell's holistic theory of empirical scientific knowledge and Quine's more radical holistic general theory of science. But it basically just reports the law as Phillipps describes it in the second paragraph of the last block-indented quotation in the previous section of this chapter. The law is the same today.

In the second paragraph just quoted from Bentham, he says that the scope of the term "evidence" includes anything which even merely *tends* to show us that something is or is not the case. This is just Keynes' view. Except for Keynes' formalizing the point, the only difference is verbal: Bentham uses "pertinent" where Keynes uses "relevant."

Concerning the second paragraph, and other Bentham texts like it, Montrose and Twining note that Bentham may be criticized for psychologizing relevance when he speaks of evidence as a tendency to produce a "'persuasion'" in "'the mind'" (Montrose 1992 / 1954: 358–59 / 538–39 quoting Bentham; Twining 1985: 29); but this need not detain us.

Montrose says that Bentham's evidence relation "has subsequently been called that of relevance" (Montrose 1992 / 1954: 349 / 529; see 358 / 538). Montrose says that Bentham:

> defines "facts" as "events or states of things," and classifies them as either "primary" or "evidentiary." Evidence is not conceived by Bentham as a concept employed only in courts of law: on the contrary, he considers that we rely on evidence in all human activities, scientific and non-scientific....Bentham's distinction between "primary fact" and "evidentiary fact" is more generally expressed as the distinction between *factum probandum* and *factum probans*. The relation between the two has subsequently been called that of **relevance**. (Montrose 1992 / 1954: 348–49 / 528–29, Montrose's italic emphasis, my boldface emphasis)

Twining concurs: "Although Bentham does not explicitly use the term in this context, the relation between the *factum probans* and *factum probandum* is normally referred to as 'relevance'" (Twining 1985: 29, Twining's emphasis). Montrose also correctly notes that Bentham is discussing evidence in general, and not just in evidence law.

Mill's Bentham says in volume 3:

> [I]t is seldom that by any one such article, standing by itself, that a persuasion, strong enough to constitute a ground for action, is constituted in the mind of the judge.
>
> By some greater number of such lots of circumstantial evidence, taken together, the fact may be said to be *proved*. Of the *probative force* of any one of them taken by itself, the utmost that can be said is, that by means of it the fact is *probabilized*:—rendered, in a greater or less degree, *probable*.

> As there are facts—evidentiary facts—by the [probative] force of which of which a fact, considered in the character of a principal fact, is probabilized; so it will generally happen that there are others by which the same fact may be *disprobabilized*:— the existence of it rendered more or less improbable.
>
> When a fact is thus probabilized, it is by the probative force of the evidentiary fact: by the strength of the inference by which, the existence of the evidentiary fact being affirmed, the existence of the principal fact is *inferred*. (Bentham 1827 vol. 3: 13, Bentham's emphasis)

Bentham also speaks of "*disprobative* force" as that which has "the opposite effect, *disprobabilization*" (Bentham 1827 vol. 3: 16 n.†, Bentham's emphasis). He says, "To probabilize any given fact will be the same as to disprobabilize its opposite" (Bentham 1827 vol. 3: 16 n.†).

Thus for an evidentiary fact to have probative force is for it to make a principal fact more probable than it would otherwise be. For an evidentiary fact to have disprobative force is for it to make an evidentiary fact less probable than it would otherwise be. (This is just like *FRE* Rule 401.) Thus it would appear that for Bentham, pertinence is relevance, and degree of probative force is degree of relevance. In any case, Dumont's Bentham's defining evidence as pertinence would be consistent with Mill's Bentham's admitting degrees of probative force. And we can and ought to understand both "pertinence" and "probative force" as meaning relevance.

Bentham says that "the degree of [probative] strength... would be capable of being expressed by numbers, in the same way as degrees of probability are expressed by mathematicians, viz. by the ratio of one number to another. But the nature of the case admits not of any such precision as that which would be given by employing different ratios (*i.e.* different pairs of numbers) as expressive of so many uniform degrees of probative force" (Bentham 1827 vol. 3: 220). Bentham says that "probative force....may be in any degree slight; and it may be strong in almost any degree short of conclusive" (Bentham 1827 vol. 3: 220). I take this to be basically the same as Keynes' view that degrees of probability cannot always be assigned determinate numbers, and basically the same as his view that certainty is an asymptote to which probability approaches.

In volume 4 of Mill's Bentham, book 9, "On Exclusion of Evidence," part 2, "View of the Cases in which Exclusion of Evidence is Proper," chapter 5, "Exclusion of Irrelevant Evidence Proper," Mill's Bentham says:

EXCLUSION OF **IRRELEVANT** EVIDENCE [IS ALWAYS] PROPER

Of the mischief liable to result from the admission of **irrelevant** evidence, no separate mention need be made: be what it may, it is resolvable *in toto* into the mischief producible by vexation, expense, and delay.

The difference between the ground of exclusion in the present case, and in those others, consists in this:—in those three cases (*i.e.* in every case where the evidence is not **irrelevant**[, but produces vexation, expense, or delay]), there is an option to make, there is a quantity of mischief, a weight in each scale: there is something to lose by the proposed exclusion,—a chance in favour of justice; [but] there is [also] a disadvantage that must be incurred by the proposed exclusion,—a probability in favour of misdecision, or perhaps a certainty [of misdecision]. But, in this case, where the information proposed to be delivered is **irrelevant**, there is nothing that can be lost by the proposed exclusion: not the least danger of misdecision is incurred by it.

In this case, then, the enquiry is much more simple than in any one of those three others: there, there are two quantities to weigh, two values to find: here, but one. Suppose the proposed evidence **irrelevant**, **exclusion** is the indisputable consequence.

Irrelevant evidence is evidence that bears no efficient **relation** to **the fact which it is brought to prove**: evidence which **proves nothing**: as well might one say, **no evidence**. (Bentham 1827 vol. 4: 571–72, Bentham's italic emphasis, my boldface emphasis)

Here Bentham says that irrelevant evidence is always to be excluded. His argument is that if evidence is irrelevant, then by definition, there *is* no relevance to weigh against such negative factors as vexation, expense, or delay. The final paragraph appears to define irrelevance in exactly the same way, and using almost exactly the same words, that Dumont's Bentham uses to define nonpertinence. Dumont's Bentham says of evidence that is not pertinent, "in a word, it is to say, that it is not evidence." Mill's Bentham says of evidence that is irrelevant, "as well might one say, no evidence." There is, of course, a difference between "it *is* to say" and "as well *might* one say." But these phrases are substantially, or if you please, functionally, the same. They might even be two renditions of the very same text in Bentham's original manuscript, the former being a translation from English to French and back, and the latter being edited by Mill. But I do not have access to the manuscript, nor do I regard this as very important to the main point, which is that Keynes could have easily learned from Bentham that evidence is relevant evidence, and that it makes the fact in issue more or less probable than it would otherwise be.

Keynes cites Bentham's *Rationale of Judicial Evidence* in his *Treatise on Probability*, Part 1, "Fundamental Ideas," chapter 2, "The Measurement of Probabilities" (Keynes 1962 / 1921: 20). Thus we know that Keynes did read Bentham on evidence, if only on the measurement of probabilities. Second, we saw that Keynes' theory was basically anticipated by Bentham. And third, Bentham expressly uses the terms "pertinent" and "irrelevant" as logical contradictories. Thus we have at least three reasons to believe that the heart of Keynes' theory may well have come from Bentham.

Thomas Starkie

Thomas Starkie (1782–1849) was a well-known evidence law writer of his time. He says in the 1839 edition of his *Practical Treatise on the Law of Evidence*:

> Sect. VII.—2dly, as to the *nature, quality*, and *quantity* of the evidence to be adduced by the parties (*l*).
> *In the first place, with respect to the *nature* of the evidence; as the business of trial is to ascertain the truth of the allegations put in issue, **no evidence is admissible which does not tend to prove or disprove the issue joined.** (Starkie 1830: 385, Starkie's italic emphasis, my boldface emphasis)

Directly to the right of this text, in the right side margin, is the header, "Evidence must be relevant" (Starkie 1830: 385). Thus Starkie appears to be equating the relevance of evidence with its tending to prove or disprove the point in issue. If there are degrees of tending to prove, as I think there must be, then this is Keynes' theory that relevance is degree of probability. Starkie is also saying that if proposed evidence does *not* tend to do this, then it is inadmissible. That all this concerns "the *nature* of the evidence" intimates that this is by definition of the term "evidence," unless "evidence" is indefinable. But whether "evidence" is definable or not, Starkie is saying that to be relevant to the point in issue, that is, to tend to prove or disprove the point in issue, is what it *is* to be evidence for the point in issue. That is Keynes' view, simply and beautifully stated 65 years before Keynes' Apostles paper on probability.

The title page says that Starkie is "of the Inner Temple." In fact, Starkie was "a lecturer in Common Law and Equity at the Inner Temple" (Twining 1994: 46). "He was a Senior Wrangler at Cambridge and [i]n 1823 he was elected to the Downing Chair at

Cambridge;" but apparently he did not actually lecture very often either at the Inner Temple or at Cambridge (Twining 1994: 46).

In 1876, Starkie's posthumous *Practical Treatise* appeared in its "tenth American from the fourth London edition. By Dowdeswell and Malcolm." The title page says that all three are "of the Inner Temple," and that Starkie was "one of Her Majesty's counsel."

George Morley Dowdeswell (1809–1893) and John George Malcolm (*The Law Times* obit. April 13, 1872)'s Starkie says:

> In the first place, with respect to the nature of the evidence; as the business of trial is to ascertain the truth of the allegations put in issue, **no evidence is admissible which does not tend to prove or disprove the issue joined....[A]ll facts and circumstances are admissible in evidence which are in their nature capable of affording a reasonable presumption or inference as to the disputed fact.** (Starkie / Dowdeswell / Malcolm 1876: 616–17, my boldface emphasis)

This gives first the negative aspect and then the positive aspect of relevance. According to the table of contents, page 617 has the sub-heading, "Must be confined to the issue," but it does not appear on the page.

Henry Roscoe

Henry Roscoe (1800–1836) says in the 1831 second edition of his *Digest of the Law of Evidence*:

> OBJECT OF EVIDENCE
> The object of evidence is to *prove the point in issue* between the parties, and, in doing this, there are three rules to be observed: 1. *That the evidence be confined to the point in issue.* 2. That the substance of the issue only need be proved; and, 3. That the affirmative of the issue is to be proved....
> EVIDENCE CONFINED TO THE ISSUE....
>   In general, evidence of *collateral* facts is not admissible....
>   Where the special damages sustained by the plaintiff is not stated in the declaration, it is not one of the *points in issue,* and evidence of it cannot be received....
>   In general, evidence as to the character of either of the parties to a suit is *inadmissible,* it being *foreign to the point in issue.*

> Where the plaintiff has delivered a bill of the
> particulars of his demand, he will be *precluded* from
> giving any evidence of demands *not contained* in his
> particular. (Roscoe 1831: 35–38, my emphasis)

This is under the heading "Object of Evidence," first sub-heading, "Evidence confined to the Issue" (Roscoe 1831: v). However, Roscoe appears to be primarily a follower of the best evidence rule (Roscoe 1831: 1–2). In 1840, he says in his *Digest of the Law of Evidence in Criminal Cases*:

> It is the first and most signal rule of evidence, that the
> best evidence of which the case is capable shall be given,
> for if the best evidence be not produced, it affords a
> presumption that it would make against the party
> neglecting to produce it, Gilb. Ev. 3. Bull. N. P. 293 (1)
> (Roscoe 1840: 1)

As you can see, he cites Gilbert on this. But while the best evidence rule may be the "first and most signal rule" for him, it is far from being the only rule, and far from subsuming the other rules under it. Roscoe says:

> *EVIDENCE CONFINED TO THE ISSUE.
> *General Rule.*] It is a general rule, both in civil and
> criminal cases, that the evidence shall be confined to the
> point in issue. (Roscoe 1840: *73)

Nothing suggests that for Roscoe, this relevance rule is a version of, implied by, or somehow subsumed under the best evidence rule.

Roscoe says on the next page, "[W]here the evidence is referable to the point in issue, it will not be inadmissible, although it may incidentally apply to another person, or to another thing not included in the transaction in question, and with regard to whom, or to which, it is inadmissible" (Roscoe 1840: 74). This is the same sort of relativity of relevance to person in issue or to matter in issue that we have seen before.

The title page says that Roscoe is "of the Inner Temple."

Richard Newcombe Gresley

Richard Newcombe Gresley (1804–1837) is a less noted evidence law treatise writer. The second edition of his *Treatise on the Law of Evidence*, edited by Christopher Alderson Calvert, appeared posthumously in 1847. Calvert's Gresley says:

Definition. *When evidence is said to be impertinent or irrelevant (which are almost synonymous terms)*, it is not intended to be understood that it does not bear upon the broad question of justice between the parties, or upon the matter in dispute, nor even that it does not support the case set forth in the pleadings, but that it does not apply to the *material* points which have been put *in issue* and which the court is prepared to decide.

Thus, *Impertinence* may be divided into several heads; First, *when the evidence relates to matters not in the pleadings;* Secondly, when it relates to matters that are *admitted* in the pleadings, and which are consequently *not in issue*; Thirdly, when it relates to issues which, although *in issue*, are *immaterial*, and therefore do not call for the decision of the Court. And to these ought perhaps be added; Fourthly, when it is needlessly prolix. (Gresley / Calvert 1847: 229 / 158, my emphasis)

This is in part 2, chapter 3, "Objections at the Hearing," section 1, "Evidence Impertinent." The header "Definition" occurs in the right margin. Calvert's Gresley adds, "In the old cases the principle of the Court seems to have been to sift the real merits in whatever way they could be discovered" (Gresley / Calvert 1847: 230 / 159). In effect, such a principle of practical utility is Benthamite. But on the whole, the book seems to emphasize the best evidence rule.

Calvert's Gresley says that impertinence and irrelevance are "almost synonymous." If so, then Bentham was speaking of impertinence as opposed to irrelevance; but impertinence would still be *almost* synonymous with irrelevance. Calvert's Gresley does not explain why he thinks these terms are not synonymous.

Simon Greenleaf

Simon Greenleaf (1783–1853) was the Royall Professor of Law in Harvard University, and taught there from 1833 to 1848. He wrote a three volume *A Treatise on the Law of Evidence*, which is considered a nineteenth century classic. He was a major influence on both sides of the Atlantic. The Simon Greenleaf School of Law in Anaheim, California is part of Trinity International University.

Greenleaf's 1842 *Treatise*, part 2, chapter 1 is entitled "Of the Relevancy of Evidence." There Greenleaf says:

§ 50....The production of evidence...is governed by certain principles....The *first* of these is, that the evidence must correspond with the allegations, and be confined to the point in issue.

> § 51....And it is an established rule, which we state as the FIRST RULE, governing in the production of evidence, that *the evidence offered must correspond with the allegations, and be confined to the point in issue.* This rule supposes the allegations to be *material* and necessary. *Surplusage*, therefore, need not be proved; and the proof, if offered, is to be rejected. The term, *surplusage*, comprehends whatever may be stricken from the record, without destroying the plaintiff's right of action....
>
> § 52. This rule excludes all evidence of *collateral facts*, or those, which are incapable of affording any reasonable presumption or inference, as to the *principal fact or matter in dispute*; and the reason is, that such evidence tends to draw away the minds of the jurors from the *point in issue*.... (Greenleaf 1997 / 1842: 58–59, Greenleaf's emphasis)

All this should be familiar by now. The chapter title shows that when Greenleaf requires that evidence "correspond with the allegations, and be confined to the point in issue," he is, in other words, requiring that evidence be relevant to the point in issue.

We see that the terms "surplusage" and "collateral fact" have different technical legal meanings for Greenleaf. We also see that he discusses both surplusage and collateral facts under the same chapter title, "Of...Relevancy..." And the meanings he gives them imply that he considers them both to be forms of irrelevancy.

The relevance rule excludes surplusage, that is, evidence that is not necessary to establish the point in issue. That falls under the heading of elegance, and is clearly analogous to elegance in the realm of deductive relevance as I discussed it in my (2015: ch. 9), which now emerges as having a similar exclusionary nature.

The rule also excludes evidence of collateral facts, or as we may as well say, of facts having no rational bearing on the point in issue. This implies that relevant evidence is rationally related to, i.e., has a minimal reasonable connection to, the point in issue.

If we allow degrees of evidence to Greenleaf, as I think we must, then we basically have Keynes' theory in 1842. Indeed, when Greenleaf speaks of "the sufficiency and weight of the evidence" (Greenleaf 1997 / 1842: 57, § 49), he admits degrees of evidence.

In 1846, the third edition of his *Treatise* appeared. It was published in both Boston and London. The title page says that the London publisher was "in Lincoln's Inn." In the included "advertisement to the first edition" of 1842, Greenleaf praises "the excellent treatises of Mr. Starkie and Mr. Phillipps on Evidence" (Greenleaf 1846: vii). He says in part 1, chapter 1, "Preliminary Observations":

§ 1. The word EVIDENCE, in legal acceptation, includes all the means, by which any alleged matter of fact, the truth of which is submitted to investigation, is established or disproved.[1] This term, and the word *proof*, are often used indifferently, as synonymous with each other; but the latter is applied, by the most accurate logicians to the *effect* of evidence, and not to the *medium* by which truth is established.[2] None but mathematical truth is susceptible of that high degree of evidence, called *demonstration*, which excludes all possibility of error....Matters of fact are proved by *moral evidence* alone; by which is meant, not [p. 60] only that kind of evidence which is employed on subjects connected with moral conduct, but also all the evidence which is not obtained either from [intellectual] intuition, or from demonstration. In the ordinary affairs of life, we do not require demonstrative evidence, because it is not consistent with the nature of the subject, and to insist upon it would be unreasonable and absurd. The most that can be affirmed of such things is, that there is no reasonable doubt concerning them.[1] The *true question*, therefore, in trials of fact, is not whether it is possible that the testimony may be false, but whether there is *sufficient probability* of its truth; that is, whether the facts are shown by competent and satisfactory evidence. Things established by competent and satisfactory evidence are said to be *proved*.

§ 2. By **competent** evidence, is meant that by which the very nature of the thing to be proved requires, as the **fit and appropriate** proof in the particular case....By **satisfactory** evidence, which is sometimes called **sufficient** evidence, is intended that **amount** of proof, which ordinarily satisfies an unprejudiced mind, beyond reasonable doubt. The circumstances which will amount to this degree of proof can never be previously defined; the only legal test, of which they are susceptible, is their sufficiency to satisfy the mind and conscience of a common man....[p. 61] Questions, regarding the **competency and admissibility** of evidence, are entirely distinct from those, which respect its sufficiency or effect; **the former being exclusively within the province of the Court;** the latter belonging exclusively to the jury.

[p. 59] 1. See Wills on Circumstantial Evid. 2; 1 Stark. Evid. 10; 1 Phil. Evid. 1.
[p. 59] 2. Whately's Logic, b. 4, ch. 3, § 1.
[p. 60] 1. See Gambier's Guide to the Study of Moral Evidence, p. 121....
[p. 61] 1. 1 Stark. Evid. 514. (Greenleaf 1846: 59–60, Greenleaf's italic and small caps emphases, my boldface emphasis)

Here Greenleaf defines evidence, as understood in law, as any means to establish or disprove matters of fact. He says that evidence in law always concerns probability, as opposed to intellectual intuition or demonstration in mathematics, and, we might add, in deductive logic. Of course, Greenleaf might still be the first to say that mathematical demonstration can play a role in a legal case. For example, a business dispute can involve a question whether certain expenses were added correctly.

The words in boldface seem to indicate talk of relevancy. Notably, all competent evidence must be "fit and appropriate." The term seems to be basically synonymous with "relevant." Also note that Greenleaf ties competent evidence, or fit and appropriate evidence, to admissible evidence. It seems that for Greenleaf, evidence is admissible if and only if it is fit and appropriate, that is, relevant. He assigns all questions of competency, i.e. of fitness and appropriateness, and of admissibility, to the judge as opposed to the jury. This is how relevance and admissibility are assigned in Anglo-American jurisdictions today.

Part 2, chapter 1 is called "Of the Relevancy of Evidence." Thus our current term is right in the chapter title. Greenleaf says:

> § 49....Whether there be any evidence, or not, is a question for the Judge; whether it is sufficient evidence, is a question for the Jury.... (Greenleaf 1846: 117)
>
> §50. The production of evidence to the Jury is governed by certain principles, which may be treated under four general heads, or rules. The *first* of these is, that **the evidence must correspond with the allegations, and be confined to the point in issue.** The *second* is, that it is sufficient, if the substance only of the issue be proved. The *third* is, that the burden of proving a proposition, or issue, lies on the party holding the affirmative. And the *fourth* is, that the best evidence, of which the case, in its nature, is susceptible, must always be produced.... (Greenleaf 1846: 119, Greenleaf's italic emphasis, my boldface emphasis)
>
> §51....And it is an established rule, which we state as the FIRST RULE, governing in the production of evidence, that *the evidence offered must correspond with the allegations, and be confined to the point in issue.* This rule supposes the allegations to be **material** and necessary. **Surplusage,** therefore, need not be proved; and the proof, if offered, is to be rejected. The term, *surplusage*, comprehends whatever may be stricken from the record, without destroying the plaintiff's right of action.... (Greenleaf 1846: 120, Greenleaf's emphasis)

> §52. This rule excludes all evidence of *collateral facts,*
> or those, which are incapable of affording any
> reasonable presumption of inference, as to the **principal
> fact or matter in dispute;** and the reason is, that such
> evidence tends to draw away the minds of the Jurors
> from **the point in issue**, and to excite prejudice, and to
> mislead them; and moreover, the adverse party, having
> had no notice of such a course of evidence, is not
> prepared to rebut it.... (Greenleaf 1846: 120–21,
> Greenleaf's italic emphasis, my boldface emphasis)

Due to the chapter title, "Of the Relevancy of Evidence," it could
scarcely be clearer that Greenleaf understands terms such as "must
correspond with the allegations" and "be confined to the point in
issue" as basically synonymous with the term "relevant."

We see again that the terms "surplusage" and "collateral
fact" have different technical legal meanings for Greenleaf; but
now he expressly discusses both surplusage and collateral facts
under the same chapter title of "Relevancy." This confirms that he
considers surplusage and collaterality to be different forms of
irrelevancy.

Note that the best evidence rule is only the fourth and last
of "four general heads." But as we shall see in a moment, "general
head" is not necessarily the same as summum genus; and even if it
were, Greenleaf would have not one but four summa genera.

Concerning the second general head, Greenleaf says in the
next chapter:

> §56. A second rule, which governs in the production of
> evidence, is, that *it is sufficient, if the substance of **the
> issue** be proved....*Thus, if, in an action for malicious
> prosecution, the plaintiff alleges, that he was acquitted of
> the charge on a certain day; here the substance of the
> allegation is the acquittal, and it is sufficient, if this fact
> be proved on any day, the time not being **material**
> (Greenleaf 1846: 126, Greenleaf's italic emphasis, my
> boldface emphasis)

I think we may as well say "relevant" in place of "material." For
the point is that if you have already been acquitted, then that is the
only relevant point, and the exact day of the acquittal is irrelevant.
Thus there is an essential relevantist aspect to the substance rule.
But here we are not finding that certain evidence is irrelevant to the
point in issue and therefore inadmissible. We are finding that
certain *language* in the *pleadings* is irrelevant to the point in issue,
and striking out the language as superfluous, i.e., as "surplusage."
Thus we may say that the substance rule is a sort of converse
relevance rule. And in that sense, it is a relevance rule after all.

The four rules do not originate with Greenleaf. Thayer writes of "Greenleaf's *Treatise on Evidence,* where he follows, with a variation, an earlier writer [in admitting] four great, fundamental rules which are said to govern the production of testimony" (Thayer 1898: 484). Thayer is right that Greenleaf presents these rules only as governing the production of testimony. Greenleaf's part 2, from whence my quotations of Greenleaf come, is entitled "Of the Rules which Govern the Production of Testimony." But the rules themselves are stated as general rules of evidence, and make perfect sense that way.

William Mawdesley Best

William Mawdesley Best (1809–1869) accepts Bentham's general concept of evidence and calls it "natural evidence." This, as we saw, is basically relevant evidence. But Best also criticizes Bentham for giving evidence law short shrift, and argues that we also need a special concept of "judicial evidence." Best holds that courts need to be concerned with *both* sorts of evidence (Montrose 1992 / 1954: 349 / 529).

Montrose quotes Best as saying, "'Judicial evidence is, for the most part, nothing else more than natural evidence, restrained or modified by positive rules of law'" (Montrose 1992 / 1954: 349 / 529). Thus Best comes very close to reducing judicial evidence to rules of admissibility.

Montrose says:

> Best did not make the distinction between natural evidence and judicial evidence the basis of his treatment of the law of evidence. The distinction, though not completely ignored, is little stressed in his subsequent exposition. The principle which he uses as the framework for the exposition is the one to which Gilbert had already attached importance, *viz.,* the best evidence rule. It is in the later work of Stephen and Thayer that basic importance is attached to the distinction; in their writing it is discussed in the language of "relevance" and "admissibility." (Montrose 1992 / 1954: 350 /530)

Thus Montrose finds that Best does not really do much with the distinction between natural evidence and judicial evidence beyond merely stating it, and says that Best finds it more important to have a substantive rule for actually evaluating evidence. And what substantive rule is it? Montrose says that Best simply follows Gilbert in making the best evidence rule the basic rule of evidence law (Montrose 1992 / 1954: 350 / 530).

Montrose overlooks that Best also has a relevance rule, which Best says is "the most universal and most obvious" rule of evidence (Best 1854: 319). In 1854, Best's *Treatise on the Principles of Evidence and Practice as to Proofs in Courts of Common Law* appeared. There Best says:

> § 245. Of all rules of evidence, *the most universal and most obvious* is this—that the evidence adduced should be alike *directed and confined to the matters which are in dispute*. [This rule's] theoretical propriety can never be matter of doubt, whatever difficulties may arise in its application...; and, anything which is neither directly nor indirectly *relevant* to these matters, ought at once to be put aside...."Frustrà probatur quod probatum non *relevat*." (Best 1854: 319, my emphasis)

This is clearly a relevance rule (*"relevat"*). And Best states that "of all rules of evidence," it is "the most universal and most obvious." By its very nature, the rule clearly belongs to natural evidence as opposed to judicial evidence. For it is universal in scope, and logically does not apply only in courtrooms. This "most universal rule" may also explain why the distinction between natural evidence and judicial evidence is logically basic to Best's framework after all. For it is logically more basic than the best evidence rule. For it is universal in its scope of application, including outside of courtrooms, while the best evidence rule is basically limited to documents, and its policy exclusion of copies in favor of originals makes it more in the nature of a rule of judicial evidence, that is, of legal admissibility. Thus these two most basic rules in Best imply the distinction between natural evidence and judicial evidence. For the relevance rule is a rule of natural evidence and the best evidence rule is a rule of judicial evidence. And if I am right, this makes natural evidence more general and logically prior to judicial evidence, which is how one would think it should be. Of course, Montrose may still be right about the text, insofar as Best does not expressly develop these points the way I just did here. And Montrose is right that the later terms for the key concepts of what Best calls natural evidence and judicial evidence are respectively "relevance" and "admissibility."

In the quoted text, "directed and confined to" the point in issue sounds just like relevance. Best even uses the term "relevant" later in the quote to repeat the rule. "Directed" sounds positive, and indicates an inclusionary rule that relevant evidence must always be admissible, absent policy exceptions ("applications"). "Confined" sounds negative, and indicates an exclusionary rule that irrelevant evidence must always be inadmissible. But this is only in contrast. If we "confine" a certain portion of water to a certain pitcher, we are not just negatively excluding it from being anywhere else. We are positively including or containing all of it in the pitcher. Thus confinement implies positive containment. If water is confined to a pitcher, then the pitcher positively contains the water. Likewise, if evidence is confined to the point in issue, then all of the evidence is positively relevant to the point in issue. (Compare the whole-part relevant containment theory of deductive inference.) Thus Best's view seems to be a biconditional ("if and only if") thesis, and both inclusionary and exclusionary. That is, it seems to be his view that absent policy exceptions, evidence is admissible if and only if it is relevant. And this implies that it is always to be excluded if it is irrelevant.

I see no attempt here by Best to reduce his relevance rule to, or to subsume it under, his best evidence rule. Since the best evidence rule is not about "best" in its ordinary general evaluative sense, but only about the most original documents available, I do not see how anyone could achieve such a reduction or subsumption. The biconditional that evidence is the most relevant if and only if it is the most original document available is absurd, and surely would not have been accepted by Best, nor even by Gilbert. I am not even invoking a principle of charity in interpretation. Granted, normally an original document is causally the most directly related one to the transaction in question. But is an original document that has nothing to do with a dispute more relevant than a copy of a document that the whole dispute is based on? Surely that is why Best presents his relevance rule as an independent basic rule that is logically unrelated to his best evidence rule, and likewise Gilbert.

The "Frustrà" maxim is often translated as, "It is useless (vain, idle) to prove that which, when proved, is not relevant." This is a species of what relevance logicians call "use-relevance."

Best was cited on relevancy by other writers of his time, as we shall see. Thus Montrose overlooks not only what Best says himself, but also how Best was understood by his contemporaries.

The title page says that Best is "of Gray's Inn."

John Pitt Taylor

John Pitt Taylor (1811–1888) was a major treatise writer. He is called John Pitt-Taylor in Edward Walford's obituary of him in the July 28, 1888 issue of *The Law Times*, and his son is called Frank Pitt-Taylor (Walford 1888: 236). But he is generally called John Pitt Taylor on the title pages of the editions of his treatise, and modern scholars such as Twining call him Taylor; so I shall follow that usage.

In 1848, the first edition of his *Treatise on the Law of Evidence, as Administered in England and Ireland* appeared. The title page says that Taylor is "of the Middle Temple."

In the Preface, Taylor expresses his great indebtedness to Greenleaf. He says his original intent was merely to produce a new edition of Greenleaf, but he eventually found that, in order to focus more on helping English and Irish lawyers with their law, it would be better to write his own treatise afresh.

The first two sentences of Taylor's preface to the first edition are, "The following Work is founded on 'Dr. Greenleaf's American Treatise on the Law of Evidence'. Indeed, when in July, 1843, my attention was first drawn to the subject of Evidence, with a view to publication, I undertook to discharge the duties of an editor only," and only later decided to write a treatise of his own. On the next page he says, "I have still, however, availed myself very largely of Dr. Greenleaf's labours, having adopted, with but few alterations, his excellent general arrangement,...and having borrowed many pages of his terse and luminous writing."

Taylor speaks of "Greenleaf's American Treatise," but in fact Greenleaf's *Treatise* was published in both Boston and London in 1842. Thus it was better known and more available in England than it might seem from Taylor.

Taylor says in volume 1, part 1, chapter 1, page 1:

> § 1. The word EVIDENCE, considered in relation to Law, includes all the legal means, which tend to prove or disprove any matter of fact, the truth of which is submitted to judicial investigation. (Taylor 1848: 1)

Thus he defines evidence as that which tends to prove or disprove the point in issue. We may as well say that he defines it in terms of probability. Later in the book, Taylor states what he takes to be the four general rules of evidence that govern the production of evidence:

> § 142. The production of evidence to the jury is governed by certain principles, which may be treated under four general rules. The *first* of these is, that the evidence must correspond with the allegations; but that it is sufficient if the substance only of the issues be proved. The *second* is, that the evidence must be confined to the points in issue. The *third* is, that the burden of proving a proposition at issue lies on the party holding the substantial affirmative. And the *fourth* is, that the best evidence, of which the case in its nature is susceptible, must always be produced. (Taylor 1848: 140)

It seems to me that Taylor presents these four rules as independent of each other, though surely he is aware that 'correspondence with the allegations' is a positive version of the more negative-sounding 'confinement to the points in issue'. But even if I am right that those two terms are logically equivalent versions of each other, the first two rules still differ in that the first permits that "the substance only of the issues be proved." In any case, Taylor presents what I have argued earlier to be two relevance rules first, and the best evidence rule last. (The first relevance rule is the first conjunct of the first stated rule: "the evidence must correspond with the allegations.") Thus, even if his order of listing the rules implies no ranking of fundamentality, it is at least clear that the best evidence rule is just one of four different main rules (or five, if we split the first rule into its two conjuncts; the "but" logically functions as an "and").

In 1878, Taylor says, in the preface to the seventh edition of his *Treatise on the Law of Evidence as Administered in England and Ireland*, that he thinks it will be his last, and indicates that it has been thirty years since the first edition appeared, meaning 1848 (Taylor 1878: v). He says in part 2, chapter 2, "Confining Evidence to Points in Issue":

> §298. The *second general rule*, which governs the production of testimony, is, that *the evidence must be confined to the points in issue.* (Taylor 1878: 283, Taylor's emphasis)

A few pages later, he says:

> §316. The rule **confining evidence to the points in issue**...excludes all evidence of *collateral facts*, which are incapable of providing any reasonable presumption as to the principle **matters in dispute**....The due application of this rule will occasionally tax to the utmost the firmness and discrimination of the judge; so that he shall reject, as too remote, every fact which merely furnishes a fanciful analogy or conjectural inference, he may admit as **relevant** the evidence of all those matters which shed a **real**, though perhaps an **indirect and feeble**, light on the **questions in issue**. (Taylor 1878: 296, Taylor's italic emphasis, my boldface emphasis)

According to the index at the end of volume 2, pages 296 and 297 are under the sub-heading "IRRELEVANT FACTS, not evidence" (Taylor 1878: 1659).

The posthumous 1897 American edition of the ninth English edition of Taylor's *Treatise* was "in part re-written by G. Pitt-Lewis" per the title page. The American editor, Charles Frederic Chamberlayne, says in the preface, "The ninth English edition embodies many extensive and painstaking improvements by G. Pitt-Lewis" (Chamberlayne 1897: iii).

Chamberlayne's Taylor distinguishes logical relevance from legal relevance:

> RELEVANCY.—**This logical relation of one fact to another, is termed "relevancy."** Of this the law furnishes no test. The test is furnished by the ordinary principles of logic **or a conscious perception of the relation**. A legal definition of relevancy was indeed courageously attempted by Sir James Fitz-James Stephen in the first edition of the "Digest of the Law of Evidence," based largely on the relation of causation. This definition was abandoned. The amended definition seems free from objection[:] Two facts are **relevant** to each other when so **related** "that, according to the common course of events, one, either taken by itself or in connection with other facts, proves or renders **probable** the past, present, or future existence or non-existence of the other" (Dig. Law of Evid. Art. 1.)
>
> The Rule Further Examined.—Such being the fundamental rule of evidence, that all evidence **logically probative** is admissible, the further law of evidence consists of excluding certain facts of the evidence otherwise admissible under this fundamental general rule [for policy reasons]....
>
> (1) LEGAL RELEVANCY.—The search for abstract truth, scientific or otherwise, is not usually limited in time. No fact at all is too remotely **relevant** to deserve consideration. No pressing necessity usually exists that the precise fact should be ascertained this year or next year, or, indeed, within the next century. Under such conditions, logic is given its unimpeded course. All facts **logically relevant** demand and receive consideration.
>
> But the course of trials in Courts of law by no means admits of such extended search into the minutiae of proof. The tribunal sits for a limited time....The proceedings are expensive....There is a recognized necessity that matters should be as speedily disposed of as the interests of justice will admit....
>
> (2) FEAR OF THE JURY.—....The average jury is composed of men selected by chance from the general community, brought together for a short time and for a limited object, with minds usually entirely untrained in the difficult art of justly balancing the weight of

conflicting statements. Jurymen, almost of necessity, are seldom given to reasoning with logical exactness....

EXCLUSIONS.—For these and similar reasons, the law of evidence excludes much evidence **logically relevant**, either (1) By applying a higher standard of relevancy than mere logic by requiring a certain high grade of probative effect, which may be called legal relevancy; and (2) By absolutely excluding certain facts both **logically** and legally **relevant**. What facts are so highly probative as to comply with the standard of legal relevancy cannot be reduced to a definite rule. (Taylor 1897: 2^6–2^8, my boldface emphasis)

We will discuss Chamberlayne and Stephen in their own sections later, and we will discuss legal relevance later. The important thing is that we see Keynes' term, "logically relevant." The 1897 edition was published in Boston and London. Keynes could have read it while he was at Cambridge University studying legal cases for his own treatise on probability. Taylor's "according to the common course of events" suggests the frequency theory of probability common at the time, which Keynes rejects. But at the same time, Taylor makes relevancy a "logical relation" known by "conscious perception." And that is just Keynes' view on the nature of the relation. The only substantive difference between Taylor and Keynes is that Taylor makes the relata of the evidence relation *facts*, instead of the propositions that *describe* the facts. This is actually better than Keynes insofar as facts, not propositions, are evidence for the obtainment of other facts, or for the truth of propositions about other facts. It is more direct, more elegant, more realistic, and more plausible. Thus here, Keynes' theory emerges as a retrograde step.

While Taylor's admission of basic elements of both the frequency theory and Keynes' sort of theory may seem confused, I find it consistent enough. The frequency theory itself is a form of logical theory of probability, insofar as "many" and "few" are notions of class theory. More than that, I find it common sense. For there would be something very wrong with Keynes' theory if in the end it did not basically find what is usually the case more probable than not. In fact, if any of the three main theories of probability were not as good at assessing probabilities as the other two, then it would be unworthier than they.

Taylor's phrases "a higher standard of relevancy" and "a certain high grade of probative effect" imply that his distinction between logical relevance and legal relevance is one of degree, not one of kind. Thus for him at bottom, there are not really two kinds of relevance, one logical and one legal. Thus the distinction is open to criticism for being a slippery slope, and for committing the fallacies of composition and division. (These fallacies are strictly deductive fallacies, and this is strictly a deductive point *about* probability. For many scintillae of evidence logically can add up to a significant probability, and one scintilla logically can be the straw that breaks the camel's back of insignificant probability.) Such a distinction of degree is necessarily inexact. It is best described as "an appreciable, but indescribable distinction" (Powell 1859: 220).

Taylor was a member of the Middle Temple, which is right next to the Inner Temple in London. He wrote the preface to the first edition of his *Treatise* on February 10, 1848, at "2, Harcourt Buildings, Temple." The Middle and Inner Temples were named after the Knights Templar, who owned the land until their order was abolished in 1312. The three Harcourt Buildings were originally built in 1703. They are located just north of the Thames, and just south of where the Strand turns into Fleet Street (if you remember Fleta). The Honourable Society of the Inner Temple, also called the Inner Temple, is one of the four professional societies called Inns of Court for judges like Taylor, and also for barristers. A current connection to Cambridge University, where Russell and Keynes were students, is that Cambridge has a companion organization for its student would-be barristers, called the Cambridge University Inner Temple Society.

Keynes was a member of the Inner Temple, admitted in 1905. Thus Keynes might have known of Taylor through the Inner Temple, but I doubt he met him. According to *The Law Times*, July 28, 1888 obituary of Taylor at books. google.com, Taylor died on July 17, 1888. It says he "was one of the oldest and most respected members of the Legal Profession," was "entered...as a student of the Middle Temple" in 1833, and "was the author of 'A Treatise on the Law of Evidence'." The obituary says he was born December 30, 1811 and "was a contemporary of Mr. Gladstone" at Eton, "from which he passed to Christ Church, Oxford."

Morgan, Starkie, and Phillipps are all of the Inner Temple. John Dawson Mayne, whose treatise on the law of damages Keynes refers to in his *Treatise* (Keynes 1962 / 1921: 25), is of the Inner Temple as well. It is hard to see how Keynes could not have known that so many great evidence law writers of his own Inner Temple were writing of the relevance of evidence. In fact, perhaps the best explanation of why Keynes does not say he takes the term logical relevance from evidence law might be that he simply regarded its use as already commonplace among readers interested in the topic.

The Honourable Society of the Inner Temple online site does not describe Keynes as having any legal credentials himself, but only as being a member who was admitted in 1905, and as being an economist. And of course it is not conclusive evidence that Keynes finished a book draft on the logical relevance of evidence in 1914, and just happened to be admitted in 1905 as a member of an Inn of English law, many of whose members had published treatises on evidence and its logical relevance. But it strains credulity to think that just after joining a world-famous legal society in which "logically relevant" was the common term for the most basic concept of evidence, Keynes magically invented the very same term for the very same concept all by himself.

Jacob R. Halsted

We have seen that Best's contemporaries were well aware that Best has a relevance rule, even though our scholars today are not. Here, Best is the very first source cited for the relevance rule.

In 1859, Jacob R. Halsted says in his *Digest of the Law of Evidence*:

> **RELEVANCY** OF EVIDENCE.
> The evidence offered in a cause must **correspond with** the allegations, and be **confined to** the point in issue. **Best's Ev. §§ 229, 248.**
> The evidence need not bear directly on the issue; it is admissible if it *tends* **to prove the issue**, or constitutes a link in the chain of proof. *Jones* v. *Van Zadt*, 2 McLean, 596....
> Evidence, having **no relation** to the allegations in the pleadings, will not be received. *May* v *Ransom*, 5 An. 424....
> *Relevancy of Evidence....*
> 42. **Irrelevant** matter may be properly excluded from the jury. *State* v. *Roper*, 3 Eng. 491.
> 52. Testimony cannot be excluded as **irrelevant** which would have a **tendency, however remote, to establish the probability or improbability of the fact in controversy.** *Trull* v. *True*, 33 Maine, (3 Red.) 367.
> 58....And it is a sufficient answer to an exception for the rejection of evidence, that it was **irrelevant.** *The State* v. *Arnold*, 13 Ired. 184.
> 67. It is error to permit testimony, not **relevant to the issue**, to go to the jury. *Maslin* v. *Thomas*, 8 Gill, 18.
> 85. The rule which requires the evidence to be **strictly confined to the point at issue**, is not violated by evidence of facts which happened before and after the principal transaction, yet which have a **direct relation** to the main subject in controversy. *Horton* v. *Reynolds*, 8 Texas, 284.

> 134. Evidence that is **pertinent**, and **applicable to the issue**, should be admitted.... *Lazare* v *Peytavin*, 9 M. 567
> 135. An instrument, **relevant** to the matter at issue and duly proved, must be admitted without inquiry into its effect.... *Livermore* v. *Morgan*, 6 N. S. 136; *Dick* v *Chew*, Ib. 396; *Gayle* v. *Gray*, Ib. 694.
> 137. Evidence having **no relation** to the allegations in the pleadings will not be received. *Colsson* v. *Consolidated Bank*, 12 Lon. 105; *May* v *Ransom*, 5 An. 424. (Halsted 1859: 95–118, Halsted's italic emphasis, my boldface emphasis)

The most striking cite is ruling #52, Trull v True. It is an astonishing anticipation of *FRE* Rule 401. *Trull* states, albeit in a negative way, that to be relevant is to have a tendency, however slight, to make the point in issue either more probable or less probable than it would be otherwise. Perhaps the negative aspect makes *Trull* even closer to Keynes' definitions of irrelevancy than it is to *FRE* Rule 401.

Halsted's citations of legal cases suggest that it is not just a few treatise writers, but also hundreds of judges making rulings in a wide variety of legal jurisdictions, who are speaking about relevance by the middle of the nineteenth century. Halsted cites 222 court rulings under his italicized sub-heading *"Relevancy of Evidence,"* though not every ruling uses the *word* "relevant." Thus it seems that to view treatise writers as the origin of the concept of relevance is to put the cart before the horse.

Halsted's language sounds quite modern, even though the American Civil War would not start for another two years.

Halsted praises "the invaluable treatises of Phillips [sic] and Greenleaf" in the Preface (Halsted 1859: iv).

Edmund Powell

In 1859, Edmund Powell (1826?–1864), in his *Principles and Practice of the Laws of Evidence*, upholds the best evidence rule for the usual reason, namely "the presumption that [an offer of] inferior evidence...arises either from fraud, or from gross negligence, which is tantamount to fraud" (Powell 1859: 41).

Concerning the substance rule, Powell says:

Chapter 19.
ON THE SUBSTANCE OF THE ISSUE.
It is enough if only the *substance* of the issue be proved.

> In other words, a party will have proved *sufficiently* his
> case if he establish *substantially* his allegations; and he
> will not be prejudiced by failing to prove matter which is
> *unnecessary* to support his claim, and which may
> therefore be disregarded as *surplusage*. But it is not
> every *unnecessary* allegation which may be treated as
> *surplusage*; for *irrelevant* matter may be so connected
> and incorporated with essential matter, as to render them
> legally inseparable; and where this is so the *irrelevant*
> matter must be proved. (Powell 1859: 187, my
> emphasis)

Thus Powell firmly connects the substance rule with the concept of
surplusage, and ties the concept of surplusage with the concept of
irrelevance. His equation of irrelevant matter with unnecessary
matter suggests that relevance is use-relevance. Compare deductive
use-relevance in chapter 9.

As we saw in the Mansfield section, earlier, Powell quotes
Mansfield's *Bristow* case of 1781:

> The distinction is that between that which may be
> rejected as *surplusage*, and what cannot. When the
> declaration contains *impertinent* matter, *foreign* to the
> cause, and which the master on a reference to him would
> strike out (*irrelevant* covenants for instance), that will be
> rejected by the court, and need not be proved.... (Powell
> 1859: 188 quoting Mansfield in Bristow v. Wright,
> Dougl. 665, 1 Sm. L. C. 223, my emphasis)

For Mansfield, surplusage is matter that is impertinent, foreign, or
irrelevant in the *pleadings*. See the Mansfield section above for a
fuller quotation.

In chapter 21, Powell equates relevancy with confinement
to the points in issue:

> Chapter 21.
> ON THE RELEVANCY OF EVIDENCE.
> As it is the object of pleading to reduce the case of each
> litigating party to one or more *substantial* issues which
> involve the *merits* of the question; and as for this
> purpose none but *material* allegations which tend to the
> raising of such issues are admissible; so it is the object of
> evidence to provide that, when such allegations have
> been made, and such issues selected, they shall be
> supported by *strictly relevant* proof. It is impossible to
> define the distinction between *relevant* and *irrelevant*
> evidence, and even the cases illustrate the difference
> unsatisfactorily. In the case of direct evidence, there is
> little difficulty in drawing the line; but, since a large

proportion of evidence is of a presumptive or circumstantial character, it requires the keenest perspicacity to distinguish between *legitimate* presumption and *irrelevant* hypothesis; and it is in observing this appreciable, but indescribable distinction, that the sense and wariness of an able judge appear. The rule is that—
> The evidence must *correspond with* the allegations, and be *confined to the points in issue.*[1]
1. Greenl. 58; Tayl. 194. (Powell 1859: 220, citing Greenleaf and Taylor, my emphasis)

This is yet another equation of relevancy with correspondence to the allegations, and with confinement to the point in issue. There are also relevantist shades of *substantial* issues, *merits* of the question, *material* allegations, and *legitimate* presumptions.

Powell sums up at the end of the chapter:

> The principles according to which the *relevancy* and *irrelevancy* of evidence are distinguished have been now explained. They are *co-extensive and identical with* the principles of presumptive evidence; and, in fact, *embrace the whole subject of legal evidence.* It is equally a condition of direct evidence as of presumptive [or circumstantial] evidence, that it should be *relevant to the issue*; and it is pre-eminently the duty of a judge to admit no evidence which he does not consider to be *relevant,* either as direct proof, or as the ground of legitimate inference. In many cases, as in the principal issues in civil cases, the *relevancy* of evidence has been *defined* by the *amount of proof* which is usually given and required to support them. In criminal cases, where practically there is no issue but the general issue, the line of demarcation has been drawn less distinctly; and the discretion of the judge requires, therefore, to be exercised with proportionable vigilance. (Powell 1859: 22, my emphasis)

Here, Powell comes close to defining evidence as what is relevant, and then defining relevance in turn as degree of "proof," not to say probability. But he does not actually leap over those narrow ditches into Keynesian theory. Possibly this is because he is concerned to report the outlines of the law, and is not a philosophical theorist at heart. Still, this looks like another striking anticipation of Keynes.

The title page says that Powell is "of the Inner Temple."

The 1904 posthumous Powell is even simpler and clearer:

Chapter 21.
THE RELEVANCY OF EVIDENCE.

[I]t is the object of evidence to provide that [allegations and issues] shall be supported by *strictly relevant* proof. The rule is that—
> The evidence must *correspond with* the allegations, and be *confined to the points in issue.*

Or as it is sometimes stated that—
> The evidence must be relevant to the issue— (Powell 1904: 441)

The synonymity of "relevant" with "corresponding with the allegations and confined to the points in issue" is too expressly stated and too obvious to need comment.

William Gillespie Dickson

In 1864, William Gillespie Dickson (1823–1876) says in his *Treatise on the Law of Evidence in Scotland*:

> § 17. The proper object in every trial being to lead the jury to a correct verdict upon the issue, it is the practice to *exclude* evidence which cannot afford an inference on some point in *favour* of either party....(*a*)....(*b*)....
> (*a*)....Wherever facts have been found *irrelevant*, they will not be allowed to be proved; M'Laren *v.* Buik, 1829, 7 S., 780.
> (*b*) This is also the English practice; 2 Starkie Ev., 313—1 Starkie Ev., 603—Haigh *v.* Belcher, 1838, 7 C. and P., 389. (W. Dickson 1864: 18, 18 n.(*a*), 18 n.(*b*), my emphasis)

Thus Dickson equates being unable to make any point 'favorable' with being inadmissible, and with being "irrelevant." This is in part 1, "General Rules Applicable to All Kinds of Evidence," title 2, "Of the Rule that the Evidence Must Be Relevant." The best evidence rule appears two titles later, in title 4, "Of the Rule Which Requires the Best Evidence." The relevance rule and the best evidence rule appear to be completely independent of each other.

In the quotation above, Dickson pushes the case law on relevance back to 1829. In the quotation below, Dickson finds a judicial ruling as early as 1810 that links the receiving of proof to:

> *tending to shew the probabilities...(x)....*
> (*x*) As in Murray *v.* Tod, 1817, 1 Mur., 225—Buchanan *v.* Buchanan, 1810, Buch. Rep., 89. *This is the constant practice in such cases.* (W. Dickson 1864: 22, 22 n.(*x*), my emphasis)

Thus, much like Halsted, Dickson shows that relevance was not just a theoretical concept found in treatises, but was "constantly" being ruled on by judges in courts.

The important thing for us is that Dickson ties relevance to probability in both directions. First, he equates evidence that does not make any point or its denial (more) probable with irrelevant evidence. Second, he equates receivability of proof with "tending to show the probabilities." And the heading at the top of the page is, "RELEVANCY OF EVIDENCE." Thus it seems that for Dickson, to be relevant, and to be receivable as evidence, is to tend to show the probabilities concerning a point in question

In the preface to the first edition, dated July 19, 1855, Dickson cites "the comprehensive and philosophical work of Professor Greenleaf" (W. Dickson 1864: vii).

John Dawson Mayne

John Dawson Mayne (1828–1917) wrote primarily on the law of damages resulting from tort (personal injury) cases. This may seem irrelevant to our topic. But it is worth looking into, since Keynes cites *Mayne on Damages*. In fact, there is much in Mayne on relevance. We will see the usual terms, such as "relevant" and "point in issue." But we will need to learn some new concepts in order to understand the full depth of Mayne on relevance: proximate cause, reasonably foreseeable cause, and remote cause.

A tort is a civil, as opposed to criminal, action for injury in some sense. Basically, a tort has four elements that must be proved. First, there must be some legal, as opposed to privately agreed upon, duty. Second, there must be some violation of the duty by a person who owed the duty to someone. Third, there must be some sort of damage or injury that results from the violation to the person to whom the duty was owed. Fourth, the injury must have been either intended or negligent. If the damage was intended, then it is an intentional tort. If the damage was unintended, but was proximately caused or at least reasonably foreseeable, then it is a negligence tort.

Historically speaking, the two main tests of negligence have been proximate causation and reasonable foreseeability. The first of these is often taken to be less clear than the second; and therefore it has often been replaced by the second.

Proximate cause and reasonable foreseeability are the two concepts of greatest interest to us here. Reasonable foreseeability implies probabilistic relevance. Proximate causation implies causal necessity. For a proximate cause is a cause. But whether an act is a proximate cause of a damage, or of anything else, may be unclear, if the concept itself is unclear.

Sometimes proximate cause is defined away as, or is understood as being or as replaced by, reasonable foreseeability. But traditionally this has not been so. "Proximate cause" is traditionally understood as direct or immediate as opposed to remote or mediated cause. But it is often taken to *imply* reasonable foreseeability. For otherwise there would not be much point in blaming anyone for the damage. So, it is often understood as immediate *and obvious* cause. Of course, "obvious," in its ordinary connotation, implies far more than just reasonably foreseeable. Being obvious would seem to equate to being clear and convincing, if not to beyond a reasonable doubt. But we could legally *define* "obvious" as meaning reasonably obvious, that is, as reasonably foreseeable. But such a definition must not be confused with the *standard of proof.* The standard of proof of a cause's being immediate and obvious may well be *less* than that of obviousness in the ordinary sense of "obvious." Typically, in a civil case such as a tort case, the standard of proof is merely preponderance of the evidence, meaning more likely than not. We may say that an event is reasonably foreseeable just in case it is more likely than not to happen, and that the standard of proof of reasonable foreseeability in a tort case is *also* preponderance of the evidence, meaning more likely than not. For example, a jury may find it more likely than not that *Smith* found or ought objectively to have found it more likely than not that his act would cause the damage. Or a jury may find it more likely than not that Smith found or ought to have found that it was *immediate and obvious* that his act would cause the damage, and find (say) for *gross* negligence.

We may say that in a negligence tort, there are four broad kinds of predictability of the damage. For the action to lie, meaning for the tort to be found, the damage must be either (1) the proximate (immediate and obvious) effect, or at least (2) the reasonably foreseeable effect. But the damage cannot be (3) a remote (not immediate and not obvious) effect, nor can it be an effect that was not reasonably foreseeable. Again, (1) and (2) have not always been distinguished, but they typically are, and certainly should be. Please note in this regard that a remote effect in one case can be more reasonably foreseeable than an immediate effect in another case, unless we define "remote" as meaning not only distant in the chain of events and not obvious, but also not reasonably foreseeable.

These four broad kinds of predictability are also four broad kinds of probabilistic relevance. Kinds (1) and (3) are also kinds of causal relevance. Kinds (3) and (4) can diminish to nullity.

In kind (2), we may further distinguish between general and specific reasonable foreseeability. For example, if you handle explosives on a railway platform filled with people, it might be *generally* reasonably foreseeable that if you handle them carelessly, they might explode and cause *some* sort of damage to *someone* there. But it might not be *specifically* reasonably foreseeable who in particular would be injured or what the particular injury would be. There might even be a *specific* chain of events no one could have possibly predicted, such that no one could have ever imagined that a certain specific person would be injured, or that she would receive the specific injury she did. Lawyers will know that I am tacitly referring to Palsgraf v Long Island Railroad Co., 248 N.Y. 339, 162 N.E. 99 (N.Y. 1928). *Palsgraf* is the leading American case on point, and is studied in every or almost every American first year torts class. But we need not be detained by *Palsgraf* here.

Black's Law Dictionary defines "proximately" as meaning

> [a] Directly or immediately. [b] Pertaining to that which in an ordinary natural sequence produces a specific result, no independent disturbing agency intervening. (H. Black 1991: 853)

Definitions (a) and (b) are not logically equivalent, insofar as (b) implies reasonable foreseeability and (a) does not. Concerning (a), directness or immediacy of cause does not imply foreseeability at all. We may be completely surprised by the effect. But in (b), the term "ordinary" seems to imply, and seems intended to imply, reasonable foreseeability. The term also seems to take into account ordinary background causal factors, at least in the negative sense of ruling out intervening causal factors. Science has long abandoned the simplistic model of bang-bang, one-one cause-effect in favor of systems of interacting variables. Strictly speaking, there is no such thing as direct or immediate causation by a single causal event. We can only say there often is one "foreground" or "triggering" event that draws our attention more than the many background factors. Thus (b) is also scientifically better than (a). Note that immediacy does not mean temporal immediacy, but only that there is no mediation by other causal factors. If all causes were temporally immediate, the universe would not last longer than an instant, even if the series of causes were infinitely many. This includes "sustaining" causes of the duration of a thing, operating immediately across temporal instants.

Black's Law Dictionary defines "proximate cause" as alternatively but somewhat repetitively meaning:

[1] That which, in a natural and continuous sequence, unbroken by any efficient intervening cause, produces injury, and without which the result would not have occurred. [2] That which is nearest in the order of responsible cause. [3] That which stands next in causation to the effect, not necessarily in time or space but in causal relation. [4] The proximate cause of an injury is the primary or moving cause, or that which, in a natural and continuous sequence, unbroken by any efficient intervening cause, produces the injury and without which the accident could not have happened, *if* the injury be one which might be *reasonably anticipated or foreseen* as a natural consequence of the wrongful act. [5] An injury of damage is proximately cause by an act, or a failure to act, whenever it appears from the evidence in the case, that the act or omission played a substantial part in bringing about or actually causing the injury or damage; *and* that the injury or damage was either a direct result *or a reasonably probable cause* of the act or omission. (H. Black 1991: 852–53, my emphasis)

Definitions (4) and (5) include reasonable foreseeability, and definitions (1)–(3) do not. Thus definitions (1)–(3) seem practically worthless, since if an injury were not reasonably foreseeable by the actor at the time, then the actor could not be reasonably blamed. In definition (4), the word "if" makes reasonable foreseeability a logically necessary condition of proximate cause, as I think it must be, if actors are to be reasonably blamed. But in definition (5), the word "or" makes reasonable foreseeability only one disjunct of two, the other disjunct being directness of result. Compare the problem I find with Stephen's disjunctive definition of relevance in the section below on Stephen. In sum, in definition (5), reasonable foreseeability is not a logically necessary condition of proximate cause, and the definition is just as worthless as the first three. I should remark that in these definitions, I do not take the terms "natural" or "order of responsible cause" to imply, and certainly not *clearly* to imply, reasonable foreseeability. For these terms appear to refer *only* to the physical order of nature, which may or may not be reasonably foreseeable to us in light of our experience and understanding. I take "order of responsible cause" to mean 'order of physical cause which results in the damage in question'. Surely a physical cause is not morally responsible for the damage. If anything, it is the actor who chooses to initiate the sequence of physical events who is morally responsible.

Definitions (4) and (5) do not even require proximate cause to be direct or immediate, and this goes against the ordinary meaning of "proximate." But we can offer technical definitions as we please, and I think that the omission of this requirement is a good thing. For as we noted a few paragraphs ago, strictly speaking there is no such thing as direct or immediate causation, but a mix of interacting variables. But even if there were such a thing, and in the ordinary sense in which we often say there is, the directness or immediacy of a result does not imply the result's foreseeability. For some sequence of several events can be more foreseeable to us in our circumstances than some direct or immediate cause. I shall not make the obvious criticism of vagueness. Yes, we can have trouble distinguishing 'immediate' cause from 'mediated' cause, depending on how we logically parse events. But "proximate cause" is a term of legal art; and as Aristotle would say, it is a mark of lack of education to expect logical precision where the nature of the subject does not allow it.

We may say that in torts, the concepts of proximate cause, immediate cause, obvious cause, and remote cause *ought* to be logically related to the concept of relevant cause, i.e., to the concept of logical relevance, in the sense of reasonable foreseeability. And this is on pain of the defendant's otherwise not being reasonably blameworthy.

In 1872, Mayne's *Treatise on the Law of Damages*, "by John D. Mayne, of the Inner Temple....THE SECOND EDITION by Lumley Smith, of the Inner Temple....," was published. Mayne and Smith say:

> In many cases of torts, no measure of damage can be stated at all.... (Mayne 1872: viii; 1894: viii)

This is the point Keynes cites Mayne for. But Mayne and Smith also have much to say that concerns logical relevance. They say more fully:

> In many cases of torts, no measure of damage can be stated at all; and the only way of approximating to such a measure, is by ascertaining what evidence could be adduced *in support of the issue*. All this has made many parts of the present work resemble a treatise on the law of Nisi Prius [i.e. of evidentiary trial by jury], rather than one exclusively appropriated to Damages (Mayne 1872: viii, ; 1984: viii, my emphasis)

They say:

> We may now proceed to the more important inquiry, as to the general rules which determine the amount of substantial damages. It will be convenient to examine in order,

I. The principles upon which damages are given in actions of contract and tort.

II. What damages are *inadmissible on grounds of remoteness.*

III. The period of time in reference to which damages may be assessed.

IV. The cases in which evidence may be given to reduce damages. (Mayne 1872: 7, my emphasis)

And:

The plaintiff was held entitled to recover the loss...as being the *direct, immediate, and necessary consequence* of the defendant's breach. (Mayne 1872: 15, my emphasis)

And:

Damage is said to be *remote*, when although arising out of the cause of action, it does not so *immediately and necessarily* flow from it, as that the offending party can be made *responsible* for it. (Mayne 1872: 26, my emphasis; see 217, 296–97, 309 for similar language)

And:

Erle, C. J.,...says that damage will be too *remote* unless it *immediately and according to the common course of events* follows from the defendant's wrong, and the two are *known by common experience* to be *usually in sequence.* (Mayne 1872: 27 n.(*n*), my emphasis)

And:

Pollock, C. B., expressed a strong doubt whether a man is responsible for all the consequences that may under any circumstances arise in respect of mischief, which by *no possibility* could he have *foreseen*, and which *no reasonable person* could be called on to have *anticipated.* He intimated that the rule was that a man is expected to guard against all *reasonable* consequences. (Mayne 1872: 37, my emphasis)

And:

[C]ould any judge leave to the jury, as *relevant* evidence, facts going to show the *collateral* liability of other parties?....

> Two cases which are frequently cited seem to
> be reducible to the same rule as to the *inadmissibility*, in
> reduction of damages, of *extrinsic* matter arising
> subsequent to the cause of action. (Mayne 1872: 68;
> 1894: 112, my emphasis)

Here we see them use the term "relevant" evidentially in the 1872
edition of the law treatise that Keynes cites in his 1921 *Treatise*.
And:

> The true measure [of an insurance claim] is the amount
> of injury the plaintiff has sustained, not exceeding the
> entire sum insured; that is, the expense, and pain, and
> loss, it may be of a limb, connected with the *immediate*
> accident; but not the *remote* consequences that may
> follow.... (Mayne 1872: 251; 1894: 343, my emphasis)

And:

> In one instance,...Lord Kenyon allowed general evidence
> of the immodest character of a woman to go in bar of the
> action. He said, that in such a case character was the
> only *point in issue*, and that *was* public opinion, founded
> on the character of the party. He *therefore* considered
> that what that public thought was *evidence*. (Mayne
> 1872: 377; 1894: 486, my emphasis, cite omitted)

And:

> Whenever an agent violates his duties [to his principal,
> t]he loss or damage need not be **directly or immediately**
> caused by the act....It will be sufficient if it be fairly
> attributable to it, as a **natural result**, or a just
> consequence. But it will not be sufficient if it be merely
> a **remote consequence**, or an **accidental** mischief; for in
> such a case, as in many others, the maxim applies, *Causa
> proxima, non remota, spectatur*. [The nearest (or
> immediate) cause, not the remote, is to be looked at
> (considered).] Mayne 1872: 411, Mayne's italic
> emphasis, my boldface emphasis)

And:

> The damages must also be the *proximate and natural*
> result of the neglect. [But the agent] is not responsible
> for *remote* consequences that may accrue....Speculative
> damages...ought never to be given; but *positive and
> direct loss*, arising *plainly and immediately* from the
> breach of orders, may be taken into the estimate. (Mayne
> 1872: 415, my emphasis)

The term "plainly" goes to foreseeability. It implies very clear and obvious foreseeability. How can that not be evidentially relevant? And:

> The law upon this point was laid down in an old case as follows: "Where the matter omitted to be inquired into by the principal jury was such as goes to *the very point of the issue*, and upon which, if found by the jury, an attaint will lie against them by the party, if they have given a false verdict, there such matter cannot be supplied by a writ of inquiry, because thereby the plaintiff may lose his action of attaint....But where the matters omitted to be inquired into by the jury did not go to *the point in issue*, or *necessary* consequences thereof, but were things *merely collateral*,...such may be inquired of by a subsequent writ of inquiry. (Mayne 1872: 441, my emphasis, cite omitted; compare 1894: 574–75)

And:

> Many of the principles upon this point are quite *unconnected* with the topics discussed in this treatise. There is one, however, *directly relevant*.... (Mayne 1894: 577, my emphasis)

And:

> Lord Kenyon said, the injury was too *remote*, and *impossible to be connected* with the cause assigned to is....Such special damage is not the *natural or necessary* consequence of the [libelous] words. (Mayne 1872: 372; 1894: 478, my emphasis)

And:

> But such libels must be shown to *relate* to the *subject-matter* of those published by the defendant....
>   Such evidence must, in any case, be *confined to the particular trait which is attacked in the libel*.... (Mayne 1872: 373–74; 1894: 480, my emphasis)

And:

> Evidence of a *mere collateral fact*...cannot be given in mitigation of damages. (Mayne 1872: 374, my emphasis; see 1894: 481)

And:

...[I]t was held to be no ground for a new trial, as it did not amount to a misdirection, not being wrong information on a matter which was *directly in issue*, or which was *substantially connected* with the finding *on the issue*. (Mayne 1872: 454–55; 1894: 582)

In 1894, the fifth edition of *Mayne's Treatise on Damages*, "by John D. Mayne, of the Inner Temple....and Lumley Smith, of the Inner Temple.....," was published. Here they add Lord Bacon's vicious infinite regress argument for the requirement of proximate cause:

Every cause leads to an infinite sequence of effects. But the author of the initial cause cannot be made responsible for all the effects in the series. In the case where a passenger, who had been set down with his wife at a wrong station, sought to recover from the railway company damages for a cold which his wife had caught by walking in the rain at night, Cockburn, C.J., said: "You must have something **immediately** flowing out of the breach of contract complained of, something **immediately** connected with it, and not merely connected with it through a series of causes **intervening** between the immediate consequence of the breach of contract and the damage or injury complained of (*k*)...."
(*k*) See Lord Bacon's maxim:—"It were infinite for the law to judge the cause of causes, and their impulsions one of another; therefore, it contenteth itself with the **immediate** cause, and judgeth of acts by that, without looking to any further degree." Bac. Max. Reg. 1, cited by Blackburn, J., in stating the rule of our law to be that the **immediate** cause, the *causa proxima*, and not the **remote** cause, is to be looked at. (Mayne 1894: 48 quoting Chief Judge Cockburn and Lord Bacon, and citing Judge Blackburn, cites omitted, Mayne's italic emphasis, my boldface emphasis)

The regress argument seems a *non sequitur*. Surely more than the most direct and immediate effect is often reasonably foreseeable, and ought to be for the law to judge. And the argument's structure is very different from that of Thomas Aquinas' "first cause" regress argument. Where the present event is damage d and its immediate cause is neglect n, Aquinas argues that there must be some uncaused or self-caused "first cause" $n + m$, where n is cause number one going backwards in time, and m is a finite number greater than zero; since if causes went back to infinity, then d (and for that matter n) would not (be caused to) exist in the first place. And n itself cannot be such an uncaused or self-caused cause, since any such cause would have always existed; and an act of neglect is not that sort of cause. In sharp contrast, Bacon is not arguing, but merely claiming, that *n* is the only cause that can be judged in law to be a cause of *d*. Aquinas wants the earliest existing cause of *d*, namely *n* + *m*, while Bacon wants the most recent, namely *n*. Or if you please, Aquinas wants God, and Bacon, immediate blame.

Collectively, all the Mayne texts paint quite a relevantist picture. Thus Mayne is very much part of the relevantist legal tradition. He even uses the terms "relevant evidence" and "directly relevant" as early as 1872. But I am not suggesting that Keynes took his own term "relevant" from Mayne. Keynes only cites Mayne as a source for his view that probabilities are rarely measurable in real life. In fact, Keynes only cites "Mr Justice Jelf" as "[h]aving referred to 'Mayne on Damages' (8th ed., p. 70)," in his *Treatise on Probability* (Keynes 1962 / 1921: 24–25). Keynes does not indicate that he himself read "Mayne on Damages," and Mayne is not listed in the index. Again, this source is only part of his discussion of his view that not all degrees of probability can be exactly or numerically measured.

But it is a small world. The 1872 and 1894 title pages say that Mayne and Smith are "of the Inner Temple." Mayne died in 1917. Smith died in 1918 at the age of 85 (*The Annual Register* 1918: 181). And Arthur Richard Jelf (1837–1917) was a member of the Inner Temple too. Thus Keynes might have got his cites to *Mayne* and Jelf from Mayne, Smith, or Jelf *in person* at dinner in the Inner Temple in 1904. Like Keynes, Smith went to Trinity Hall, Cambridge, and was ninth Wrangler in 1857 (*The Annual Register* 1918: 181). Per the 1894 title page, Smith was "One of Her Majesty's Counsel, Judge of the Westminster County Court, Late Fellow of Trinity Hall, Cambridge." Later, Smith was "Judge of the City of London Court" (*The Annual Register* 1918: 181).

Alexander James Edmund Cockburn (1802–1880) of the Middle Temple "was Lord Chief Justice of England,...was educated at Trinity Hall, Cambridge, of which he was elected a fellow, and afterwards an honorary fellow[.] Lord John Russell[, Bertrand Russell's grandfather,] appointed him solicitor-general in 1850 and attorney-general in 1851" (Fact-Index.com 2015). Lord Justice Colin Blackburn (1813–1896) went to Trinity Hall, Cambridge too, and was of the Inner Temple. This too goes to the small world, even if Keynes could not have dined with them in 1904.

James Fitzjames Stephen

James Fitzjames Stephen (1829–1894) wrote the Indian Evidence Act "almost entirely on his own" (Twining 1994: 53); it is still the evidence law of India today (Twining 1994: 54). In

England, he was quite famous for this. Later he served as a judge. "Stephen was called to the Bar by the Inner Temple on 26 January 1854" Hostettler 2013: 148).

Twining says that like Gilbert, Stephen tried to subsume all evidence law under a single principle; but Gilbert "unhelpful[ly]" chose the best evidence rule, while Stephen chose the relevance rule, which was deeper and more plausible, and was a "fruitful failure" in stimulating further work on the concept of relevance (Twining 1994: 56–57). We saw that earlier that Twining is wrong about Gilbert; we are about to see he is wrong about Stephen too. For just as Best has a relevance rule which Best does not subsume under the best evidence rule, so Stephen has a best evidence rule which Stephen does not subsume under the relevance rule, though Stephen certainly regards the best evidence rule as less important.

It might be objected that it all depends on what we mean by "subsume under." But if we mean 'show to be a version or aspect of', 'logically derive from', 'explain in terms of', or even just 'find to be intellectually illuminated by', I find no subsumption of either of these two rules under the other in Gilbert or Stephen, or in any other law treatise writer that I discuss in this chapter. If we mean 'classify under' in a species-genus relation, then we need to be able to state what the genus is and what the difference is according to the law treatise writer in question. And beyond that, I am not sure what else we might reasonably mean by "subsume under." Even 'find to be intellectually illuminated by' is not enough in my opinion. For analogies often illuminate but fail to suffice for classification, much less explanation, derivation, aspecthood, or versionhood. And really the burden is on the authors who use the word "subsume" to explain what precisely *they* mean by it. I can only suggest the only plausible meanings that *I* can think of.

Murphy says, "The concept of relevance was developed in the nineteenth century, and refined principally by Sir James Fitzjames Stephen" (Murphy 2008: 9). Murphy finds that Stephen's work was eventually superseded (Murphy 2008: 9).

Stephen makes Best's distinction between natural and judicial evidence basic to evidence law, which Montrose says Best himself did not do (Montrose 1992 / 1954: 350 / 550). Stephen deems Best's natural evidence, which was Bentham's evidence in general, to be *(logically) relevant* evidence, and he deems Best's judicial evidence to be *legally relevant* evidence. Thus Stephen admits a basic dualism in relevance: there is logical relevance, and there is legal relevance. Legal relevance is generally narrower than logical relevance, and functions to exclude some logically relevant evidence as legally irrelevant. No doubt Chamberlayne's Taylor gets his distinction between logical relevance and legal relevance from Stephen (Taylor 1897: 2[6]–2[8]).

In fact, Stephen was going in the right direction, deeming the legal rules of evidence to be basically exclusionary (Twining 1994: 54). What he failed to see was that they were not *evidentiary* in nature at all, since they are not *relevant* to the point in issue at all. Instead, they are rules that exclude natural evidence (which *is* evidentiary and *is* relevant) as *legally inadmissible* for various general *policy* reasons which may or may not have anything to do with evidentiary concerns. The rule against admitting hearsay is largely based on the evidentiary unreliability of hearsay in general. But the rule against self-incrimination is largely a protection against forced confession regardless of the evidentiary reliability of torture or other coercion.

In 1872, the year Russell was born, Sir James Fitzjames Stephen wrote in the Preface to *The Indian Evidence Act* that "On the 5th March, 1872, in moving that the 'Indian Evidence Act' should be taken into consideration by the Legislative Council, I said" (Stephen 1872: v):

> "The subject is one which reaches far beyond law. The law of evidence is nothing unless it is founded upon a rational conception of the manner in which truth as to all matters of fact ought to be investigated." (Stephen 1872: v, quoting his own speech to the Legislative Council on March 5, 1872)

This is natural evidence. In the Introduction, under the heading "Fundamental Rules of English Law of Evidence," Stephen says:

> That part of the English law of evidence which professes to be founded upon anything in the nature of a theory may be reduced to the following rules:—
> (1) Evidence must be *confined to the matters in issue.*
> (2) Hearsay evidence is not to be admitted.
> (3) In all cases the best evidence must be given....
> Each of these rules is very loosely expressed. The word 'evidence', which is the leading term of each, is undefined and ambiguous.
> It sometimes *means* the words uttered and things exhibited by witnesses before a court of justice.
> At other times, it *means* the facts proved to exist by these things....
> Again, it is sometimes used as *meaning* to assert that a particular fact is *relevant* to the matter under inquiry. (Stephen 1872: 3, my emphasis)

We see that Stephen places the relevance rule first, the hearsay rule second, and the best evidence rule third, and that he does not reduce any of these rules to any of the others. Instead, he says that any part of English evidence law that is capable of theoretical treatment "may be reduced to" those three rules, which he treats as equally logically fundamental, *pace* Twining. Stephen does not explain exactly what he means by 'reduce', but surely it must be a logical relation of *some* sort, in the broad sense of intellectual or conceptual relation.

We also see that Stephen makes relevance one of the three *meanings* that can be expressed by the word "evidence." When the word "evidence" is used with that meaning, this of course makes the thesis that evidence is relevant into a tautology, as opposed to an informative logical analysis. Thus it makes rule (1) tautological, insofar as to be relevant is to be confined to the matters in issue.

Stephen regards the relevance rule as the most important one. He says, "[T]he question, 'what facts are relevant',...is the most important of all the questions that can be asked about the law of evidence" (Stephen 1872: 4).

Stephen discusses relevancy further on pages 9–11. He distinguishes facts in issue from relevant facts. He says:

> (1) [Facts such that] the existence of the disputed right or liability would be a legal inference from them....may be called facts in issue...." (Stephen 1872: 9)

Then he says:

> (2) Facts, which are not themselves in issue in the sense above explained, may *affect the probability* of the existence of facts in issue, and be used as the foundations of inferences respecting them; such facts are described in the Evidence Act as *relevant* facts.
>
> All the facts with which it can in any event be necessary for courts of justice to concern themselves, are included in these two classes.
>
> The first great question, therefore, which the law of evidence should decide is, what facts are *relevant*. (Stephen 1872: 9–10, my emphasis)

All the foregoing is from the introductory chapter 1. The discussion is very logical and very modern. Note that in provision (2), he defines (or essentially describes) relevance in terms of probability. The definition is basically the same as American *FRE* Rule 401.

Chapter 2, "Induction and Deduction," occupies pages 13–51. The final header is "Degrees of Probability" (Stephen 1872: 51).

Chapter 3, "The Theory of Relevancy, with Illustration[s]," occupies pages 52–128. After some argumentation, he concludes:

> The rule, therefore, that facts may be regarded as relevant which can be shown to stand either in the relation of cause or in the relation of effect to the fact which they are said to be relevant, may be accepted as true, *subject to* the caution that, when an inference is to be founded upon the existence of such a connection, every step by which the connection is made out must be proved, or be so probable under the circumstances of the case that it may be presumed without proof. (Stephen 1872: 53–54, my emphasis)

Here he wisely requires not only that there be a causal relation, but also that it be provable or at least probable. That is to say, he is requiring that the causal relation be evidentially relevant. My only criticism is that we should be going by probability alone, since in some cases we may not be able to make any *specific* causal relation probable. For example, suppose three people conspire to murder a fourth. They load three physically identical guns, one with bullets and two with blanks. They pick up the guns at random and shoot at the victim at the same time in a firing squad in front of hundreds of witnesses and video cameras. They then destroy the guns in a vat of molten steel. Supposing that this describes all the evidence, no one shooter is the probable *specific* agential cause of the murder, since there is only a one third chance any one of them shot the victim. Even they have no idea who did it. But that there *was* a murder, not to mention a conspiracy to murder, would seem very probable indeed. No doubt there are indefinitely many cases where one person puts another in harm's way, and the harm is inevitable in one way or another, but the specific cause of the harm is unknowable. For example, one could lock another in a room with ten bombs hidden in locations where the prisoner would inevitably go, and in such a way that any bomb would destroy all the evidence.

Whether we accept Stephen's definition or not, we may still agree with him that:

> These sections [on relevancy] are by far the most important, as they are the most original part of the Evidence Act, as they affirm positively what facts may be proved, whereas the English law assumes this to be known, and merely declares negatively that certain facts shall not be proved. (Stephen 1872: 55)

But I am not sure I agree with the "whereas." Looking to what we have reviewed so far, I think he might be a bit harsh on English law as discussed by his predecessors.

In 1876, Stephen's summary *Digest of the Law of Evidence* appeared. He says in the Introduction:

> The arrangement of the book is the same as that of the Indian Evidence Act, and is based on the distinction between relevancy and proof....The neglect of this distinction, which is concealed by the ambiguity of the word evidence (a word which sometimes means testimony and at other times relevancy) has thrown the whole subject into confusion, and has made what was really plain enough appear almost incomprehensible....
>
> The facts which may be proved are facts in issue, or facts relevant to the issue.
>
> Facts in issue are those facts upon the existence of which the right or liability to be ascertained in the proceeding depends.
>
> Facts relevant to the issue are facts from the existence of which inference as to the existence of the facts in issue may be drawn.
>
> A fact is relevant to another fact when the existence of the one can be shown to be the cause or one of the causes, or the effect or one of the effects, of the existence of the other, *or* when the existence of the one, either alone or together with other facts, renders the existence of the other highly probable, or improbable, according to the common course of events. (Stephen 1876: viii–x, my emphasis)

The disjunctive "or" definition of relevance in the last paragraph is very different from the conditional "subject to" definition in the *Act*. I have three criticisms of this new disjunctive definition.

First, if it suffices for relevance that a fact make a fact in issue highly probable, or even merely more probable than it would be otherwise, then the alternative disjunct, making a causal relation a sufficient condition of relevance, is needless. And if the causation was improbable, then it is irrelevant. Of course, if a fact is shown to be either a cause or an effect of a fact in issue, then we have a causal proof. I mean by "causal proof" that if a fact F is proved to exist, and is proved to be either the cause or an effect of fact G, then the existence of fact G is proved. But the question is whether we can give such a causal proof in the situation at hand. Fact F may indeed *be* the cause or an effect of fact G. But fact F is *relevant evidence* for fact G only if we can *show* that it is the cause or an effect of G.

Second, not every cause or effect of a fact is relevant to a matter in issue. My shooting a person may cause someone else to be sad, but the sadness is evidentially irrelevant to whether I shot the person. Of course, one can validly argue that (1) the sadness exists and (2) the sadness was caused by my shooting the person, therefore (3) I shot the person. That would be a valid causal proof. But premiss (2), that the sadness was caused by my shooting the person, begs the question on whether I shot the person. Thus, considered by itself, a sadness that is later in time is not evidence. We might not even be able to infer that *any* act in particular made the person sad, much less that it was my act. It might have been just a wave of sadness caused by the brain. This is not to mention remote causes or remote effects, or more to the point, unlikely causes or effects.

Third, the very same cause or effect may be relevant or irrelevant depending on how it is described. As we know, causation is referentially opaque (Føllesdal 1971: 53–54). "I shot the hooded man" does not imply "I shot my brother." Thus if evidential relevance is causal, then it is referentially opaque.

These three criticisms also apply to the disjunctive definition (5) of proximate cause in *Black's Law Dictionary* which I criticized in the section on Mayne. Of course, *Black's* is correct as a mere report of Stephen's usage.

One might object to the third criticism that evidence is referentially opaque in any case. For one and the same body of evidence can always be described in different ways. For example, "Witnesses saw that I shot the hooded man" makes it less probable that I shot my brother than does "Witnesses saw that I shot my brother." My reply is that all evidence as such is already under a description. For evidence is always relative to cognitive beings and to their points of view. That is, evidence is *our* evidence, and our evidence is always our evidence *as we understand it.* If there were no conscious beings, then there would be no evidence either. Not so for causation, which is there in the world independently of how we think of or describe the world. But because our understanding of the evidence *is* essential to what the evidence is, evidence cannot be described in *essentially* different ways and remain the evidence it is. (Of course, it can be described in *accidentally* different ways, such as "the evidence that I collected last night.") What is evidence for me might not be evidence for you, or for some super-scientist. To sum up, evidence is *essentially not* referentially opaque. It belongs to the world of seeming as opposed to the world of being. Specifically, it is rational or relevant seeming. In contrast, facts in issue belong to the world of being. And we try to use our rational seemings to prove what happened in the world of being. This is not at all to say that seemings are subjective. Rational seemings are objective to the extent that they are rational. Also, seemings can be shared, or public. Then they are relative to the public understanding of the world.

One might further reply that what evidentially seems to be the case is what is given, and what is given is preconceptual, predescriptive "pure" experience. Therefore evidence is essentially preconceptual and predescriptive, and thus cannot be referentially opaque, since it cannot be described at all, much less in different ways. My reply is that the premiss may be true, but the implied conclusion does not follow, that *evidence* is pure experience. Perhaps evidence includes or ultimately involves pure experience, but evidence for something is not pure experience. It is a concept, and a highly abstract concept at that. Evidence is ultimately perception as opposed to pure experience, and as such it is often describable. Thus the way out is to distinguish essential description from accidental description of evidence. Evidential seemings are perceptions as opposed to pure experience, and often describable. In contrast, pure experience is nameable by logically proper names; this includes naming sense-qualities. Even in a scientific study of what colors we saw, which might be evidence for what chemical was used to murder someone, the colors must be perceptually established as factually the case. I shall return to this point shortly.

Russell gives two arguments that there must be a pure datum of sense if there is to be any perception at all, and an argument that can be rewritten as a vicious regress argument for the same conclusion. These arguments are given in my (2015: ch. 4) as:

(Psychological) Argument #3. Perception cannot be pure interpretation, that is, interpretation that is *of* nothing. Therefore there must be something perceived which is not nothing (IMT 124–25).

(Epistemological) Argument #4. There must be a pure datum. For data cannot be conceptualization alone. Conceptualization must be *of* something (HK 167–70).

(Epistemological) Argument #5. Each datum has its own evidential weight which is not nothing. Otherwise knowledge will be impossible due to a vicious epistemic regress (IMT 124–25; see HK 157, 189–90). This weight is intrinsic, hence preconceptual.

I accept arguments #3 and #4 as clear and convincing, though not as absolutely certain, partly because I am not absolutely certain what absolute certainty is.

I take argument #5 as rewritable for a different conclusion as follows. If, every sensation were a conceptualized percept, then it would have a conceptual component and a sensation component. But then the sensation component would be a percept in turn, and would have its own conceptual component and sensation component. And so on to infinity. But the regress is vicious, since if there were no sensation, there could be no perception. Thus there must be a "first" sensation which is purely sensational. We may call this argument #5a. The first thing to note is that Russell goes not give it. But I think he might be very sympathetic to it, since he gives the *similar* #5, and since he gives #4 for the same *conclusion* as that of #5a. The second thing to note is that #4 arguably states the basis of #5a. I mean that #5a argues that the regress must stop because percepts must include sensations; and that it is intuitively plausible to say that the deeper *reason* it must stop, besides the mere definitional fact that percepts must include sensations, is that conceptualization must be *of* something; and in a percept, the conceptualization could only be of a sensation.

One might object that an infinite series of sensation components guarantees not just one, but infinitely many sensations, albeit conceptualized ones. My reply is that this is contrary to the phenomenology of perception. We are simply not presented with any such series in perception. When we are presented with a perceptual object, we are presented with just one such object, and it is presented through sensation. That we may *focus* on, say, the redness of an apple, and then ask ourselves about its conceptual component and its sensation component, does not detract from this point. Quite the opposite. That we have to change our focus to single out another percept, the apple's redness as opposed to the red apple, is actually further proof of the point.

Still, I favor arguments #3 and #4 as better than #5a, partly because of the difficulty of evaluating regress arguments, and partly because #3 and #4 are simpler, clearer, deeper, and more direct.

The large literature on the "given" is beyond the scope of this book. Briefly, it is plausible to analyze an ordinary perceptual object into a sensation component and a conceptual component; and it seems from arguments #3 and #4 that this is what the 1940–48 Russell does. In 1912 *Problems*, the perception of an ordinary thing involves sense-data given in acquaintance, and a description that goes beyond that immediate experience. The description involves a universal, and "a universal of which we are aware" is a concept (PP 52). Thus there is a pure sensation and a conceptual component in *Problems* as well.

Of course, for the 1912 Russell, *physical* evidence can only be known by description. This is consistent with the 1912 Russell's views that *sense-data* are self-evident (PP 114), and that we cannot have physical evidence *without* sense-data; they are a necessary condition.

The deepest rejoinder to my reply, that all evidence as such is already under an essential description, would be that this is simply not true. We often have good evidence based on our experience that we are simply unable to describe. I agree with a point very much like this one in note 4 to this book. There I hold that we cannot always describe our reasons for our views; and that is pretty much the same thing. For our evidence is our reason to believe. My reply is to distinguish description from conceptualization. That is, perceptual evidence is essentially *conceptualized*, but we may not always be able to *describe* it, that is, to state our reasons for believing some view. Thus I amend my reply so as to say that all evidence as such is already under an essential *conceptualization* (but not necessarily under any *description*). And that is enough to make all evidence as such already *conceptually opaque*, as opposed to causation that is out there in the world. I need not add that conceptualizations, as such, are not linguistic like descriptions.

A final objection to my view is that if all evidence is conceptualized, then pure sensations are not evidence. My reply is that this is generally true. There may be exceptions where we are doing a frequency prediction of occurrences of pure sensations, or predicting a pure sensation such as a phenomenal after-image, or the like. But in ordinary life, typical science, and typical courts of law, our evidence is never or almost never pure, uninterpreted sensation. Courts want witnesses to report only the facts and not add their own opinions; but these facts are already conceptualized ordinary things. Again, even in a scientific study of what colors we saw, which might be evidence for what chemical was used to murder someone, the colors must be perceptually established as factually the case.

Murphy has noticed that Stephen closely anticipates *FRE* Rule 401. Murphy says:

> In *DPP* v *Kilbourne* [1973] AC 729 at 756 Lord Simon of Glaisdale said:
>
>> Evidence is *relevant* if it is *logically probative or disprobative* of some matter which requires proof. It is sufficient to say, even at the risk of etymological tautology, that *relevant* (*i.e., logically probative or disprobative*) evidence is evidence which makes the matter which requires proof *more or less probable.*
>
> This is, perhaps, a simpler and more satisfactory, if less comprehensive definition of relevance, than the classic formulation in Stephen's *Digest*, according to which the word signified that:[22]

> any two facts to which it is applied are
> so *related* to each other that according
> to the common course of events, one
> either taken by itself or in connection
> with other facts *proves or renders*
> *probable* the past, present or future
> *existence or non-existence* of the
> other.

Neither attains the appealing simplicity of the American Federal Rule of Evidence 401, whereby the term "relevant evidence"

> means evidence having any tendency
> to make the existence of any fact that
> is of consequence to the determination
> of the action *more probable or less*
> *probable than it would be without the*
> *evidence.*

Thus, relevant evidence is evidence which has probative value in assisting the court or jury to determine the facts in issue. *Relevance is not a legal concept, but a logical one, which describes the relationship between a piece of evidence and a fact in issue....If the evidence contributes in a logical sense, to any extent, either to the proof or the disproof of the fact in issue, then the evidence is relevant to the fact in issue. If not, it is irrelevant.* It is a fundamental rule of the law of evidence that...evidence must be relevant in order to be admissible. The converse, however, is not true, because much relevant evidence is inadmissible under the specific rules of evidence affecting admissibility.
22. *Digest of the Law of Evidence*, 12th ed., art. 1. The definition was somewhat different in earlier editions, but this seems to be the author's mature view. (Murphy 2008: 29, my emphasis, except for case and book titles)

I take it that the following is a definitional logical equivalence for Stephen, Lord Simon, Murphy, and *FRE* Rule 401 alike: Evidence is relevant if and only if that evidence, "taken by itself or in connection with other facts," makes the fact in issue more or less probable "than it would be without the evidence." Here, relevant evidence logically can, but need not be, intrinsically relevant.

By updating our account to the 1936 twelfth edition of the *Digest* (Murphy 2008: 29 n.22; Stephen 1936), Murphy shows us that the posthumous Stephen avoids the problems I raised with his 1876 disjunctive definition of "relevant."

It seems that for Stephen, probabilistic relevance is implicitly grounded in the modality of epistemic necessity. Stephen says:

> ARTICLE 8.
> FACTS *NECESSARY* TO EXPLAIN OR INTRODUCE *RELEVANT* FACTS.
> Facts *necessary* to be known to explain or introduce a fact in issue or *relevant* fact, or which support or rebut an inference suggested by a fact in issue or *relevant* fact, or which establish the identity of any thing or person whose identity is at issue or relevant to the issue, or which fix the time and place at which any fact in issue or relevant fact happened, or which show that any document produced is genuine or otherwise, or which show the relation of the parties by whom any such fact was transacted, or which afforded an opportunity for its occurrence or transaction, or which are *necessary* to be known in order to show the relevancy of other facts, are *relevant in so far as they are necessary* for those purposes respectively. (Stephen 1876: 11, my emphasis)

The key phrase is "relevant in so far as they are necessary for those purposes." This implies that for the purposes mentioned, evidence is relevant if and only if it is necessary. The twice-used phrase "necessary to be known" bases relevance on *epistemic* necessity. But it seems trivial that to provide evidence, it is also *logically* and *essentially* necessary to provide relevant facts, since evidence is essentially relevant. Correspondingly, in deductive logic, that a premiss is necessary to prove a conclusion is a strict sense of what Anderson and Belnap (1992; 1975) and others call use-relevance. A looser sense would be that the premiss is necessary to *some* proof, which cannot succeed without it, but there are or may be alternative proofs which do not need to use it, in order to succeed. One would think there is a corresponding looser sense for probabilistic evidence as well.

Might Keynes have known of Stephen on evidence law simply because Stephen was famous? John Hostettler says:

> In the early 19th-century vast areas of India were controlled by the East India Company...It is difficult to overestimate Stephen's impact on the English political scene following his Indian experiences. For years he had used his pen in England to write numerous articles in popular journals and engage in controversy with the most important people of the day. His name was everywhere. Disraeli was later to write Lord Lytton in 1881, "It is a thousand pities that J F Stephen is a Judge;

he might have done anything and everything as a leader
of the future Conservative party." (Hostettler 2013: 151)

The young Keynes actually worked in the India Office, the office in
Great Britain that controlled all Indian affairs, while working on his
theory of probability. How could he not have known one of the
most famous names of British India?

Keynes and Russell might at least have heard of Stephen as
a major conservative critic of John Stuart Mill, Russell's godfather.
Stephen's major critique of Mill, *Liberty, Equality, and Fraternity*,
was published in 1873, the year after Russell was born (Hostettler
2013: 152). But Stephen also greatly praises Mill for updating
logic. The days of Locke's being the main philosophical inspiration
for legal writers on evidence are now gone (Twining 1994: 52).
This is not mention the inspiration of Bentham, especially in Mill's
edition.

James Bradley Thayer

James Bradley Thayer (1831–1902) was Royall Professor
of Law at Harvard, and later Weld Professor. He gave us the view
we accept today, but not at first. This is not well known. Montrose
and Twining omit Thayer's early view.

The 1880–81 "early" Thayer accepts both logical relevance
and legal relevance. He says in an essay called "Bedingfeld's
Case—Declarations as a Part of the Res Gesta":

> Whatsoever is irrelevant may, of course, be rejected;
> whatsoever, also, though in strictness relevant, is, as the
> case stands, clearly inadequate, and so immaterial;
> whatsoever, though relevant and not quite immaterial,
> yet, having regard to the bearing of it in other parts of
> the case or the use that is likely to be made of it, is really
> colorable. No doubt the exercise of these functions is a
> delicate matter; but the right to exercise them points to a
> difference between parts of the *res gestae*, which are
> **legally admissible**, and other parts. We are to consider,
> then, that just as **there is a relevancy which is logical
> but not legal,**—so that when we talk in a **legal**
> discussion, we mean **legal relevancy,**—so in a **legal**
> discussion about evidence the expression, "a part of the
> *res gestae*," means such a part of it as is **admissible in
> evidence**, having regard to all the rules. (Thayer
> 1880–81: 285, Thayer's italic emphasis, my boldface
> emphasis)

Thus Thayer admits both "a relevancy which is logical but not legal" and "legal relevancy"—and equates legal relevancy with the legal admissibility of evidence. But the distinction appears to be one of degree, with the degrees ranging from "immaterial" to "not quite immaterial" and beyond. Compare Chamberlayne's Taylor.

Material relevance is indeed relevance to the point in issue, but it is conceptual and legal as opposed to evidentiary and empirical in nature. It does not prove anything or make anything probable.

The popular Perry Mason phrase "incompetent, irrelevant, and immaterial" is confused. Nothing can be all three. *Witnesses* are competent if they are qualified to *testify*. *Evidence*, including the testimony of witnesses, is relevant if it helps establish some *fact*. A *fact* is material if it conceptually relates to some legal issue, i.e., if it *would* help establish the legal issue if there *were* evidence for the fact. The popular phrase is best left to television shows.

The 1898–1900 "later" or "mature" Thayer admits logically relevant evidence, but sees that what is called legal relevance is not evidentiary in nature at all, but is merely a grab bag of unrelated policy restrictions on the *admissibility* of logically relevant evidence. "It was Thayer who demonstrated most fully the basic distinction between" logical relevance and admissibility" (Montrose 1992 / 1954: 351 / 531). Wigmore follows Thayer, and so does the world of Anglo-American evidence law today.

In one of the most influential passages on evidence law, Thayer says in his 1898 (the book says "copyright 1896, 1898" on the title page, but was first published in 1898) *Preliminary Treatise on Evidence*:

> There is a principle—not so much a rule of evidence as a presupposition involved in the very conception of a rational system of evidence, as contrasted with the old formal and mechanical systems—which forbids receiving anything *irrelevant, not logically probative.* How are we to know what these forbidden things are? Not by any rule of law. The law furnishes no test of relevancy. For this it tacitly refers to logic and general experience....
>
> There is another precept which should be laid down as preliminary...namely, that *unless excluded by some principle or law, all that is logically probative is admissible.* This general admissibility, however, is not, like the former principle, a necessary presupposition in a rational system of evidence; there are many exceptions to it....These rules of exclusion [and] their exceptions [are] the chief part of the law of evidence. (Thayer 1898: 264–66, my emphasis)

We see two principles here. First is the negative principle that what is irrelevant is inadmissible. Second is the positive precept that what is relevant is admissible unless it is excluded by some rule of exclusion. Thus, in order for evidence to be admissible, it must pass a two prong test. First, it must be logically relevant. Second, it must not be excluded by any of the exclusionary policy rules (Thayer 1898: 266). As Thayer says later in the book:

> In all cases, upon offering evidence, two questions may arise: one of its *logical relevancy*, and another of its admissibility, under the excluding rules of evidence. [These respectively involve] the *logical principle of relevancy,* and the excluding operation of the general rules of evidence.... (Thayer 1898: 468–69, my emphasis; see 514–15)

Thayer says, "This excluding function is the characteristic one in our law of evidence" (Thayer 1898: 264).

Thus Thayer no longer admits two types of relevance, logical and legal. He admits only logical relevance. He finds it confusing to consider the grab bag of exclusionary rules to amount to legal relevance, or even to an evidentiary concept at all. He says:

> [I]t is a question of where lies the balance of practical advantage. To discuss such questions...even if we introduced *the poor notion of legal relevancy, as contrasted with logical relevancy*—tends to obscure the nature of the inquiry. There is in truth no rule of law to apply [consistently to the huge and confusing mass of court opinions on when to exclude relevant evidence]. Thayer 1898: 517, my emphasis)

Thayer dislikes the best evidence rule. In his first sub-title in chapter 11 on the best evidence rule, Thayer calls it "A large and vague thing" (Thayer 1898: xii). The whole chapter is a sustained critique of the best evidence rule which I will not describe here.

Thayer sums up his views in chapter 12, "The Present and Future of the Law of Evidence." Four sub-titles are: "Its principles few, but its rules many and perplexed.—Much of it is really a mistaken expression of doctrines of the substantive law.—Excluding rules.—Relevancy" (Thayer 1898:xii).

Thayer finds the concept of legal relevance confused for two reasons. First, where probability is concerned, any concept of relevance makes sense only as an evidentiary concept. But the so-called concept of legal relevance is not an evidentiary concept at all. It really concerns policy reasons for *not* admitting evidence that *is* relevant. Thus it is really the concept of admissibility. Second, there is one thing that logical relevance is. Namely, it is the general relation of being objective, rational evidence for something. And as such, it belongs to logic, not to law. But there is no one thing that so-called "legal relevance" can be. For the term refers to a grab bag of unrelated policy reasons for excluding evidence. Some such reasons do indeed have an evidentiary aspect, such as excluding hearsay; but even here the policy reason is not merely that hearsay is unreliable, but also that it can be misleading or even prejudicial.

In his brief 1900 paper, "Law and Logic," Thayer replies to a critic of his 1898 *Preliminary Treatise*. Thayer says the thesis of his book is that:

> [O]ur law of evidence is a *rational* system[;] that in admitting evidence in our law, it is always assumed to be logically probative, i.e., probative in its own nature.—according to the rules that govern the process of reasoning; that the considerations determining this logical quality are not fixed by the law, and that, so far as legal determinations do proceed merely on such considerations, they do not belong to the domain of law; that the law of evidence, however, *excludes* much which is logically good, that is to say, good according to the tests of reason and general experience; and that the rules of exclusion make up the main part of the law of evidence. The reasons for these views...are indicated in the book....
>   **Now this book uses the word "relevancy" merely as importing a logical relation, that is to say, a relation determined by the reasoning faculty. The word "admissibility" is the term which it applies to the determinations of the law of evidence.** (Thayer 1900: 307–8, Thayer's italic emphasis, my boldface emphasis)

This is another deeply influential passage from Thayer. Except for Thayer's not admitting logical relevance as a timeless Platonic entity in metaphysics, the first boldface sentence is Keynes exactly. The second boldface sentence sounds the death knell of legal relevancy.

Today everyone or almost everyone rejects the confusing distinction between logical relevance and legal relevance, which makes it sound as if there were two kinds of evidentiary relevance: one being the general rational kind, and the other being a specific kind peculiar to law. Today we find it correct to distinguish between logical relevance and legal *admissibility* of evidence, which is what talk of "legal relevance" was really about. Admissibility is not a kind of relevance, but is a laundry list of *curbs on* relevant evidence due to various policy reasons. Compare the very modern Murphy (2008: 29–33). See also *Federal Rules of Evidence*: Article 4, "Relevancy and Its Limits," encompassing Rules 401–415, on many topics; Article 8, "Hearsay," encompassing Rules 801–806, on the admissibility of hearsay; Rule 105 on limited admissibility, and so on. Finally, I am honored to cite the treatise of my University of Michigan School of Law professor, Rick Lempert, *A Modern Approach to Evidence* (2011: ch. 3, "Relevance," ch. 4, "Relevant But Inadmissible," and elsewhere). I took his course in 1995 and helped correct the treatise draft (Lempert 2000: vi).

Concerning logical relevance, Taylor and Thayer agree that mere or bare logical relevance is not enough, and basically for the same reason:

> The law of evidence undoubtedly requires that evidence to a jury shall be clearly relevant, and not merely slightly so; it must not barely afford a basis for conjecture, but for real belief; it must not merely be remotely relevant, but proximately so. (Thayer 1898: 516)

That is, evidence must be not only logically relevant but clearly relevant, weighty enough to be a basis for real belief, and proximately (foreseeably) relevant as opposed to remotely relevant. That would be a departure from philosophical theory of relevance. In fact, it is technically an exclusion of relevant evidence, and is thus a kind of inadmissibility. Arguably, it also falls under *FRE* Rule 403's "exclusion of relevant evidence...by considerations of undue delay, waste of time, or needless presentation of cumulative evidence." But the important point is that logical relevance is the proper *locus* for this sort of difference in degree ("slightly so," "barely afford"). That is in the sharpest terminological difference from calling a higher degree of logical relevance "legal relevance," as if it were different in kind.

Shapiro appears to disagree with me on Thayer. She says:

> Although most early and mid-nineteenth century treatises emphasize the similarity between legal reasoning and evidence and ordinary reasoning and evidence, it must be admitted that James Thayer's influential *Preliminary Treatise on Evidence at the Common Law* represents a departure from this position....Thayer appears to be of several minds whether, or to what degree, legal evidence and reasoning differ from evidence and reasoning in other fields of inquiry. At one point he differentiates between legal evidence and historical and religious evidence and insists that legal evidence is concerned with what is admissible, not what is logically probative. Yet he also admits that the rules of legal argument are

"mainly an affair of logic and general experience, not legal precept," and they do not call "into play any different faculties or involve any new principles or methods."....Thayer thus represents something of a departure from previous thinkers. On the one hand he differentiates legal from mathematical reasoning on the traditional ground that the law does not deal with demonstration. On the other hand, unlike most of his predecessors, he distinguishes legal reasoning from other types of evidence that deal with probabilities. (Shapiro 1991: 38–39)

Granted, Thayer is of two minds, "early" and "later." And the early Thayer is confused and needs correcting, certainly according to the later Thayer. But Shapiro gives no indication that she is aware of the early Thayer. And her statement is a misdescription of the later Thayer from start to finish. The sentence beginning "At one point" misdescribes Thayer's view that the so-called legal "evidence rules" for excluding evidence concern admissibility. The sentence beginning "Yet he also" misdescribes his view that all reasoning from evidence is based on general principles of logic and general experience in every field, and that there is no special rational faculty or special rational method for law, or for that matter, for any field. The sentence beginning "On the one hand" misdescribes his view that mathematics is a deductive science while law concerns inductive logic. And the sentence beginning "On the other hand" misdescribes the fact that he chiefly differs from his predecessors in that he holds that the so-called legal evidence rules are not rules for assessing the specific evidentiary value of specific evidence, but for excluding evidence for various policy reasons that have nothing in common with each other, and that range from excluding hearsay as unreliable in general to protecting the rights of the accused.

Thayer is the culminating flower of the assimilative tradition of making evidence in law just like any other evidence. He is the fulfiller of Bentham's general concept of evidence, which Best calls natural evidence. He says that general or natural evidence is the only kind of evidence there is, in law or elsewhere. He denies that general evidence is a genus with a legal species. He finds that general evidence is not a genus at all, since it has no species. He says that the so-called "evidence rules" in law are really admissibility rules.

Though Thayer was an American legal scholar, Keynes could have easily read him, not to mention hearing about him or his ideas, as far as dating is concerned. Thayer was writing of logical relevance in a way that involves degrees of logical relevance at least six years before Keynes read Moore's book in 1904. Taylor was even earlier, and lived and worked as a judge in London. Keynes could have read even the posthumous Taylor quite easily, and have taken from him his concept of logical relevance, which would have been the only one of interest to Keynes. There is no reason why Keynes would have been interested in legal relevance as opposed to logical relevance. And Keynes could have learned all this at lunch in the Inner Temple from lawyers who read Thayer, and who knew Taylor personally for many years.

Charles Frederic Chamberlayne

Charles Frederic Chamberlayne (1855–1913) studied under Thayer at Harvard Law School, and "was recommended by Thayer to be the American editor of Best's *Principles*[. He wrote the] American notes for three editions of that work, which was commended by Thayer 'as the most authoritative and reliable treatise on the subject of evidence in the English language'" (Twining 1994: 61 quoting Thayer). And as we saw earlier, Chamberlayne also wrote the notes to the 1897 edition of Taylor. The first volume of Chamberlayne's own treatise appeared in 1911.

Chamberlayne knew Thayer and his work well. No doubt he knew Thayer wrote of logical relevancy as early as 1880/81.

In 1883, Chamberlayne uses the terms "logical relevancy" and "logically relevant" in a note in his 1883 American edition of posthumous Best. Chamberlayne says in his note 1 to Best's § 251:

> §251. **Of all rules of evidence, the most universal and the most obvious is this,**—that the evidence adduced should be alike **directed and confined to the matters which are in dispute,** or which form the subject of the investigation.[1]
>
> 1. *Facts in Issue.* —The "facts in issue" in any action are those so constituted by the pleadings or the nature of the investigation. Facts which **logically** and obviously tend to determine the existence, extent, or nature of the right, liability, or disability asserted or denied in any such action, are facts **relevant** to the issue....Conf. Steph. Dig. Law. Eviden., 3d ed., Art. 1;....
> *Relevancy.*—Mr. Justice Stephen in his third edition **defines relevancy** in an unexceptionable manner. Two facts are said to be **relevant** to each other when so related "that, according to the common course of events, one, either taken by itself or in connection with other facts, **proves or renders probable** the past, present, or future existence or non-existence of the other." (Dig. Law Evid., Art. 1) **This is relevancy,—in a logical sense. Legal relevancy**, which is essential to admissible

evidence, requires a higher standard of evidentiary force. It includes **logical relevancy**; and for reasons of practical convenience, demands a close connection between the fact to be proved and the fact offered to prove it. **All evidence must be logically relevant,**—that is absolutely essential. The fact, however, that it is **logically relevant**, does not insure admissibility; it must also be **legally relevant**. A fact which "in connection with other facts renders probable the existence" of a fact in issue, may still be rejected, if in the opinion of the judge and under the circumstances of the case it be considered essentially misleading or too remote. U.S. *v.* Ross, 92. U.S. 281, 284, per Strong, J.; Morrissey *v.* Ingham, 111 Mass. 63; Jones *v.* State, 26 Miss. 247. See § 90, supra....

    Relevancy not Sole Test of Admissibility.— **Logical relevancy** is assumed by Mr. Justice Stephen throughout the Digest of Evidence to be the **sole rational test of admissibility**; that the two, relevancy and admissibility, are or ought to be coextensive and interchangeable terms. This is certainly a mistake. Public policy considerations of fairness, the practical necessity for reaching speedy decisions, these and similar reasons cause constantly the necessary rejection of much evidence entirely relevant, and they must continue to do so. All admissible evidence. as has been said supra, is relevant; but all relevant evidence is not therefore admissible. A communication to a legal adviser, or a criminal confession improperly obtained, may, undoubtedly, be relevant to a high degree. They are none the less inadmissible. Conf. § 33, n. 1, *supra*. (Best 1883: 257 main text; Chamberlayne 1883: 257–58 n.1 note to main text, Chamberlayne's italic emphasis, my boldface emphasis)

Mr. Justice Stephen is James Fitzjames Stephen, and the *Digest* is the third edition of Stephen's *Digest*.

I cannot say this is the first use of the terms "logical relevancy" and "logically relevant" in an evidence law treatise. But it does show that those terms were used in a major evidence law treatise in 1883, over twenty years before Keynes read Moore. Again, the 1880–81 Thayer was basically already using them:

> [T]here is *a relevancy which is logical* but not legal.... [W]hen we talk in a legal discussion, we mean legal relevancy,... (Thayer 1880–81: 285, my emphasis)

The text is remarkable for other reasons too. Chamberlayne starts by distinguishing logical relevancy from legal relevancy. He not only considers *both* kinds of relevancy to be evidentiary in nature, but says, "Legal relevancy...requires a *higher* standard of evidentiary force" (my emphasis). Thus, as with Chamberlayne's Taylor and the early Thayer, the difference is really one of degree. But by the end of the quoted text, he has replaced "logically relevant" with "relevant," and has replaced "legally relevant" with "admissible" with respect to "public policy considerations." These replacements are, in effect, the later Thayer's critique of the theory that there are two kinds of relevancy, logical and legal, in a nutshell. But here Chamberlayne slides from the one pair of terms to the other pair as if it made no difference.

The policy reasons why logically relevant evidence may be inadmissible include violations of attorney-client confidentiality, and improperly obtained confessions. This is quite modern.

Unlike some recent commentators who believe that Best chiefly subscribes to the best evidence rule, Chamberlayne knows that Best says that "the most universal and the most obvious" rule of evidence is that evidence "should be alike directed and confined to the matters in dispute." Chamberlayne immediately identifies being "directed and confined" with being "logically relevant." "Directed" sounds positive and "confined" sounds negative, but I argued earlier that confinement implies positive containment. If water is confined to a pitcher, then the pitcher positively contains the water. Likewise, if evidence is confined to the point in issue, then all of the evidence is positively relevant to the point in issue.

Chamberlayne says that in his editing, he consulted the treatises of Greenleaf and of Francis Wharton (1820–1889), and Stephen's "eminently useful Digest" (Chamberlayne 1883: iv). He says, "Especially is the editor under a sense of deep obligation to Professor James B. Thayer of the Harvard Law School, without whose kindly encouragement the present work would certainly not have been undertaken, and to whose exact scholarship, patient research, and well-known devotion to the Law of Evidence, such value as it may be found upon examination to possess should perhaps be more justly ascribed" (Chamberlayne 1883: iv–v). This too suggests that in writing his notes on Best, Chamberlayne was basically following Thayer's views—by which I mean the early or 1880–81 Thayer's views. In particular, it seems to me that when Chamberlayne distinguishes between logical and legal relevance, he is following the early Thayer, since that is the early Thayer's view. And the same can be said of Chamberlayne's 1897 edition of Taylor, but with the irony that Thayer had changed his view by 1896. The mature or 1896–1900 Thayer rejects legal relevance as practically a contradiction in terms, since relevance is evidentiary and legal relevance is not. Thus while Chamberlayne's editing of

Best was timely, his editing of Taylor was outdated, at least insofar as the editings were intended to reflect Thayer's views.

The seventh English edition of Best crossed the Atlantic quickly. Chamberlayne wrote the preface to the American edition of it in Cambridge, Massachusetts on June 1, 1883. J. M. Lely had written the preface to the seventh English edition at The Temple in December, 1882, just half a year earlier. For his part, Lely "most thankfully acknowledges his obligations to the exhaustive work of Mr. Pitt-Taylor and the well-known Digest of Mr. Justice Stephen" (Lely 1883: viii). Thus this edition of Best was well-known in legal circles on both sides of the Atlantic by 1883.

I omit Chamberlayne's own treatise (1911) as published too late to have influenced the 1906 Keynes. An anonymous reviewer says in *Oklahoma Law Journal*, "[T]his work is the production of a Specialist on this most important branch of the law," and "the work of a master in the whole field of the law," who "has stood for years as an authority...." (Anon. 1911: 468). Chamberlayne was a judge for some years, and a member of the Boston bar.

Frank Sumner Rice

In 1892, Frank Sumner Rice's (1850–1898) *General Principles of the Law of Evidence* appeared. Chapter 12, "Relevancy," occupies pages 488–524. The chapter starts with a survey of definitions of relevancy. One is from the Trull v True case that was cited by Halsted (Rice 1892: 489). Rice discusses Stephen the most, and praises some of Stephen's formulations (Rice 1892: 490–81, 492–93). Rice quotes Chamberlayne's commentary on Best's *Principles of the Law of Evidence* as using, in a criticism of Stephen, the term "'Logical relevancy'" (Rice 1892: 492 quoting Chamberlayne). Rice says:

§ 252. **Relevancy not the Sole Test of Admissibility.**
a. **Dissenting View.**—Mr. Chamberlayne, in his commentary upon Best's Principles of the Law of Evidence, vigorously dissents from some conclusions reached by Sir James Stephen. His assault upon the English jurist...has...had the effect of emphasizing a distinction it is highly proper to observe, and but too frequently overlooked. The learned commentator said: "Logical relevancy is assumed by *Mr. Justice* Stephen throughout the Digest of Evidence to be the sole rational test of admissibility; that the two, relevancy and admissibility, are or ought to be co-extensive and interchangeable terms. This is certainly a mistake. Public

policy, considerations of fairness, the practical necessity for reaching speedy decisions, these and similar reasons cause constantly the necessary rejection of much evidence entirely relevant, and they must continue to do so. All admissible evidence, as has been said, *supra*, is relevant; but not all evidence is therefore admissible. A communication to a legal adviser, or a criminal confession improperly obtained, may, undoubtedly, be relevant, in a high degree. They are none the less inadmissible." Best, Ev. 251, *note*, Chamberlayne's ed. (Rice 1892: 492, Rice's emphasis; see ch. 7, "Relevancy")

This is pure Thayer. What is more, Rice says that *Stephen* assumes that "logical relevancy" is "the sole rational test of admissibility" "throughout the *Digest of Evidence.*" I think that is quite correct. Thus Rice not only uses the term "logical relevancy" in 1892, but he finds that logical relevancy is basic to the 1876 Stephen, and to the 1872 Stephen by implication, since the *Digest* is precisely a digest of Stephen's views in *The Indian Evidence Act*.

In the next section of the same chapter, Rice says that the United States Supreme Court has "greatly simplified" the question of what relevancy is:

§ 252. **Relevancy not the Sole Test of Admissibility.**
a. **Dissenting View.**—Mr. Chamberlayne....
b. **Views of United States Supreme Court.**—The entire question has been greatly simplified by an unmistakable formula from the United States Supreme Court. It is impossible to misconstrue such language as the following: "It is well settled that if the evidence offered conduces in any reasonable degree to establish the probability or improbability of the fact in controversy, it should go to the jury....*Hart* v. Newland, 3 Hawkes, 122...." *Home Ins. Co.* v *Weide*, 78 U.S. 11 Wall. 438, 20 L. ed. 197. (Rice 1892: 492–93, Rice's emphasis)

He means "it should go to the jury" because it is relevant. I omit the usual exclusionary exceptions to the general relevance rule.

Rice praises Best, Phillipps, Taylor, and Starkie, but says they are now out of date, and agrees with Greenleaf that their writing is too massively detailed to study easily (Rice 1892: iii–iv).

Rice was admitted to the bar in 1877 in Saratoga Springs, New York. Keynes is not very likely to have read him. But Rice helps to show that the term and concept of logical relevance were the cutting edge of Anglo-American evidence law over twenty years before Keynes read his 1904 paper on probability to the Apostles.

John Henry Gillett

In 1897, John Henry Gillett (1860–1920) sees Stephen and Best as consistent with each other insofar as that they both admit both a relevance rule and a best evidence rule (Gillett 1897: § 51). I myself see Stephen and Best as inconsistent with each other at most in their claims as to which rule is primary. Let us pretend that Stephen seeks to reduce all evidence law to the sole principle that all evidence must be relevant in some sense, while Best seeks to reduce it to the sole principle that all evidence must be the best evidence in some sense. If so, there is no logical conflict in the sense that either reduction can be used, if indeed both are logically possible. Compare reducing the operators of propositional logic to the Sheffer stroke as the sole primitive operator, or to the Quine dagger. The statement, "All the operators of propositional logic can be reduced to either the stroke or the dagger," is logically consistent. In fact, it is far more than logically consistent. It is true. We can also either define conjunction in terms of negation and disjunction, or disjunction in terms of negation and conjunction. In Frege's logic, we can define either (1) functions in terms of objects and thoughts, (2) objects in terms of thoughts and functions, or (3) thoughts in terms of objects and functions. All these examples are technical and trivial. It would be more interesting to ask if "the best evidence" and "the most relevant evidence" are interdefinable, or if we can define any one of the following terms using the other two: "relevant fact," "probable," and "fact in issue."

Augustus Straker

In 1899, S. Augustus Straker says in his *Compendium of Evidence*, chapter 1, "Definition and Division":

> Definitions. Evidence is...."That which tends to render evident or to generate proof." *Best on Ev.*, p. 10. (Straker 1899: 22, my emphasis)
>   Primary evidence is the *best* evidence which goes to prove the true [state] of fact to which it *relates*. In saying the best evidence, we mean the highest quality of evidence attainable. (Straker 1899: 23, my emphasis)

Thus Straker says Best *defines* ("Definitions") evidence in general as relevant evidence. Thus it appears that for Best, that evidence is relevant is definitional, while the best evidence rule that evidence ought to be the best is not. Straker in effect defines *primary* evidence as having two elements. It is the best evidence, and it also "relates" to the fact in issue. It is only *primary* evidence that is the best. Thus for Straker, if not also for Best, relevant evidence is the genus, and best evidence is the primary species.

Straker appears to find the terms "relevant evidence" and "competent evidence" logically equivalent, if not synonymous:

> Competent evidence is that which by the general rules of evidence is properly to be admitted in proof of the facts alleged. This distinction is adopted, to prevent the admission of testimony *not properly relating* to the subject matter to be investigated. It is akin to *relevant* evidence, and the difference is so small as to make it a *distinction without a difference.*
>
> It is important in trials to restrict the testimony to its competency, so as to prevent that which does not elucidate the fact and make single the issue as well as to hinder confusion in the minds of the Jury and lead them off into strange paths. (Straker 1899: 25, my emphasis)

This is about competent evidence, not competent witnesses.

John Henry Wigmore

In 1899, the sixteenth edition of Greenleaf's *Treatise on the Law of Evidence* appeared. Its editor was to become perhaps the greatest treatise writer on evidence law, John Henry Wigmore (1863–1943). The first edition of Wigmore's four-volume *Treatise on the System of Evidence in Trials at Common Law* was published in 1904, the year Keynes met Russell, read Moore's *Principia Ethica*, wrote his first paper on probability as a response to Moore, and read it to the Apostles (see Skidelsky 1986: 152–53, 183–84). Wigmore adopts Thayer's views on relevance, but goes far beyond Thayer by writing a comprehensive study of all aspects of evidence law, which Thayer never did. Wigmore's *Treatise* is arguably still the best Anglo-American work on evidence law today.

I shall discuss Wigmore's edition of Greenleaf first, and then Wigmore's own treatise.

Wigmore notes that Greenleaf "died on October 6, 1853, and that "fifteen editions of the first volume [were published in] 1842, 1844, 1846, 1848, 1850, 1852, 1854, 1856, 1858, 1860, 1863, 1866, 1876, 1883, and 1892" (Wigmore 1899: v). Wigmore says that Greenleaf wrote the first seven editions, and that the next eight were posthumous (Wigmore 1899: vi). Wigmore says:

> In none of these posthumous editions was there any attempt to deal with the text, except in a few instances, chiefly by the insertion of brief references to statutory

changes. But for the present edition a different treatment seemed to have become necessary. The broad statutory changes in the past two generations, the detailed development of many doctrines, the numerous novel applications of established principles, required not only many additions which could not be conveniently relegated to cumbrous notes, but also the omission of some portions of the text rendered obsolete by statutory abolitions. Moreover, in the expositions of principles, account could not fail to be taken of the new epoch in the understanding of the rules of evidence, due to the historical studies of Professor James Bradley Thayer, the great master of the law of evidence. No book purporting to represent the present state of our knowledge could omit to recognize and make use of his results, in the exposition of the principles of evidence. (Wigmore 1899: vi)

Here Wigmore testifies that the torch has passed from Greenleaf to Thayer, "the great master" who has introduced "the new epoch" in evidence law. But Wigmore also has high praise for Greenleaf:

On the other hand, it was necessary to leave the original text still available in its classical integrity. The profession has long been accustomed to rely on this work. In the opinions of every Court for the last fifty years there occur references to its sections; and, even of the errors that are to be found in its pages, it may often be said that they have become law in many jurisdictions because they were put forth in these pages (Wigmore 1899: vi)

Wigmore's Greenleaf says in chapter 1:

§ 1. **Definitions**. The word EVIDENCE, in legal acceptation, includes all the means by which any alleged matter of fact, the truth of which is submitted to investigation, is established or disproved.[1] This term, and the word *proof*, are often used indifferently, as synonymous with each other; but the latter is applied by the most accurate logicians to the effect of evidence, and not to the medium by which truth is established.[2] None but mathematical truth is susceptible of that high degree of evidence, called *demonstration*, which excludes all possibility of error....Matters of fact are proved by moral evidence alone; by which is meant not only that kind of evidence which is employed on subjects connected with moral conduct, but also all the evidence which is not obtained either from intuition, or from demonstration. In the ordinary affairs of life, we do not require

demonstrative evidence, because it is not consistent with
the nature of the subject, and to insist upon it would be
unreasonable and absurd. The most that can be affirmed
of such things is, that there is no reasonable doubt
concerning them.[3] The true question, therefore, in trials
of fact, is not whether it is possible that the testimony
may be false, but whether there is sufficient probability
of its truth....
1. See Wills on Circumstantial Evid. 2; 1 Stark. Evid.
10; 1 Phil. Evid. 1; [compare Thayer, Preliminary Treatise on Evidence, ch. 6]
2. Whately's Logic, b. 4, ch. 3, § 1.
3. See Gambier's Guide to the Study of Moral Evidence,
p. 121. (Greenleaf 1899: 3–4, Greenleaf's emphases,
Wigmore's square brackets for his addition of material
to Greenleaf)

The general picture is much the same as in Locke. Here, evidence,
as understood in law, is defined as any means to establish or
disprove matters of fact. Evidence in this sense is very clearly said
to concern probability, as distinguished from intuition or
demonstration in mathematics, and, one might add, deductive logic.
Of course I am sure Wigmore would be the first to say that
demonstration can sometimes play a role in a legal case. A business
dispute could involve a question whether certain expenses were
added correctly. But that would only be arithmetic, not evidence in
the sense with which Wigmore is concerned. Of course, Wigmore's
definition of evidence makes evidence essentially relevant to the
matter alleged.

Chapter 5 is entitled "Relevancy; Circumstantial Evidence." Wigmore's Greenleaf says:

It is not the law which furnishes the test of relevancy, but
logic. Probative value, or capability of supporting an
inference, is a matter of reasoning, and the modes of
reasoning must be the same in a court-room as in a
laboratory; it is only the subject-matter which differs.
Whatever rulings upon relevancy are found in our
precedents are mere applications of logic by the
Court....In other words, there is a law of relevancy,[3]
consisting of those rulings which declare when one fact
may be received in a court as the basis of inference to
another....Thus a marked feature of our [Anglo-
American] system of evidence, distinguishing it radically
from the Continental system, and historically due to the
separation of function between judge and jury, is the
distinction between admissibility and proof. Our law of
evidence leaves it usually to the jury to say what
constitutes proof or demonstration [in the probabilistic

sense]; and the rules of relevancy aim only to determine whether a given fact is of sufficient probative value to be admissible at all....
3. Professor Thayer, in 3 Harv. L. Rev. 143, 145, seems to take a contrary view. Yet, at any rate, the fact remains that such decisions exist, and whether they be termed logical or legal rulings, trials will be conducted according to them, and the profession must take note of them. See Cushing, C[hief] J[ustice], in State *v.* Lapage, 57 N. H. 288. (Greenleaf 1899: 36, Greenleaf's emphasis, my square bracket additions of material)

Wigmore's Greenleaf is very Thayerian here, *pace* note 3, which concerns only the banner under which the work is done ("whether they be termed"). Wigmore's Greenleaf goes on to say:

The degree of strength..., *i.e.* the test of probative value for purposes of admissibility, can hardly be stated except in terms so general as to be practically of little use. It us usually said that the fact [must indicate the fact to be proved] with a fair or reasonable degree of probability. Only rarely can anything more precise be attempted in the way of a general formula.... (Greenleaf 1899: 36, Greenleaf's emphasis, cite omitted)

In the context of the chapter, this is a frank equation of degree of relevance with degree of probability. Wigmore expressly identifies relevance with probative value on the next page. Wigmore says, "[A fact may have probative value or relevancy, and still be excluded for collateral reasons, *i.e.* reasons independent of its probative value...." (Greenleaf 1899: 37, Wigmore's beginning square bracket for his addition of new material to Greenleaf, Wigmore's emphasis). The vagueness of degree of probability in the block indented quotation is, of course, completely Keynesian as well, and antedates Keynes on probability by five years.

I proceed to discuss Wigmore's own *Treatise*. The *Treatise* was published in Boston and is dedicated to the memory of two Americans, Charles Doe and James Bradley Thayer. It had a great impact on all major later Anglo-American legal theories of evidence, and shows a thorough knowledge of American, English, and Canadian law.

Wigmore discusses Thayer and Stephen on relevance, and is also well versed on Greenleaf and Starkie. Wigmore says:

Its one master, now passed away, James Bradley Thayer, set the example and marked the lines for all subsequent research....It was part of the aim in this work to fill out the missing places, accepting the results already reached by him. Portions of this remaining history, as here set forth, had been seen and accepted by him; [but the rest] lost the good fortune of his friendly perusal and possible concurrence. (Wigmore 1904: xii)

Wigmore identifies "Relevance" with "Probative Value" (Wigmore 1904: § 12 / p. 38). He considers Thayer and Stephen to be "two of the most original thinkers in the law of evidence" (Wigmore 1904: § 27 / p. 88). He sides with Thayer against Stephen by distinguishing logical relevance from admissibility and holding that there is no such thing as legal relevance, unless it be "a mere difference of phraseology" or "nomenclature only" from admissibility (Wigmore 1904: § 12 / pp. 38–39). Logical relevance is not a legal concept, and concerns the nature of all evidence. Wigmore says the concept of *"rational probative value* [applies regardless of] whether [the evidence is] practical or scientific, coarse and ready[,] or refined and systematic" (Wigmore 1904: § 9 / p. 31, Wigmore's emphasis; see § 27 / p. 88). Wigmore expressly admits degrees of probative value, and requires that evidence presented to a jury be of more than minimum probative value.

Wigmore says:

[Courts] require a generally higher **degree of probative value** than would be asked in ordinary reasoning. The judge, in his efforts to prevent the jury from being satisfied by matters of slight value, capable of being exaggerated by prejudice and hasty reasoning, has constantly seen fit to exclude matter which does not rise to a clearly sufficient **degree of [probative] value**. In other words, legal relevancy [i.e. **logical relevancy as admissible in law**] denotes, first of all, something more than a minimum of probative value. **Each single piece of evidence must have a plus value.**[1]

1. **The degree of admissible probative value** is more particularly considered, for circumstantial evidence, post, § 38, and for testimonial evidence, post, §§ 475–478. (Wigmore 1904: § 28 / p. 91, Wigmore's italic emphasis, my boldface emphasis)

This is the heart of Keynes and of *FRE* Rule 401. But the sentence, "Each single piece of evidence must have a plus value," implies that every item of evidence, considered entirely by itself, must make a significant difference to what the evidence would otherwise be. This is liable to the criticism of slippery slope, and commits the fallacies of composition and division. There is no conceptual room for the accumulation of "mere scintillae" of evidence, or for one scintilla to be the straw that breaks the camel's back. This is also called the problem of the heap in the logical literature. (By extension, this is a problem with Rule 401 as well, if that rule is so interpreted. But it is clear to me that Rule 401 is *not* best so interpreted, since it speaks of "*any* tendency" to make the point in issue "more probable or less probable than it would be" otherwise. At least Wigmore makes it clear that for him, "legal relevancy" is really just a high degree of "logical relevancy," so that for him, the difference in degree is really within its proper *locus*, logical relevance.

Wigmore says on the next page:

> [The function of judges], in determining Relevancy, is not that of final arbiters, but merely of preliminary testers, *i.e.* that the evidentiary fact offered does not need to have strong, full, superlative, probative value,...but merely to be worth consideration by the jury. It is for the jury to give it the appropriate weight in effecting persuasion. The rule of law which the judge employs is concerned merely with admitting the fact through the evidentiary portal. The judge thus warns the opponent of the evidence that he is not entitled to complain of its lack of demonstrative power; **a mere capacity to help is enough for its admission.** (Wigmore 1904: § 29 / p, 92, Wigmore's italic emphasis, my boldface emphasis)

But evidently, an item's "capacity to help" is its "plus value."

Wigmore's *Treatise* was published in Boston in 1904, the same year Keynes wrote his first paper on probability, but two years before Keynes' more serious work on probability.

Courtenay Peregrine Ilbert

In 1902, the tenth edition of the *Encyclopaedia Britannica* appeared. It consisted of the ninth edition plus some new volumes. Volume 28, the fourth of the new volumes, included an article on "Evidence, Law of" by Courtenay Peregrine Ilbert (1841–1924), who became Clerk of the House of Commons the same year. The article is perhaps the best brief general summary of the history of English evidence law up to 1900 ever written. And it was written by a specialist at the end of that period. Thus the present section will be something of a brief review of the period.

Ilbert says of early English law, "Early Teutonic procedure knew nothing of evidence in the modern sense....The court had no desire to hear or weigh conflicting testimony. To do so would have been to exercise critical faculties, which the court did not possess, and the exercise of which would have been foreign to the whole spirit of the age" (Ilbert 1902: 331).

In Europe, interest in evidence began with Pope Innocent III and the Inquisition. But the standard of "full proof" was so high that almost nothing was ever fully proved. Thus there came to be a premium on confession, and thereby a premium on torture. "'Every safeguard of innocence was abolished or disregarded; torture was freely used. Everything seems to have been done to secure a conviction'" (Ilbert 1902: 331 quoting without citing the author). Nonetheless, there were rules of evidence, however poor and unused they may have been. "The rules of evidence attempted to graduate the weight to be attached to different types of testimony and almost to estimate that weight in numerical terms" (Ilbert 1902: 331).

Ilbert says:

> The first systematic treatise on the English law of evidence appears to have been written by Chief Baron Gilbert, who died in 1726, but whose Law of Evidence was not published until 1761. In writing it he is said to have been much influenced by Locke. It was highly praised by Blackstone [but severely criticized by Bentham]. (Ilbert 1902: 331–32, citation to Locke omitted)

Ilbert says:

> Bentham wrote his *Rationale of Judicial Evidence, Specially Applied to English Practice*, at various times between the years 1802 and 1812. By this time he had lost the nervous and simple style of his youth, and required an editor to make him readable....The manuscript...was edited for English reading, and to a great extent rewritten, by J. S. Mill, and was published in five volumes in 1827. [So edited, the book was] always shrewd and often profound. Bentham examined the practice of the courts by the light of practical utility. Starting from the principle that the object of judicial evidence is the discovery of truth, he condemned the rules which excluded some of the best sources of evidence. The most characteristic feature of the common-law rules of evidence, was, as Bentham pointed out, and, indeed, still is, their exclusionary character. They excluded and prohibited the use of certain kinds of evidence which would be used in ordinary inquiries. (Ilbert 1902: 332)

Ilbert beautifully states his criticism of Stephen's work:

> Its most original feature, but unfortunately also its weakest point, is its theory of relevancy. Pondering the multitude of "exclusionary" rules which had been laid

down by the English courts, Stephen thought he had discovered the general principle on which those rules reposed, and could devise a formula by which the principle could be expressed. "My study of the subject," he says, "both practically and in books has convinced me that the doctrine that all facts in issue and relevant to the issue, and no others, may be proved, is the unexpressed principle which forms the centre of and gives utility to all the express negative rules which form the great mass of this law." The result was the chapter on the Relevancy of Facts in the Indian Evidence Act, and the definition of relevancy in s. 7 of that Act. This definition was based on the view that a distinction could be drawn between things which were and things which were not causally connected with each other, and that relevancy depended on causal connexion. Subsequent criticism convinced Stephen that his definition was in some respects too narrow and in others too wide, and eventually he adopted a definition out of which all reference to causality was dropped. But even in their amended form the provisions about relevancy are open to serious criticism. The doctrine of relevancy, *i.e.* of the probative effect of facts, is a branch of logic, not of law, and is out of place both in an enactment of the Legislature and in a compendium of legal rules. The necessity under which Stephen found himself of extending the range of relevant facts by making it include facts "deemed to be relevant," and then narrowing it by enabling the judge to exclude evidence of facts which are relevant, illustrates the difference between the rules of logic and the rules of law. Relevancy is one thing; admissibility is another; and the confusion between them, which is much older than Stephen, is to be regretted. Rightly or wrongly English judges have, on practical grounds, declared [as] inadmissible evidence of facts, which are relevant in the ordinary sense of the term, and which are so treated in non-judicial inquiries. Under these circumstances the attempt so to define relevancy as to make it conterminous with admissibility is misleading, and most readers of Stephen's Act and Digest would find them more intelligible and more useful if "admissible" were substituted for "relevant" throughout. Indeed it is hardly too much to say that Stephen's doctrine of relevancy is theoretically unsound and practically useless. (Ilbert 1902: 333)

This criticism is basically the same as Thayer's. Ilbert agrees with Thayer that relevance belongs to logic as opposed to the law, and is not to be confused with legal admissibility. Ilbert agrees with Thayer that there is only logical relevance, that there is no such thing as legal relevance, and that talk of legal relevance ought to be replaced with talk about admissibility.

Ilbert mentions Thayer three times elsewhere in the article (Ilbert 1902: 331, 334, 342). Ilbert says that "among modern text-writers,...the late Professor Thayer, of Harvard, was perhaps the most independent, instructive, and suggestive" (Ilbert 1902: 334). At the end of the article, Ilbert cites Thayer's *Preliminary Treatise on Evidence at the Common law* as a principal source on "the history of the English law of evidence" (Ilbert 1902: 342). Thus Thayer was well-known in the English evidence law literature as early as 1902, and was even in the 1902 *Encyclopedia Britannica*, where any educated person with access to the *Encyclopedia* could read Ilbert's brief and clear advocacy of the theory that relevance belongs to "the rules of logic" and not to "the rules of law."

Despite agreeing with Thayer that Stephen overreaches on the concept of relevance, Ilbert accepts the same four basic rules of evidence law that Stephen does:

> The rules will be found, as might be expected, to be vague, to overlap each other, to require much explanation, and to be subject to many exceptions. They may be stated as follows:—(1) Facts not relevant to the issue cannot be admitted as evidence. (2) The evidence produced must be the best obtainable under the circumstances. (3) Hearsay is not evidence. (4) Opinion is not evidence. (Ilbert 1902: 336)

Ilbert finds the first rule, the relevance rule, to have been "laid down [in England] by Baron Parke in 1837 (Wright v Doe and Tatham, 7 A. and E. 384), when he described 'one great principle' in the law of evidence as being that 'all facts which are relevant to the issue may be proved'" (Ilbert 1902: 336 quoting Parke). The relevance rule is, of course, far older than 1837 in England. Baron James Parke (1782–1868) was a member of the Inner Temple, and went to Trinity College, Cambridge.

Ilbert continues:

> Stated in different forms, the rule has been made by FitzJames Stephen the central point of his theory of evidence. But relevancy, in the proper and natural sense, as we have said, is a matter not of law, but of logic. If Baron Parke's dictum relates to relevancy in its natural sense it is not true; if it relates to relevancy in a narrow and artificial sense, as equivalent to admissible, it is tautological. (Ilbert 1902: 336)

Ilbert holds that *not* "'all facts which are relevant to the issue may be proved'," due to the many policy rules that exclude much relevant evidence from being admissible, Ilbert says:

> Such practical importance as the rule of relevancy possesses consists, not in what it includes, but in what it excludes, and for that reason it seems better to state the rule in a negative or exclusive form. (Ilbert 1902: 336)

And as we saw, Ilbert does just that. His first rule is that whatever is irrelevant is to be excluded. But the contrapositive of this is that whatever is to be included as evidence is relevant, which seems awkward and unhelpful. Do we not also want a positive rule that, in the absence of issues of admissibility, whatever is relevant is to be included?

Ilbert now comes very close to Keynes indeed:

> But whether the rule is stated in a positive way or in a negative form its vagueness is apparent. No precise line can be drawn between "relevant" and "irrelevant" facts. The two classes shade into each other by imperceptible degrees. (Ilbert 1902: 336)

Is it possible that Keynes took his theory of degrees of probability as often unmeasurable from the *Encyclopedia Britannica*?

Ilbert says that the best evidence rule, which is the second of his own four foundational rules of evidence law, and which first came into prominence in the pronouncements of "Chief Justice Holt about the beginning of the 18th century," and in Lord Chief Baron Gilbert's book soon after, "does not seem to be more than a useful guiding principle which underlies, or may be used in support of, several rules" (Ilbert 1902: 337).

Ilbert and Stephen knew each other well. Ilbert succeeded Stephen as Law Member of the Council of the Governor-General of India / East India Company, in which capacity Stephen prepared the India Evidence Act. The Charter Act of 1833 created a Law Member for the Council of the East India Company (Hostettler 2013: 149). Thomas Babington Macaulay was the first Law Member. Stephen was the second, being appointed in July 1869 (Hostettler 2013: 150). "Sir Courtenay Ilbert...succeeded Stephen as Law Member," praising Stephen's work for its "strong will," if not always agreeing with Stephen (Hostettler 2013: 151).

Ilbert was a member of Lincoln's Inn.

Elliott and Elliott

Byron Kosciusko Elliott (1835–1913) was a judge on the Indiana Supreme Court for twelve years; William Frederick Elliott (1859–1927) was his son, law partner, and co-author (Graydon 1927: 142–43). I discuss the Elliotts not because Keynes was likely to have read them, but because they deepen and illuminate the intellectual history of logical relevance in evidence law.

Almost every legal writer today understands Thayer's view and accepts it. But at the time Thayer wrote, not everyone agreed with him. The Elliotts argue for a concept of legal relevance in addition to the concept of logical relevance, even in the face of the later Thayer. Like the early Thayer, Chamberlayne's Taylor, Chamberlayne, and Wigmore, they make legal relevance a higher degree of logical relevance, i.e., different only in degree. But that is not all they do.

In 1904, the Elliotts argue in their *Treatise on the Law of Evidence* that there is still room for a concept of legal relevance, as a sort of halfway-house between logical relevance on the one hand and legal admissibility on the other. They begin by agreeing with me that there is more to Best than the rule of best evidence:

> § 143. Generally—Views of older text writers.—The older text writers treated the rule requiring evidence to be relevant as one of the four great rules of evidence, and as, perhaps, the most important of all. Thus, Best says: "of all the rules of evidence the most universal and the most obvious is this—that the evidence adduced should be alike directed and confined to the matters which are in dispute, or which form the subject of investigation."[1] So, Greenleaf says: "We state as the first rule governing in the production of evidence, that the evidence must correspond with the allegations, and be confined to the point in issue."[2] Frustra probatur, quod probatum non relevat. Stephen goes even further and makes the admissibility of evidence depend almost entirely upon the question of relevancy, using the term "relevant" so as to be practically synonymous with "admissible."
>
> 1. 1 Best Ev. (Morgan's Ed.) § 251.
> 2. 1 Greenleaf Ev. § 51. See, also, Ferguson, &c. Co. v Manhattan Trust Co. 118 Fed. 791, 795; Edd v. Union, &c. Co. 25 Utah, 293, 71 Pac. 215. (Elliott 1904: 198)

All these authors identify the term "confined to" the point in issue as another way of saying that something is relevant to the point in issue. I translated the Latin earlier.

The Elliotts say in chapter 8, "Relevancy," under their boldfaced heading, "**Meaning of the term**":

> [F]acts relevant to the issue are facts from the existence of which inferences as to the truth of existence of the facts in issue may be justly drawn. As a general proposition, therefore, it may be said that *any* evidence that tends in *any reasonable* degree to establish the probability or improbability of a fact in issue, *no matter how slight* its weight may be, is relevant.[4]
> 4.....Indeed, it is said that "it is relevant to put in evidence any circumstance which tends to make the proposition at issue either more or less probable." 1 Wharton's Ev. § 21.... (Elliott 1904: 199, my emphasis)

This is very much like *FRE* Rule 401 and Keynes Perhaps the word "justly" is too legal, though it may simply mean "fairly." The main connection is that of relevance to probability. The Elliotts also say on the same page, "As a general rule,...there must be a *logical relation* between the evidentiary fact and a fact in issue" (Elliott 1904: 199, my emphasis). Like many writers before them, they allow that often a fact is relevant to a point in issue only in combination with other facts, as "a link in the chain of evidence tending to prove the issue by reasonable inference" (Elliott 1904: 199). Thus we see here a fourfold equation of (1) relevance, (2) confinement to the point in issue, (3) making the point in issue more or less probable (than it would be otherwise), and (4) there being a (nondeductive) logical (in the broad sense of rational) relation between the evidentiary fact and the point in issue.

The Elliotts say that so far, they have been basically discussing logical relevancy. They say, "If there is such a thing as legal relevancy distinct from logical relevancy it is at least based upon logical relevancy, for evidence cannot well be relevant in any sense unless it is logically relevant," since "no evidence is admissible unless it is logically relevant" (Elliott 1904: 200). After a preliminary discussion of the issues, they present Thayer's view, and then argue for legal relevancy. I think it is worth presenting their argument at length:

> **§ 147. Theoretical Objections.**—Professor Thayer says that the law furnishes no test of relevancy, but tacitly refers to logic and general experience for the test....He denies that there is any law or rule of legal relevancy[. He holds that] there are no rules of evidence that fix the limits and determine what is relevant....It is true that the law furnishes no very definite general rule for determining the relevancy of evidence in all cases, and that the admissibility of evidence is determined, in the

main, by logic or modes of reasoning which are peculiar
only in respect to the subject matter to which they are
applied....But, in applying such reasoning and rules of
logic to concrete cases, the courts have laid down rules
or established precedents that may well be considered as
constituting a law of relevancy, and we are not left
wholly without a guide....

§ 148. **Legal relevancy.**—Some of the authorities deny
that there is any such thing as legal relevancy, and
Professor Thayer calls it a "poor notion." Others draw a
distinction between logical relevancy and legal
relevancy, and consider that the term legal relevancy
applies only to such matters as are not only logically
relevant, but are not rendered inadmissible by any of the
excluding rules of evidence. It seems to us that *a third
view may be taken* which is more helpful and more
nearly correct than either of the others. We have already
intimated that, in our opinion, there is such a thing as
legal relevancy or a law of relevancy, although few
attempts have been made to define it, and it is probably
incapable of exact definition. In one case it is said:
"Legal relevancy includes logical relevancy and requires
a higher standard of evidentiary force. A fact logically
relevant may be rejected, if in the opinion of the judge
and under the circumstances of the case, it is considered
essentially misleading or too remote." *It is, perhaps, not
strictly accurate to say that legal relevancy requires "a
higher standard of evidentiary force," but the statement
quoted indicates the distinction we would draw.* If there
were no rules of evidence and no established system,
everything bearing in the *slightest* degree upon the
controversy might well be admitted as logically relevant.
But owning doubtless to our jury system, and the
separation of functions of judge and jury, and also in
part to reasons of convenience, it is for the court to say
whether a matter is of *sufficient probative value* to be
admissible or is too remote and conjectural to furnish
any aid to the jury consistent with the practical
administration of justice under our system; and it is for
the jury to determine its weight or effect as proof where
admitted. We think it may be said, therefore, that [for]
evidence to be legally relevant, [it] must, in general,
reasonably tend to establish the probability or
improbability of a fact in issue....

§ 149. **Legal relevancy—rules of exclusion.** As
intimated in the last preceding section, it seems to us to
be of little practical use, if not indeed misleading, to say
that nothing is legally relevant if it comes within any rule
of exclusion. If this view is taken[,] the term legal
relevancy would seem to mean nothing more nor less
than admissibility. Is it true that many matters are

excluded that are logically relevant, but are they excluded because they are not legally relevant? Hearsay is excluded, but certainly not because it has no probative value....In these and other cases, evidence that would probably be of high probative value or effect if admitted, is excluded by some rule of exclusion based on convenience, policy, or some other consideration that may have nothing to do with the question as to whether it has any *reasonable* probative value or not. It seems to us a misuse of terms to say that evidence which is proximately connected with a fact in issue, and is of sufficient probative value as tending to prove it, is not relevant. If it is logically relevant, not too remote to furnish assistance in getting at the truth of the matter in controversy, and, except for some rule of exclusion based on other grounds, would be received by the courts in accordance with established rules, it is legally relevant, no matter whether it is inadmissible upon some other ground or not....To be legally relevant it must, we think, as a general rule at least, *reasonably* tend to render a fact in issue more or less probable or improbable [than it would otherwise be]. (Elliott 1904: 201–4, the Elliotts' boldface emphasis, my italic emphasis, cites omitted)

To sum up, the Elliotts may be said to define evidence as legally relevant just in case the evidence: (1) is logically relevant, (2) is of sufficiently high probative value to aid the jury; (3) reasonably tends to make a point in issue more or less probable than it would be otherwise; and (4) is not excluded as inadmissible by any of the exclusionary policy rules.

Conjunct (1) is in effect the genus, and conjuncts (2)–(4) are in effect three conjoined differences (differentiae). In contrast, the early Thayer, Chamberlayne's Taylor, Chamberlayne, and Wigmore make conjunct (2) the sole difference (differentia). No doubt there are indefinitely many ways to make such a dialectical move by adding new differences (new limiting conjuncts) to the genus, but I shall discuss only the conjuncts the Elliotts themselves add.

I have already argued earlier against conjunct (2) that it is a slippery slope (is a version of the problem of the heap), and commits the fallacies of composition and division.

Conjunct (3) contains the Elliotts' beautifully chosen key term, "reasonable." No better general term could be chosen. No other term could better express the essential vagueness which is needed here. As Aristotle says, it is a mark of lack of education to expect precision in a subject whose nature does not allow it. Yet the term only postpones the problems I have detected with conjunct

(1). For conjuncts (1) and (2) are logically equivalent, and the reason they are is that for the Elliotts, the term "reasonable" means or mutually implies "sufficiently high probative value." For they are not going to apply either term unless they apply the other. Thus all the problems with conjunct (1) are also problems with conjunct (2).

I turn now to conjunct (3). For the Elliotts, legal relevance is a species of logical relevance. And not violating the exclusionary rules could be a differentia. But since these policy rules are not evidentiary in nature, they are really admissibility rules as opposed to evidentiary rules, just as the later Thayer says.

For the Elliotts to succeed, they need to use *evidentiary* rules in their definition of legal relevance. For if legal relevance is not essentially *evidentiary*, then legal relevance is *not* a species of evidentiary relevance. But on their own account of the exclusionary rules, all they are entitled to speak of is *policy* rules.

One might object that for the Elliotts, legal relevance is evidentiary because its genus is evidentiary, not to mention conjuncts (2) and (3). My reply is that this is correct, but legal relevance is really a hybrid concept, since conjunct (4) concerns the concept of policy admissibility, while the rest concerns the concept of evidence. And perhaps that is not so bad, if we waive the problems with conjuncts (1) and (2). Perhaps such a concept of legal relevance may even be useful. But it is a hybrid concept for all that. To that extent we have left the realm of evidence behind. Conjunct (4) is properly a mere scope restriction, not a difference of a genus. It would be like saying that brown is a difference of the genus cat. Yes, "brown cat" excludes nonbrown cats from its scope. But brown is nothing like a difference. For brown cat is nothing like a species of cat. "Brown cat" fails to state the essence of a species of cat. Brown cat is not what any species of cat is. The color of a cat is accidental.

The Elliotts are right to note that the exclusionary rules of evidence law always or almost function *as a matter of fact* to raise the bar of relevance, that is, to raise the degree of relevance, or at least the degree of clarity of relevance. But that is an accidental as opposed to essential function of theirs. It is not their essential reason for being. It is not their essential purpose. It is not why we have them. They are not rules or guidelines of inductive logic. They are not axioms or theorems of probability theory. They are not scientific theories or even guidelines. They are not essential to evaluating the evidence qua evidence. They do not function to evaluate the evidence as such at all. Strictly speaking, such rules have no impact on the specific evidentiary situation, and only a logically accidental impact on the level or quality of evidence admitted in a court. The reasons we have them are *simply not evidentiary reasons* for judges' deciding what evidence the jury may or may not consider.

Let us use the Elliott's own example. Why do we generally exclude hearsay? Is it because hearsay is not probative? No. To quote the Elliotts themselves again, "Hearsay is excluded, but certainly not because it has no probative value" (Elliott 1904: 203). And they explain why it *is* excluded: "In these and other cases, evidence that would probably be of high probative value or effect if admitted, is excluded by some rule of exclusion based on convenience, policy, or some other consideration that may have nothing to do with the question as to whether it has any reasonable probative value or not" (Elliott 1904: 203).

Assume now that the hearsay rule prohibits all hearsay in general for the reason that hearsay in general is not very *reliable evidence.* This would make the rule essentially concerned with evidentiary relevance on a *general* level. But the rule would still not function to weigh the *specific* probative value of each particular item of hearsay evidence. And if the rule *were* essentially concerned with weighing probative value, then that is what it *would* do in individual cases of hearsay. That is, it would function to evaluate cases of hearsay on whether or not they are members of the hearsay species of logically relevant evidence.

To sum up, if hearsay is excluded by policy, then hearsay evidence is much like brown cat. There is a general scope restriction. But when hearsay is excluded by policy, it is being excluded from being a *species* of evidence, or more precisely a difference. It is really a species (or difference) of the genus of inadmissible items. And policy exclusions do not, as such, state either what evidence is or what it is not. Policy is not what evidence is. Policy is not even part of what evidence is. Logically relevant is what evidence is. The genus of inadmissible items includes both logically irrelevant items and policy-excluded logically relevant items. Cases of hearsay can belong to either of those two types of inadmissible items, so it is a cross-classification relative to those two sub-categories.

The Elliotts recognize the relativity of both relevance and admissibility, and even what may be called their multiple relativity:

> [Evidence] may be relevant to one issue or fact in issue. although not to another....Evidence may be relevant and admissible upon one issue or for one purpose or as against one party, although it would be irrelevant or inadmissible for some other reason upon another issue in the case or for another purpose or against another party. (Elliott 1904: 204)

Evidence can be relevant not only to certain issues, but to certain parties, and to certain purposes. Other things being equal, a bloody knife with Smith's name on it is more relevant to a stabbing than to a theft, more relevant to Smith than to Jones, and more relevant to showing who owned the knife than showing who used it. And the relativity of relevance may be more multiple than that. Keynes, we know, holds that the probability of an event is always relative to the body of evidence we have.

    This concludes my review of Anglo-American evidence law on the topic of relevance. The following two charts of the history of Anglo-American evidence law show the main trends:

History Chart of Relevance Rules

Evidence must (be):
Today: logically relevant, that is, tend to make more or less probable (Am.; Eng.)
1985 Cross: logically relevant (Eng.)
1958 Cross: relevant (Eng.)
1941 James: logically relevant (Am.)
1921 Keynes: logically relevant (Eng. philosopher-economist)
1906 Keynes: relevant (Eng. philosopher-economist)
1904 Elliott and Elliott: logically and legally relevant (Am.)
1900 Thayer: logically relevant; there is no legal relevance (Am.)
1899 Straker: ascertain the fact or point in issue, for or against (Am. citing Eng.)
1898 Thayer: logically relevant; there is no legal relevance (Am.)
1897 Chamberlayne's Taylor: logically and legally relevant (Am.)
1894 Mayne: relevant
1883: Chamberlayne's notes in Best: logically and legally relevant (Am.)
1880–81 Thayer: logically and legally relevant (Am.)
1876 Stephen: relevant (Eng.)
1876 Starkie: tend to prove or disprove the point in issue (Eng.)
1872 Mayne: relevant
1868 Phillipps: relevant; confined to points in issue (Eng.; Am. ed.)
1864 Dickson: not be irrelevant (Scot.)
1859 Phillipps: relevant; confined to points in issue (Eng.; Am. ed.)
1859 Halsted: relevant and pertinent; tend to prove the issue; confined to the issue (Am.)
1859 Powell: relevant; confined to the points in issue; correspond with the allegations (Eng.)
1854 Best: directed and confined to the matters in dispute; directly or indirectly relevant (Eng.)
1852 Burke: relevant (Eng. philosopher)

1847 Calvert's Gresley: relevant and pertinent to the issue (Eng.)
1842 Greenleaf: relevant; confined to the point in issue; correspond
    with the allegations (Am.)
1842 Taylor: confined to the points in issue; tend to prove or dis-
    prove the matter of fact under investigation (Eng.)
1839 Starkie: tend to prove or disprove the issue (Eng.)
1838 Phillipps: approximate to the allegations (Eng.)
1837 Parke: "all facts which are relevant to the issue may be
    proved" (Eng.)
1831 Roscoe: confined to the issue (Eng.)
1830 Starkie: tend to prove or disprove the point in issue; ascertain
    the truth of the allegations (Eng.; Am. ed.)
1827 Bentham: pertinent; add / contribute to discovery of the truth;
    tend to produce a persuasion for or against (Eng.)
1824 Peake: relate or connect to issue in dispute (Eng.; Am. ed.)
1822 Phillipps: bear upon / confined to the point in issue (Eng.)
1820 Phillipps: relate / refer to / ascertain the facts in issue (Eng.;
    Am. ed.)
1817 Buller: relate or connect to the issue; prove no more than the
    substance of the issue (Eng.)
1816 Phillipps: confined to facts or points in issue (Eng.; Am. ed.)
1791 Gilbert: relevant to the cause of action; relevant to the point
    under judicial inquiry; relevant to the point in issue; relate
    to the subject in dispute
1789 Morgan: ascertain the very point in issue (Irish pub.)
1785 Buller: prove no more than substance of point in issue (Eng.)
1772 Buller: prove no more than substance of issue (Eng.)
1768 Blackstone: ascertain the very point in issue (Eng.)
1739 Duncombe: agreeable to the issue; not collateral, surplusage,
    or a variance (Eng.)
1726 Gilbert: admit degrees of proof (Eng.)
1717 Nelson: answer the issue / maintain the issue (Eng.)
1717 Blount citing Coke: make evident the point at issue (Eng.)
1690 Locke: admit degrees of probability (Eng. philosopher)
1666 Eure: answer the issue / prove the issue / make evident the
    point in issue to the jury (Eng.)
1628 Coke: make evident the point in issue to the jury (Eng.)

These are not dates of rule creation, but dates of reports of already
well-established rules. All the rules are older. Modern evidence law
begins "[b]y the 1500s" (Wigmore 1913: 2). *Contra* Langbein's 'I
found no earlier cites, therefore there are none' logical fallacy of
appeal to ignorance (1996: 1171–1172), "*Most* legal discussion of
evidence in the early Tudor period [1483–1558] concerns relevance
and conformity to the issue" (Baker 2003: 363, my emphasis).
    A chart of broad time periods follows:

History Chart of Common Terms for Relevance

Evidence must (be):
1880–81–today: logically relevant
1791–today: relevant
1830–today: conform with / ascertain the allegations
1772–today: be confined to / prove no more than (the substance of)
    what is in issue
1690–today: admit of degrees of probability / proof / certainty
1628–today: (help) ascertain / make evident the point in issue

Again, these are dates of reports of already well-established rules.

Keynes appears to belong to all five of these general phases of the Anglo–American legal tradition, expressly or implicitly.

Here is a third chart of special interest on Keynes and the origins of his theory that probability is degree of logical relevance:

Relevantist Members of the Inner Temple

John Maynard Keynes (1883–1946)
Arthur Richard Jelf (1837–1917)
Lumley Smith (1833?–1918)
John Dawson Mayne (1828–1917)
James Fitzjames Stephen (1829–1894)
John George Malcolm (obit. 1872)
Edmund Powell (1826?–1864)
Colin Blackburn (1813–1896)
George Morley Dowdeswell (1809–1893)
Henry Roscoe (1800–1836)
James Parke (1782–1868)
Thomas Starkie (1782–1849)
Samuel March Phillipps (1780–1862)
John Morgan (fl. 1789)
William Nelson (fl. 1717)
Giles Duncombe (fl. 1702)
Thomas Blount (1618–1679)
Samson Eure (d. 1659)
Edward Coke (1552–1634)
Thomas Littleton (ca. 1415–1481)

Anglo-American Relevance Law Today

Today logical relevance is the heart of Anglo-American evidence law, as any good English or American law school course on evidence law will teach, and as any good English or American treatise on evidence law will explain (Lempert 2011; Cross 1985). The rule that only logically relevant evidence is admissible applies in courts having jurisdiction over hundreds of millions of people.

Thayer's arguments for logical relevance and against legal relevance are the basis of American state and federal evidence law today. Thayer is praised in the Advisory Committee's Note to *Federal Rules of Evidence* Rule 402, and in George F. James' 1941 article, "Relevancy, Probability, and the Law" (James 1992 / 1941: 389–90 / 701–5), which the Advisory Committee's Note to Rule 401 cites.

Federal Rules does not expressly speak either of "logical" relevance or of "legal" relevance. But *Federal Rules* certainly does not speak as if there were two kinds of relevance; and Rule 401 clearly has logical relevance in mind. It basically defines "relevant evidence" as Thayer and Keynes understand it. Rule 401 says:

Rule 401. Definition of "Relevant Evidence"
"Relevant evidence" means any evidence having any tendency to make the existence of any fact that is of consequence to the determination of the action more or less probable than it would be without the evidence. (West 1995: Rule 401)

Granted, Rule 401 reverses Keynes and defines relevance in terms of probability instead of the other way around. But the basic implication of either definition is that the two terms are logically equivalent. Then in modern classical logic, either term can be formally used to define the other. For Frege or Russell, there would be nothing *formally* wrong either with Keynes or with Rule 401, even though the definitions go in opposite directions. Formally speaking, the choice of definition would be logically arbitrary. It would be no different from defining equilateral as equiangular or vice versa. Either way, we eliminate a term and logically guarantee truth-preservation. But I suggest that in philosophy, we want more than that. We want theoretical definitions that state what a thing is, if at all possible. We want to illuminate what things are. And my own logical intuition is that it is intellectually more illuminating to use the (intuitively) *relatively* clearer notion of relevance to explain the relatively more obscure notion of probability.

I grant that the whole history of logical relevance, both in deductive and in inductive logic, shows that the notion of relevance is problematic. But the problems with relevance are basically technical issues in logic, as can be seen in my (2015: ch. 9). No one doubts that relevance exists in the sense that *some* evidence is relevant to a given issue and other evidence is not. We may say that ordinary probabilistic relevance, in some sense or senses, *exists*. Of course, one may object that there is no one concept of relevance, if there is no one thing that is appropriately called relevance. But the situation is different for probability. There the problem is precisely whether there is *any* such thing, that is, whether we can develop a plausible theory of probability such that *anything* is probable, even if the word "probability" is taken to be both ordinary and univocal. That is Hume's problem of skepticism.

One might well object that if Hume denies probability, then he would deny probabilistic relevance as well. He would only admit patterns of impressions. And conversely, if Keynes admits synthetic *a posteriori* logical relevance, then he would admit probability as well. My reply is that this only shows that the two concepts stand or fall together. And that only shows that they are interdefinable after all. Thus we come back to my original intuition, which is only that if the two concepts are logically equivalent, which is all the objector is pointing out, then it is more illuminating to define probability in terms of relevance than the other way around. And even if there is a battle of conflicting intuitions on the point, I am not clearly wrong.

Let us assume for the sake of the argument that I am right that in philosophy, it is best to define probability as relevance, and not the other way around, so as to illuminate the true nature of things. From that, it does not follow in the least that *outside* of philosophy, there logically cannot be good reasons for going in the opposite direction and defining relevance as probability. Now, the Advisory Committee's Note to Rule 401 suggests two *practical* reasons for defining relevance in terms of probability in the field of evidence law. The Note says:

> Compare Uniform Rule 1(2) which states the crux of relevancy as "a tendency in reason," thus [1] perhaps emphasizing unduly the logical process and ignoring the need to draw upon experience or science to validate the general principle upon which relevancy in a particular situation depends....
>
> Dealing with probability in the language of the rule has the added virtue of [2] avoiding confusion between questions of admissibility and questions of the sufficiency of the evidence. (Advisory Committee's Note to Rule 401, my square bracket numbering of the reasons)

Clearly, any such practical reasons would not apply to a theoretical definition in philosophy. As to practical reason (1), Keynes makes relevance a purely logical relationship between propositions, yet can very easily and correctly note that experience and scientific findings are precisely what we ordinarily assert in our evidentiary premisses. Thus for Keynes, there is no undue emphasis of logic over experience in our understanding of probability. As to practical reason (2), Keynes' theory does not even appear to confuse either the concept of probability or the concept of evidentiary relevance with the concept of legal admissibility. For that matter, neither do the frequency theory or Ramsey's theory. Philosophical theories of probability, as such, have nothing to do with the legal admissibility of evidence.

Yet these two practical reasons may be very useful indeed for attorneys. The very fact the Advisory Committee saw fit to state them practically tells us what many attorneys are prone to do.

The Advisory Committee in effect agrees with Keynes that "Relevancy is not an inherent characteristic of any item of evidence but exists only as a relation between an item of evidence and....the fact to be proved" (Advisory Committee's Note to Rule 401). The Committee also agrees with Thayer that, in the rationalist tradition of evidence theory, to which Keynes belongs:

> The provisions that all relevant evidence is admissible, with certain exceptions, and that evidence which is not relevant is not admissible are "a presupposition involved in the very conception of a rational system of evidence" Thayer, Preliminary Treatise on Evidence 264 (1898). (Advisory Committee's Note to Rule 402)

These similarities between Keynes and the Advisory Committee are structurally deeper than the issue whether logical relevance is best defined in terms of probability or vice versa. See Twining (1994: ch. 3, "The Rationalist Tradition of Evidence Scholarship"; 1986: ch. 1, "The Rationalist Tradition of Evidence Scholarship".

For a more detailed discussion of various rival definitions of legal relevance than I can offer here, see Hunt (2012).

Continental Evidence Law

What is Continental European evidence law like? Mirjan R. Damaška finds that in "legal systems outside the [Anglo-American] common law world, we find that relevance so understood plays hardly any role in legal discourse. In the Continental tradition[,] the probative value of information is seldom discussed apart from the credibility of its carrier" (Damaška 1997: 55). Damaška asks, "Why is a conceptual tool so central in Anglo-American procedure without importance in other systems?" (Damaška 1997: 55). He answers that the Anglo-American system bifurcates the court into judge and jury, where the judge is the gate-keeper of admissibility and the jury weighs degree of relevance or probative value. But in Continental unitary courts, judges handle everything, so to them "the need to express these two aspects of evidence processing by two separate conceptual categories appears as a barren theoretical impulse" (Damaška 1997: 56). My reply is that this only shows that the concept of relevance does not matter in *practice* in Continental law. It matters in *theory* to everyone. For theory is general. And it advances the theoretical analysis to distinguish relevance from admissibility. Anglo-American logical niceties, such as the distinction between direct and indirect relevance, and relatedly, among levels of (interim, penultimate, and ultimate) probanda (T. Anderson 2005: ch. 2–3), advance the analysis even further, but need not detain us here. Within the theory of Anglo-American evidence law, our mission is a simple one. We need only point out that Damaška, and Continental evidence law in general, overlook the obvious. Namely, Bentham's general concept of evidence, its survival in Best's concept of natural evidence, and its development in Stephen as relevance and in Thayer as logical relevance, is precisely a concept of *evidence in general*, which both intends to and succeeds in going beyond not only Anglo-American law in particular, but all law in general. Thus to say there is no "Anglo-American" concept of relevance on the Continent is to say that there is no *general* concept of evidence on the Continent. The only sense in which the concept of logical relevance is Anglo-American is the historical sense in which it was developed by Anglo-American thinkers. And ironically, even in this historical sense, the logical theory of probability was originally Continental. As we saw near the beginning of this book, Leibniz and a host of other early modern Continental thinkers developed this theory. And perhaps Continental jurists do not think they need a general logical concept of evidence. But on the theoretical level, that is their loss. Was it not traditional Continental philosophy of education that professionals in every field should have at least some under-standing of the philosophical foundations of their subject?

Panayot Butchvarov argues that there is no general concept of evidence because there is nothing all the things we deem to be evidence have in common (Butchvarov 1970: 283–87). And even if the general concept of evidence is that of logical relevance, I think Butchvarov might well reply in turn that there is no one thing that all the things we deem to be *logically relevant* have in common. My reply is that on my own theory, there is something they all have in common, something phenomenological: objectively seeming to be the case. See note 4 in the notes section of this book.

Langbein says:

> The great chasm that separates the modern Continental
> legal systems from the Anglo-American systems is
> largely about the conduct of fact-finding. On the
> Continent, professional judges take the main respons-
> ibility for investigating....Prototypically, our trial judge
> sits with a jury....
>   Sit in one of our trial courtrooms, civil or
> criminal, and you hear counsel interrupting incessantly
> to raise objections founded upon the rules of evidence.
> These incantations are so familiar that they have passed
> into the popular culture. Close your eyes and you can
> hear Perry Mason or the protagonists of "L.A. Law" or
> similar television fare bound to their feet, objecting
> fiercely: "Immaterial!" "Hearsay!" "Opinion!" "Leading
> question!"
>   Cross the Channel, enter a French or an Italian
> or a Swedish courtroom, and you hear none of this. Over
> the past two decades I have had frequent occasion to
> observe German civil and criminal proceedings. I have
> heard much hearsay testimony, but never a hearsay
> objection. No one complains of leading questions, and
> opinion evidence pours in without objection. (Langbein
> 1996: 1168–69)

Langbein duly cites Damaška, but quotes "a famous dictum in the
Berkeley Peerage Case in 1816" to show that English judges have
long been aware that Continental judges felt free to admit hearsay
because they considered themselves objective professionals and
trusted their judgment, while in England this could not be done. In
England, an exclusionary rule was found by experience to be
needed because the jury decides what the facts are, and they are
ordinary laypersons unpredictably swayed by hearsay (Langbein
1996: 1169). Hearsay, of course, is just one example of a policy
objection to admitting relevant evidence.

Langbein is right that Damaška's view, that evidence law
as Anglo-American lawyers know it does not exist in Continental
law due to the absence of the jury system, is far from new. The
major writers agree with the *Berkeley* dictum. Thayer says in 1898:

> It seems, then, that our law of evidence, while it is,
> emphatically, a rational system, is yet a peculiar one. In
> the shape it has taken, it is not at all a necessary
> development of the rational method of proof; so that,
> where people did not have the jury, or, having once had
> it, did not keep it, as on the continent of Europe,
> although they, no less than we, worked out a rational
> system, they developed under the head of evidence, no
> separate and systematized branch of the law. (Thayer
> 1898: 270)

Wigmore's Greenleaf says in 1899:

> Thus a marked feature of our [Anglo-American] system
> of evidence, distinguishing it radically from the
> Continental system, and historically due to the separation
> of function between judge and jury, is the distinction
> between admissibility and proof. Our law of evidence
> leaves it usually to the jury to say what constitutes proof
> or demonstration [in the probabilistic sense]; and the
> rules of relevancy aim only to determine whether a given
> fact is of sufficient probative value to be admissible at
> all.... (Greenleaf 1899: 36)

Ilbert says in 1902:

> It was by reference to trial by jury that the English rules
> of evidence were originally framed; it is by the
> peculiarities of this form of trial that many of them are to
> be explained; it is to this form of trial alone that some of
> the most important of them are exclusively applicable.
> The negative, exclusive, or exclusionary rules which
> form the characteristic features of the English law of
> evidence, are [precisely] the rules in accordance with
> which the judge guides the jury....These rules of
> exclusion are peculiar to English law and to systems
> derived from English law. (Ilbert 1902: 333)

And the Elliotts say in 1904:

> But, owing doubtless to our jury system, and the
> separation of the functions of judge and jury, and also in
> part to reasons of convenience, it is for the court to say
> whether a matter is of sufficient probative value to be
> admissible...consistent with the practical administration
> of justice under our system.... (Elliott 1904: 202)

No doubt there are earlier statements.

Why is there no real Continental jury system? It is because
Continental evidence law is basically inquisitorial and descends
from the papal Inquisition. Ilbert says:

> Modern Continental procedure, as embodied in the most
> recent codes, has removed the worst features of
> inquisitorial procedure....[But] the French Code of
> Criminal Procedure...still retains some of the features of
> the unreformed procedure which was condemned in the
> 18th century by Voltaire and the *philosophes*. Military
> procedure is in the rear of civil procedure, and the trial
> of Dreyfus at Rennes presented some interesting

> archaisms. Among these were the weight attached to the
> rank and position of witnesses as opposed to the intrinsic
> character of their evidence, and the extraordinary
> importance attributed to confession even when made
> under suspicious circumstances and supported by flimsy
> evidence. (Ilbert 1902: 331, Ilbert's emphasis)

Again, the inquisitorial standard of proof was so high, it rarely could be met. The result was that torture to gain confessions was used well into the nineteenth century, until Cesare Beccaria (1738–1794) awakened the conscience of Europe with his *On Crimes and Punishents* (Beccaria 1963 / 1764). But even with torture abolished and other improvements, the Continent remained inquisitorial and never adopted the jury system as a safeguard of human rights. Of course, the Continental democracies have many other safeguards of human rights, and are very democratic on the whole. In some ways, they may be more democratic than Anglo-American nations.

3

Impact on Keynes and Russell

The Modern Logic Background

In everyday use, legal use, and Keynes' use alike, "logical" means much the same thing as 'rational' or 'reasonable'; and "relevant to" means much the same as 'significant for' or 'related to'. Thus "logically relevant to" simply means 'rationally related to as evidence'. This meaning is so general that either deductive logic, inductive logic, or both might well be meant. But while Keynes and some lawyers today use "logically relevant" in this broad way, some nineteenth century legal writers discuss evidence in a specific way that casts inductive logic in the garb of deductive logic.

To explain what many nineteenth century legal theorists have in mind, I will use an example. Where a lawyer might offer a simple probability argument from two particular facts to a third:

(A)   1. In bloody murder #1, DNA identified people on scene.
        2. In bloody murder #2, DNA identified people on scene.
        3. Therefore probably, in bloody murder #3, DNA will identify people on scene.

Stephen, Taylor, and Thayer would first generalize to a universal statement:

(B)   1. In bloody murder #1, DNA identified people on scene.
        2. In bloody murder #2, DNA identified people on scene.
        3. Therefore probably, in all bloody murders DNA will identify people on scene.

They would then use universal statement (B3) as the major premiss of this *formally valid deductive* argument:

(C)   1. Probably, in all bloody murders DNA will identify people on scene. (inductive general principle as major premiss)
        2. Bloody murder #3 takes place (evidence as minor premiss).
        3. Therefore probably, in bloody murder #3 DNA will identify people on scene (material fact to be proved).

While argument (C) is a deductive argument in form, that is just window dressing, since our only evidence for (C)'s major premiss (1) is described in the premisses of inductive argument (B). (B) and (C) taken together are a way of saying what argument (A) says, but with (C) in deductively valid syllogistic form. The benefit is that we are forced to articulate a universal statement which will be both the conclusion (3) of (B) and the major premiss (1) of (C). Often there is no one best way of doing that, since there are different generalizations we might make about the earlier bloody murders. Thus we are forced to articulate exactly which probable universal statement we are basing our conclusion on, and that may affect how good our argument is. This is what I meant when I spoke of the analytically helpful but superficially deductive, frankly syllogistic format of such arguments earlier in this chapter.

Probabilistic syllogisms were studied in the eighteenth century by Johann Heinrich Lambert. Lambert argued in 1764 that "three quarters of the A's are B's; C is an A, therefore with probability 3/4, C is a B" (Hailperin 1988: 144); compare Wigmore (1904: § 30). For a recent discussion, see Murphy (2008: 5–6).

The probabilistic syllogism is due to Aristotle. Richard Sorabji says of Aristotle's *Posterior Analytics*:

> [Aristotle recognizes] that in natural science it is not always possible to obtain exceptionless generalisations. Often a predicate will attach to members of the kind only for the most part. In An. Post., he is not confident that broadness of leaf, or coagulation of sap, will have its effect of making the leaves fall in every instance. Twice, therefore, he discusses degenerate scientific syllogisms in which the predicates attach only for the most part to their subjects (An. Post. I 30, 87*b*19–27; II 12, 96*a*8–19). In these syllogisms, the thing to be explained will be a truth that holds for the most part, and the explanatory premises will be neither necessary nor universal, but again true only for the most part. (Sorabji 1980: 50)

I omit the subtleties of Sorabji's discussion (Sorabji 1980: 50–51).

Paul Slomkowski points out that in Aristotle's *Topics*, topoi of the greater, lesser, or like degree include syllogisms about greater, lesser, or similar probabilities or likelihoods (Slomkowski 1997: 147 quoting Aristotle, *Topics* 115a6–8; Aristotle 1960: 373).

I myself could point out that Aristotle says in the *Rhetoric*:

> Again, conclusions that state what is merely usual or possible must be drawn from premises that do the same, just as 'necessary' conclusions must be drawn from 'necessary' premises; this too is clear to us from the *Analytics*.[13]

13. *An. Pr.* 1. 8, 12–14, 27. (*Rhetoric* 1357*a*25–30 / Aristotle 1968c: 1332, note 13 by the editor)

Thus Leibniz was unfair to disparage Aristotle for lacking any logic of probability (Leibniz 1966 / 1765 / 1704: 466).

Again, Anglo-American evidence law did not develop a logical interpretation of probability so much as a logical framework for analyzing probability arguments. Legal scholars came to see that inductive arguments can always be rewritten as deductive arguments, and that while that could not alter the strength of an argument, it could articulate more precisely what the induction was. The deductive arguments were conceived as Aristotelian syllogisms whose major premises describe general principles arrived at inductively, whose minor premises describe items of evidence, and whose conclusions describe the probability that certain material facts obtain or fail to obtain. In this way, evidence law maintained a connection between formal deductive relevance and probabilistic relevance, though merely as a matter of format.

As Shapiro documents so well, the early modern tradition of evidence law sought to assimilate evidence law to logic at virtually every turn (Shapiro 1991: 30). In the eighteenth century, lawyers often cited the 1724 Isaac Watts, *Logick, or the Right Use of Reason in the Inquiry after Truth* (Shapiro 1991: 31). In the nineteenth century, they often cited the 1807 Richard Kirwan, *Logick, or an Essay on the Elements, Principles, and Different Modes of Reasoning*. Kirwan recommends that logic be carefully studied in all countries using the jury system, and often cites legal matters. Shapiro says:

> Indeed Kirwan appeared to have considered lawyers and prospective jurors as his primary audience....
>   It is thus not surprising that David Hoffman should recommend Kirwan's *Logick* and [Thomas] Reid's *Essays* to students of law or that other writers on legal evidence should recommend logical or epistem-ological oriented treatises such as those of Locke, Hartley, Reid, Abercrombie, Kirwan, and others.... [L]ater writers favored Kirwan, [Whately], and John Stuart Mill over earlier works. (Shapiro 1991: 32)

James Glassford, Daniel McKinnon, and William Wills treated evidence law as based on, if not literally part of, logic. This view became quite common by the nineteenth century. Indeed, most eighteenth and nineteenth century scholars saw nothing special about legal reasoning (Shapiro 1991: 34, 228, 232–33). As Murphy says in his *Murphy on Evidence*, sect. 1.3, "Philosophical Basis for Use of Evidence":

> Twining draws attention to the fact that, despite a wide divergence of opinion as to the detail of both the science

> and the law of evidence, every writer on the subject
> since it began to be the subject of methodical study in
> the eighteenth century has agreed, either explicitly or
> implicitly, on a philosophical basis for evidence....The
> basic tenet...is that the drawing of rational inferences
> from evidence is capable of leading to correct
> knowledge of past events, and is the only, or the only
> known, method of arriving at correct knowledge of past
> events. (Murphy 2008: 3–4, cites omitted)

In contrast, early modern legal scholars were generally against applying the mathematical probability calculus of Laplace, partly because criminal convictions required the beyond a reasonable doubt standard, but chiefly because outside of actuarial situations, early attempts to apply the calculus were unworkable. Numbers simply could not be assigned to the contractual risks and evidentiary likelihoods that triers of fact had to weigh (Shapiro 1991: 253–55; Franklin 1991: 123–44). And that is just what Mayne and Keynes say. Keynes resolves the problem by holding that not all degrees of probability, i.e., degrees of logical relevance, can be assigned numbers. In this way, Keynes crowns the assimilative tradition by assimilating evidence law and the probability calculus alike to Russell's logic in *Principles*. But he is far from original on whether probabilities can always be assigned numerical values.

When Did Keynes First Write of Relevance?

So far, I have mainly discussed only whether Keynes might have learned of relevance from Burke, Bentham, or Mayne. These are all plausible sources of his view. I shall shortly discuss what I think the main possibilities are. But first we must briefly discuss *when* Keynes first acquired the concept of logical relevance, so as to set an upper time limit to our time line of possible origins.

Again, 1904 is the year Keynes read Moore, wrote his first paper on probability, and read it to the Apostles. There is no doubt that Keynes read Moore's book carefully. Skidelsky says, "The inside covers of Keynes' own copy of *Principia Ethica* are covered with pencilled notes" (Skidelsky 1986: 146).

In 1906, Keynes wrote the first version of his fellowship dissertation on probability; it was deemed unready for submission. In 1907, he wrote the second and final version, which he submitted. Vincent Barnett says:

> In the autumn of 1905, [Keynes] sketched out a draft
> outline for a project called a "Scheme for an Essay on

the Principles of Probability." In December 1907, he submitted as a fellowship dissertation to King's College a work entitled "The Principles of Probability." Thus, between the end of 1905 and the end of 1907, he had continued working on [probability.] (Barnett 2013: 24)

Barnett says a few pages later:

> Chapter 16 of Keynes's 1907 dissertation on "The Principles of Probability" was entitled "The relation of Probability to Ethics, and the Doctrine of Mathematical Expectation." This was directly connectable to the chapter in Moore's book entitled "Ethics in Relation to Conduct." [Thus] his early interest in probability was linked to his early interest in ethics. (Barnett 2013: 32)

Of course, ethics and probability were linked for Moore as well. Keynes writes in chapter 1 of his second or revised dissertation on probability, which he submitted on December 12, 1907:

> In the ordinary course of thought and argument we are constantly asserting that the truth of one statement, while not [deductively] *proving* another, is nonetheless *some ground* for believing the second. We assert that, with the evidence at our command, we *ought* to hold such and such a belief. We expressly say we have *rational* grounds for assertions which are, in the usual logical sense, unproved. We allow, in fact, that statements may be unproved, without for that reason being unfounded. Nor does reflexion show that it is information of purely psychological import which we wish to convey when we use such expressions as these....We are in fact claiming to **cognize** correctly a **logical connexion** between one set of propositions which we call our evidence and which we take to be true, and another set which we call our conclusions and to which we attach more or less weight according to the grounds supplied by the first. We recognise that *objectively* evidence can be *real* evidence and yet not *conclusive* evidence....I do not think I am straining the use of words in speaking of this as the **probability** relation or the relation of **probability**. (Skidelsky 1983: 183 quoting Keynes 1907: ch. 1, Keynes' italic emphasis, my boldface emphasis)

Thus Keynes states a logicist theory of probability as early as 1907. Keynes' dismissal of "psychological import" is much like Frege's and Husserl's anti-psychologism. Keynes continues:

> The idea of a premisses's having *some* weight to
> establish a conclusion, of its lying *somewhere* between
> cogency and [total] *irrelevancy*, is altogether foreign to a
> logic in which the premiss must either prove or not prove
> the alleged conclusion. This opinion is, from the nature
> of the case, incapable of positive proof. The notion
> presents itself to the mind, I feel, as something
> independent and unique....
>   Yet that 'probability' is, *in the strict sense*
> indefinable, need not trouble us much; it is a
> characteristic which it shares with many of our most
> necessary and fundamental ideas.... (Skidelsky 1983:
> 184 quoting Keynes 1907: ch. 1, my emphasis)

This text includes most of his basic ideas in just a few words. All that is missing is the relativity of probability to one's body of evidence. Most importantly for our purposes, Keynes uses the term "irrelevancy" as a term applicable in logic, though not in formal deductive logic. That is, for him the *locus* of relevance is in logic. Of course, his Platonic theory of logic as timelessly real, and its attendant theory of cognition of abstract logical entities, goes beyond evidence law and comes from Russell, if not also from Moore. For a premiss to be *totally* irrelevant to a conclusion is for it to have to have *no* logical connection with that conclusion at all. Evidently it is only later that he understands there to be degrees of logical relevance which are degrees of probability. But the texts do imply that there is a theoretical continuum between deductive logic and inductive logic, with deductive logic at the extremes and inductive logic covering everything in between. Deductive implication and total irrelevancy are opposite extremes, with what he calls "partial relevancy" years later in the *Treatise* covering everything in between.

The only improvement I would make to Keynes here would be to say that not just "many," but by definition of "fundamental," *all* of our logically fundamental ideas are indefinable. But he does not appear to be using the word "fundamental" in this way, since he writes of "our *most* fundamental ideas," thus allowing for *degrees* of fundamentality, while my more usual definition of "fundamental" as meaning 'logically indefinable' would not. He also qualifies his talk of "indefinable" by saying "*in the strict sense* indefinable," just as he does in the *Treatise*. Thus he appears wisely to allow that a term can be indefinable in one sense and definable in another sense. This is just what allows him to offer a theoretical definition of probability as degree of logical relevance. This is his logically informative analysis of one term as logically equivalent to a clearer term. Such analyses are basic to modern classical logic. Beyond than that, probability, or logical relevance, is a logically primitive logical relation which either we intuit or we do not.

To sum up, it seems that we have a window of three years at most, from 1904 to December 12, 1907, in which Keynes first starts to use the term "relevance," or more precisely, one of its negative grammatical forms, "irrelevancy," to describe his theory of probability as belonging to logic. For he uses the term in this way on December 12, 1907. Of course, he may have used the term earlier than that.

Stephen and Ilbert as Possible "India Connections"

Keynes was working in the India Office while working on his theory of probability. Might Keynes have personally known or at least heard of Stephen or Ilbert through an "India connection"?

Stephen and Ilbert do not seem to have had any personal communication with Keynes. They are not named in the indexes to the three volumes of Skidelsky's *John Maynard Keynes* (Skidelsky 1986; 1994; 2001), nor in the index to Harrod (1951), nor in the index to Moggridge (1992). Nor is it likely that Keynes met them. Stephen died in 1894. And while Ilbert was in London as Clerk of the House of Commons starting in 1902, Keynes was merely one of ten junior clerks over in the India Office. Keynes worked first in the Military Department starting on October 16, 1906, and then in the Revenue, Statistics and Commerce Department, ending with his resignation on June 5, 1908, or if you prefer, with his final day of work on July 20, 1908. (Skidelsky 1983: 175, 177, 186). These particular departments would scarcely be old stamping grounds for Ilbert, a lawyer who worked on evidence law and legal statutes. And for all I know, Ilbert might never have visited the India Office after 1902 at all.

But we cannot completely rule out the possibility that Keynes somehow learned of relevance in the India Office, and learned of it as it was discussed by Stephen, Ilbert, or both. The head of the Military Department was Sir Thomas Holderness. The Secretary of State, who was in charge of the India Office, meaning he was in charge of India, was John Morley. And the Permanent Under-Secretary was Sir Arthur Godley (Skidelsky 1983: 176). Keynes knew all three; they knew him; and on the whole they were indulgent on his working on probability theory in his spare time, which was most of his time at work. "Keynes seems to have had the utmost sympathy and understanding of his superiors" (Skidelsky 1983: 177). Any one of these three superiors might have known of Stephen and Ilbert, and might have mentioned their legal work on relevance to Keynes. And it is precisely during this period in the

India Office that he seems to have been writing of probability as relevance (Skidelsky 1983: 184). Skidelsky agrees with Elizabeth Johnson that Keynes "expanded" his relationship with the India Office in the years after he left it (Skidelsky 1983: 186); but we are looking for 1907 or earlier origins of Keynes' talk of probability as logical relevance.

In any case, Keynes might well have learned of Stephen, Ilbert, or both through his job at the India Office, and thereby learned of their major contributions on relevance in evidence law. It might have been one of the first things his superiors told him, once they learned that he was interested in probability theory.

There might be an indirect India connection of Keynes to Stephen through Mayne. We know Keynes knew of Mayne, since Keynes mentions Mayne in his *Treatise on Probability*. Mayne's Wikipedia article says "he is remembered as the author of *Mayne's Hindu Law*[,] regarded as the most authoritative book on the Indian Penal Code." Stephen knew the Indian Penal Code well. He praised it highly, and even worked on it a little. Leslie Stephen says of his brother Fitzjames, "In regard to the famous Penal Code, of which he always speaks with enthusiasm, his action was confined to filling up a few omissions" (L. Stephen 1895: 266). Macaulay, Stephen's predecessor as Law Member of the Council, had been in charge of the Indian Penal Code; Stephen apparently did some final editing. It is possible that Mayne and Stephen knew or knew of each other through an India Penal Code connection. In any case, both did years of legal work in India. But it is unlikely that they had a significant personal connection with each other, since Mayne is not mentioned in Leslie's biography of Fitzjames.

Lytton Strachey and Thoby Stephen as Possible Indirect "India Connections"

If I were looking for a possible indirect "India connection" between Keynes and Stephen on relevance in evidence law, I would look to Keynes' early friendship with (Giles) Lytton Strachey, who was later the author of *Eminent Victorians*, and to Keynes' early friendship with Stephen's nephew, (Julian) Thoby Stephen.

Keynes biographers Harrod, Skidelsky, and Moggridge all discuss the Strachey family in their biographies of Keynes. Harrod says, "Among the undergraduates who arrived at Trinity in the year 1899, five soon became intimate friends. When Maynard went up five years later, he found them there, a close circle, and was adopted by them. These men [included] Thoby Stephen, Clive Bell,...Leonard Woolf and Lytton Strachey" (Harrod 1851: 81–82).

Thus Keynes was "adopted" by both Lytton and Thoby in 1904. I shall discuss Lytton first, and then Thoby.

Barbara Caine's *Bombay to Bloomsbury: A Biography of the Strachey Family* explores the deep roots of the Strachey family in India during the British Raj. Lytton's parents were Richard and Jane, and his uncle was John Strachey. Richard was a military officer. John was chairman of the East India Railway; he "retired and returned to England in the 1870s" (Caine 2005: 33). Richard and John spent many years in India. Jane and Lytton did not, though Jane did visit. "Like other Raj families, the Stracheys took it for granted that school-age children should remain in England" (Caine 2005: 38).

Lytton was anti-imperialist and wanted nothing to do with the Raj of his father's generation. "Lytton...absolutely rejected the idea of Indian or any other form of imperial service" (Caine 2005: 4). But the question here is how much Lytton *knew* about India from his family, and in particular, if Lytton had heard about Stephen's evidence code and its relevance rule connecting relevance with probability, and if Lytton might have passed this on to Keynes.

My evidence is only circumstantial. Caine says the Strachey family discussed all sorts of things in great detail, and says the Raj was central to the family history (see Caine 2005: Introduction and chs. 1–3 generally). Caine says:

> At least a decade before the controversy over the Ilbert Bill, a measure that would have given Indian magistrates the capacity to preside over cases involving British men and women, John Strachey was in no doubt of the impossibility of giving Indian magistrates any form of authority over British settlers and clearly his sympathies lay with his own countrymen. Both he and Richard ultimately adhered closely to the views of *John's great friend, Fitzjames Stephen* concerning the need to ensure that all positions of authority in India were held by Europeans. Caine 2005: 48, cite omitted, my emphasis)

This is a "smoking gun" text. James Fitzjames Stephen, the famous evidence law writer, was Lytton's Uncle "John's great friend."

In addition, John, Richard, and Jane Strachey all had a close friend in Lord Lytton. Caine says:

> John's very close relationship with Lord Lytton was also important. The friendship between them was intense: Lytton once told Richard Strachey that of all the men he know, John Strachey was the one he would most like as a brother. (Caine 2005: 30)

Caine adds:

> Although Jane engaged in amateur theatricals with Lord
> Elgin in the early 1860s, the viceregal family to whom
> she became closest were the Lyttons. She was not the
> only member of the Strachey family for whom this was
> the case. Lytton had worked closely with John Strachey
> from the time he (Lytton] arrived in India as viceroy in
> 1875 and the two men became very close friends. Lytton
> courted Richard Strachey when he went out to purchase
> the land for the East India Railway in 1877 and when
> Jane went out a year later to join her husband, she and
> the viceroy became very close friends. (Caine 2005: 37)

Thus John, Richard, and Jane Strachey were all close friends with
Lord Lytton—who was a supporter of James Fitzjames Stephen.
Again, Stephen's *Indian Evidence Act* was enacted in 1872, and his
Digest of the Law of Evidence came out in 1876. Could it be
possible that Lytton Strachey's parents were unaware of Stephen
and his theory that evidence is what is relevant? And if they *were*
aware, how likely would it be that Lytton Strachey knew of that
theory too, and passed it on to Keynes? I can only say the Strachey
family was famous for its prodigious intellectual discussions. And
ironically, in light of his anti-imperialism, I suspect that Lytton
Strachey was named after Lord Lytton. That might speak volumes
about an India connection between Keynes and Stephen through
the two Lyttons: Lytton Strachey and his namesake, Lord Lytton,
with this possible "Lytton connection" mediated in turn by Richard
and Jane Strachey, if not also by Uncle John.

The very possible "Thoby connection" between Keynes
and Stephen would be even more direct.

Thoby was the "son of Leslie Stephen" (Harrod 1951: 82).
And Leslie Stephen (1832–1904) was James Fitzjames Stephen's
brother. Leslie wrote a biography of Fitzjames, as he calls him,
including some brief words on Fitzjames' theory of evidence law,
which I shall quote shortly. Leslie thanks "Sir John Strachey" for
providing "information as to the Indian career" of Fitzjames (L.
Stephen 1895: vii–viii). Leslie says that Fitzjames "made some
valued friends in India; chief among whom, I think, was Sir John
Strachey, of whom he always speaks in the warmest terms, and
whose friendship he especially valued in later years" (L. Stephen
1895: 245). This proves beyond doubt that John Strachey knew and
was a good friend of Thoby's uncle, James Fitzjames Stephen, the
evidence law writer.

As a sort of preface to the quote to come, I would like to
note the general picture of the human connections involved. Leslie
Stephen says that James Mill, John Stuart Mill's father and the

"foremost" "disciple" of Jeremy Bentham, "upon whom Bentham's mantle had fallen, held a leading position at the India House, and his evidence before a parliamentary committee had an important influence in determining the outlines of the new system" for managing India (L. Stephen 1895: 246–47). Bentham was against the common law as a judge-made morass, and favored the utility of law codes that were relatively simple and easy to use. Following Bentham, James Mill favored codification as well (L. Stephen 1895: 246, 247). The first such law code for India, the penal code of 1834, "was an accomplishment of Benthamite aspirations" (L. Stephen 1895: 247). Leslie says the penal code "served as a model for all the later Indian codes" (L. Stephen 1895: 248). Fitzjames' evidence code was also Benthamite in this sense. It was a great simplification of the morass of common law on evidence. But while Bentham wanted to abolish all legal rules for evidence, and simply rely on science and common experience, Fitzjames felt that the gist of the historical common law development of rules (or, we may say, of the common law experience) was worth preserving in a simplified form as a law code (see L. Stephen 1895: 272–73, not mentioning Bentham). Thus we see at least an indirect connection between Stephen's evidence code and evidence law philosopher Bentham, a connection reported by Stephen's brother Leslie.

Now we come to the text which shows that Leslie Stephen basically understood his brother Fitzjames' work on relevance in evidence law, and thus could have easily explained it to his son Thoby, who could have just as easily explained it in turn to his friend Keynes. Leslie Stephen says:

> The English system, although the product of special historical developments, had resulted in laying down substantially sound and useful rules. They do in fact *keep inquiries within reasonable limits*, which, in courts not guarded by such rules, are apt to ramble step by step into *remoter* and *less relevant topics*, and often end by accumulating masses of useless and irritating scandals. Moreover, they would protect and guide the judges, who, unless you prohibited all rules whatever, would infallibly [I think he means inevitably] be guided by the practices of English courts. To abolish the rules of evidence would be simply to leave everything 'to mere personal discretion'. Moreover, the rules have a 'real though a *negative*' value as providing tests of solid truth. The best shoes will not enable a man to walk nor the best glasses to see; and the best rules of evidence will not enable a man to reason any better upon the facts before him. It is a partial perception of this which has caused the common [and the Benthamite] distrust of them. But they do supply *'negative' tests,* warranted by long experience,

upon two great points. The first is that *when you have to make an inference from facts, the facts should be closely connected in specified ways with the fact to be decided.* The second is, that whatever fact has to be proved, should be proved by the best evidence, by the actual document alleged, or by the man who has seen with his own eyes or heard with his own ears the things or the words asserted to have occurred.

If, however, these rules are substantially the expression of sound common sense, worked out by practical sagacity, it is equally true that 'no body of rules upon an important subject were ever expressed so loosely, in such an intricate manner, or at such intolerable length'. (L. Stephen 1895: 272–73, presumably quoting James Fitzjames Stephen, my emphasis)

We see at the start the rejection of Bentham's rejection of "judge-made law." We see at the end the endorsement of Bentham's complaint that common law was a hopeless morass, which was the reason for Bentham's rejection of judge-made law—a sort of cleansing of the Augean stables, if you will. In the middle, we see the positive relevance rule itself, and also its negative gate-keeping function. The term "closely connected" expresses the concept of relevance, though perhaps not as clearly as we might like. Of course, the concept of relevance is by its nature not perfectly determinate. And this is a work intended to be a popular biography written by a legal amateur. For the sort of book he is writing, I think Leslie is doing well on the topic of relevance.

The term "specified ways" indicates a general requirement that it must be specified (and therefore must be specifiable), for each piece of evidence, just what its close connection is to the point in issue. I suggest that the implicit principle here is that if there is no specifiable connection, then there is no relevant connection. If so, then my criticism is that evidentiary connections are not always specifiable in the sense of being describable in language. Of course, my criticism concerns evidence in general, not evidence in law.

Leslie Stephen is also well aware of Ilbert, and of Ilbert's comments on Fitzjames' work. (L. Stephen 1895: 246n., 279, 280, 378, 379, 461). Thus Leslie could have discussed Ilbert with Thoby as well.

It is hard for me to believe that Keynes would not have known of Thoby's father Leslie, or would not have known about Leslie's biography of Fitzjames, by the end of 1904. In fact, Keynes might possibly have met Leslie, who died on February 22, 1904 (Harrod 1951: 172). Harrod says that Leslie had been a tutor at Trinity Hall in Cambridge, and that "Thoby had already been bringing his friends to Hyde Park Gate," Leslie Stephen's home until he died (Harrod 1951: 172–33). However, Keynes may have come on the scene after Leslie's death. Also, "Towards the end [Leslie] Stephen became very deaf, and in his last two years was ill with cancer" (Harrod 1951: 173). Thus even if Keynes met Leslie, Leslie might not have communicated very much to him. Thoby died from typhoid fever in 1906 (Skidelsky 1994: 16); but he is still in the window for Keynes' having learned of relevance by December 12, 1907.

There is a more general and indirect "Bloomsbury Group" connection between Fitzjames Stephen and Keynes. Thoby and his sisters Vanessa and Virginia were children of Leslie's second marriage. Vanessa married "one of Thoby's best friends at Trinity, Mr. Clive Bell" (Harrod 1951: 173). Virginia married Leonard Woolf, another of Thoby's best friends. Vanessa Bell and Virginia Woolf were "part of the central core" of the Bloomsbury Group (Harrod 1951: 175). Moore's philosophy of ethics fit well with the agnosticism of Leslie Stephen and the later free thinking of the Bloomsbury group (see Harrod 1951: 180). Regardless of whether everyone liked each other (Skidelsky 1994: 15), it was a small intellectual world, and it intellectually included both Keynes and three of Leslie Stephen's children. Skidelsky says, "Intellectual life in Victorian Cambridge was shaped by the crisis and eventual decline in religious belief. The 1860s were the decade when Cambridge men lost their religious belief, [including] Leslie Stephen, Henry Sidgwick, [and the economist] Alfred Marshall.... The decade opened with the consequences of Darwin's *Origin of Species*, published in 1859" (Skidelsky 1986: 26). This was the climate for the later Bloomsbury Group, and was the climate in which Moore wrote his ethics book.

Certainly Keynes was reading Leslie Stephen by 1924. On November 6, 1924, Keynes gave the Sidney Ball lecture at Oxford, "The End of *Laissez-Faire*" (Skidelsky 1994: 225). An "essay version" "was published in 1926;" "An important source was Leslie Stephen's *English Thought in the Eighteenth Century*" (Skidelsky 1994: 225).

It was an even smaller world than that. On April 26, 1902, the Council of the Senate of Cambridge University "received a memorial from 126 members of the Senate" (Moggridge 1992: 91). "A Syndicate, including...Neville Keynes..., was appointed" to expand economics "and associated branches of Political Science" (Moggridge 1992: 91). "Neville Keynes did not sign the Memorial," but "Bertrand Russell,...Leslie Stephen,...John Venn and James Ward" signed it; and so did historian of early English law "F. W. Maitland" (Moggridge 1992: 91n.). Thus it seems likely that Keynes' father Neville, Fitzjames Stephen's brother Leslie, and Russell all knew or knew of each other as early as 1902. An India connection could have come through Neville, or even Russell. As a smaller world yet, Fitzjames Stephen was an Apostle, or member of the Cambridge Conversazione Society, and so was his son Thoby—and so were Keynes, Russell, and Moore. Leslie Stephen says:

> In October 1847 my brother [Fitzjames] went into residence at Trinity College, Cambridge....
>
> My brother became intimate with several very able men of his own age, and formed friendships which lasted for life. He met them especially in two societies, which influenced him as they influenced many men destined to achieve eminence. The first was the 'Union'....
>
> The other society was one which has included a very remarkable number of eminent men. In my undergraduate days we used to speak with bated breath of the 'Apostles'—the accepted nickname for what was officially called the Cambridge Conversazione Society. It was founded about 1820....
>
> [Fitzjames was elected] at an unusually early part of his career....
>
> [Henry Summer] Maine brought Fitzjames into the apostles in his first term.[2]
>
> [Fitzjames] visited Cambridge in later years and was my guest, and long afterwards the guest of his friend Maine, at certain Christmas festivities in Trinity Hall. He speaks in warmest terms of his appreciation of the place, 'old and dignified, yet fresh and vigorous.' Nearly his last visit was in the autumn of 1885, when he gave a dinner to the apostles, of whom his son James was then a member.
>
> 2. He was proposed by Maine on October 30, and elected November 13, 1847. (L. Stephen: 1895: 91, 98, 99–100, 101, 102, 102 n.2, 110)

Thus not only was Fitzjames' nephew Thoby an Apostle, but so was Fitzjames' own son James, as well as Fitzjames himself. Could there be *three* Stephen family members who were Apostles, Fitzjames, James, and Keynes' dear friend Thoby, with Thoby being a member at the very same time Keynes was, and Keynes not learn that Fitzjames characterized probable evidence as relevant evidence? We see that Fitzjames gave a dinner to the then-current Apostles in 1885, almost forty years after he became a member. In doing so, he seems to have been keeping up something which was already a tradition when he became a member himself. Leslie says that when Fitzjames joined the Apostles, "Old members...

occasionally attended meetings" (L. Stephen 1895: 102). And the 1885 visit was not his last, though it was "Nearly his last visit."

It was a smaller world yet. Leslie Stephen says, "In January 1876, Lord Lytton was appointed Governor-General of India. In February, Fitzjames dined in his company at Lord Arthur Russell's" (L. Stephen 1895: 386). Lord Arthur Russell (1825–1892) was a nephew of Lord John Russell (1792–1828); both served in Parliament. Lord John, Bertrand Russell's grandfather, was the one who appointed Lord Lytton to be Viceroy and Governor-General of India. At that time, Lord John was Prime Minister of the United Kingdom for the second time. (Lord Lytton arrived in India in 1876. One of his first official acts was to proclaim that Queen Victoria was Empress of India. The vast ceremony took place on January 1, 1877 in Delhi with all or nearly all the princes of India in attendance.) Lord John had been elevated to the peerage as the first Earl Russell and as Viscount Amberley in 1861. Some fourteen years earlier, in 1847, Queen Victoria had given Pembroke Lodge to Lord John and his second wife, Lady John, née Lady Francis Anna-Maria Elliott-Murray-Kynynmound, as a place to live. That was during the first time Lord John was Prime Minister, while he was still only Lord John. Lord and Lady John were living in retirement at Pembroke Lodge when Russell was sent there by court order to live with them at the age of three (see Russell 1987: 12). Lord John died on May 26, 1878, when Russell was six. Russell briefly recalls his grandfather in his *Autobiography* (Russell 1987: 15). Thus it appears that Arthur Russell, nephew of Bertrand Russell's grandfather John, not only knew Fitzjames Stephen, but invited him to dinner. Of course, this is not a Keynes connection but a Russell connection. I cannot take it seriously, but it is dimly possible that Russell himself somehow knew about Fitzjames Stephen on relevance and told Keynes. But if anything, it would be more likely that Russell somehow learned of it from Leslie.

I am not expecting there to be a thread on logical relevance going specifically from Fitzjames Stephen through Lord Arthur or Lord Lytton to Lord John, and then somehow to Bertrand Russell and / or Keynes. Russell was only six when his grandfather died, and Keynes' interest in probability started in 1904, some twenty-six years later. I am noting only that it was a small world. I mean to show only that if Keynes' terminology of relevance originated somehow from Fitzjames Stephen, then there could have been any number of ways that could have happened through a small group of people who socially knew each other very well. Fitzjames Stephen dined with Lord Arthur, the nephew of Russell's grandfather Lord John. And as public figures, all three of them must have known many hundreds of people who would have known Stephen's view, in the then-famous Indian Evidence Act, that evidence must be relevant. And many of those people might have been able to tell Keynes about that, either at Cambridge while Keynes was a student there, or in the India Office while Keynes was a junior clerk there. Once Keynes mentioned that he was making a major study of probability, it would have been a very natural thing to tell him. The Stephen family and the Strachey family are only the more obvious possibilities.

The Economists Edgeworth and Marshall

Of course, there might have been a personal connection on logical relevance in evidence law between Keynes and someone other than the people I have just described. For example, it might have been Francis Ysidro Edgeworth. Though Edgeworth did not practice law, he was admitted to the bar in the Inner Temple in 1877. Lluís Barbé says that Edgeworth said "he had 'studied Law' at the Inner Temple of London, just like his grandfather, and had been called to 'the English Bar' in 1877" (Barbé 2010: 65 quoting Edgeworth, "Report to the Council of King's College, submitted in June of 1988").

Barbé says that Edgeworth "was called to the Bar by the Inner Temple. This meant he had successfully completed his studies in law at the professional level. However, by then he had decided not to pursue a legal career" (Barbé 2010: 85). Charles R. McCann, Jr. says of Edgeworth, "Called to the Bar in 1887 (while never having practised law, he described himself in his early writings as Barrister-at-Law)" (McCann 1996 / 1922: xii). Stephen M. Stigler says that Edgeworth "undertook the study of commercial law....[H]e was called to the bar in 1877, but well before 1877 he must have realized that a career as a barrister could not satisfy either his intellectual curiosity or his ambition for recognition as a scholar" (Stigler 1986: 305).

Edgeworth and Keynes' father Neville knew each other well. Alfred Marshall wrote to John Neville Keynes that he (Neville) was preferred by "*'Everyone'*" to be the first editor of *The Economic Journal* (Harrod 1951: 10 quoting Marshall's letter to Neville Keynes dated February 8, 1889, Marshall's emphasis). Neville Keynes rejected the offer, and the first editor was Edgeworth (Harrod 1951: 158; Moggridge 1992: 208).

Maynard Keynes knew Edgeworth well and cites him often in the *Treatise*. Edgeworth was the first editor of the *Economic Journal* from 1891 to 1912; Keynes was his immediate successor as the second editor from 1912 to 1944. From 1919 to 1926, Keynes and Edgeworth were joint editors of *The Economic Journal* because Keynes was so involved in the post-war "peace-making" process (Harrod 1951: 151 n.1). Edgeworth reviewed Keynes' *Treatise* in 1922, and Keynes wrote Edgeworth's obituary in *The Economic Journal* in 1926. Keynes published two letters in the *Journal of the Royal Statistical Society* in 1910 and 1911; Edgeworth was president of that society in 1912–14.

Keynes was reading Edgeworth on economics as early as 1905 (Moggridge 1992: 95). Edgeworth, as one of Keynes' examiners, criticized an essay Keynes wrote on index numbers in 1909. Keynes felt Edgeworth's criticisms to be "*hopeless*" and to show a "*closed* mind" (Harrod 1951: 148 quoting Keynes' letter of May 10, 1909 to Duncan Grant, Keynes' emphasis). But Harrod adds:

> On 13th February [1926,] F. Y. Edgeworth, Keynes' collaborator in editorship of the *Economic Journal,* died, and Keynes wrote one of his charming obituary notices. Despite his early rage at Edgeworth's obtuseness on the subject of index numbers, he had come to appreciate the qualities of that great man. The appreciation was reciprocal. Edgeworth could not say too much in praise of Keynes. (Harrod 1951: 373)

In any case, the timing was right for Edgeworth to have influenced Keynes' theory of probability at any time from 1905 to 1921.

Edgeworth wrote on probability years before Keynes read Moore. Edgeworth begins promisingly in his article, "Probability and Calculus of Probabilities," in R. H. Inglis Palgrave's *The Dictionary of Political Economy*. His first sentence is, "Probability means a greater or less degree of credibility" (Edgeworth 2003 / 1899: 495). This sounds just like Keynes. But his second sentence is, "The probability of an event is measured by the frequency with which it has occurred in past experience" (Edgeworth 2003 / 1899: 495), and he cites "Venn, *Logic of Chance*" as the source of his view. Thus Edgeworth is just a Venn frequentist. Still, the first sentence does sound like the view Keynes adopted years later.

In his review of Keynes' *Treatise*, Edgeworth declines to discuss Keynes' philosophical theory of probability. He seems uninterested in philosophical theories of probability in general, and in Keynes' logical theory of probability in particular, throughout his lifetime of publications. Edgeworth says in the review:

> We cannot now follow him to the speculative heights.... This is not the place to enquire...in what sense there is a degree of belief which is "rational,": the conclusion standing in an "objective" relation to the premisses.... (Edgeworth 1996 / 1922: vol. 1, 152)

This is consistent with Stigler's careful summation of Edgeworth's contributions, in which no philosophical theory of probability is even mentioned by Stigler (Stigler 1986: ch. 9).

I found no philosophical theory of probability in the three volumes of Edgeworth's *Writings in Probability, Statistics, and Economics*, certainly not a developed one (Edgeworth 1996/ 1922). However, as we saw, Edgeworth briefly indicates that he is a Venn frequentist in his 1899 article on probability.

Keynes does not cite Edgeworth on relevance. Edgeworth might not have studied evidence law at all, since he specialized in business law. But evidence law is the sort of thing which every good lawyer needs to know something about. Even in business cases, how could Edgeworth have expected to present evidence for anything without knowing the basics of evidence law?

There seems to be no Edgeworth-Russell connection, Russell does not mention Edgeworth in his *Autobiography*, and Russell is not mentioned in Barbé's biography, *Francis Ysidro Edgeworth: A Portrait with Family and Friends*.

No doubt like most economists, Edgeworth's colleague Alfred Marshall too "was basically uninterested in what he called 'philosophical economics'" (Moggridge 1992: 17 possibly quoting Marshall). D. E. Moggridge adds that Marshall "was unhappy with [Keynes' father] Neville Keynes' sharp distinctions and attempts at classification, and tried to blur them wherever possible" (Moggridge 1992: 17). Thus Marshall seems even less likely than Edgeworth to have told Keynes about relevance in evidence law. Again, both Edgeworth and Marshall were primarily economists.

Keynes Dines at the Inner Temple

The best and most direct link of Keynes to evidence law might be through Arthur Spokes. Phyllis Deane says that after John Maynard Keynes received his undergraduate degree on June 20, 1904:

> he could take his time weighing up and choosing between different career options. Always risk-averse, Neville instantly introduced an outside possibility by arranging for them (Maynard and Neville] to lunch with Arthur Spokes—his [Neville's] University College contemporary, now a well-established barrister—who could sponsor Maynard's entry to the Inner Temple. However unenthusiastic the latter may have felt about the examination-ridden route to the Bar, he embarked cheerfully on the traditional programme of "eating dinners" with members of the legal fraternity. Within a

week of his graduation, the Diary reported with
satisfaction that he had "now eaten two dinners at the
Inner Temple." Deane 2001: 272–73 quoting Neville
Keynes' diary)

Thus Keynes dined *at least* twice in the Inner Temple in 1904,
since he dined there twice in a single week. Neville Keynes had
known Arthur Spokes at least since 1872 (Deane 2001: 13). Spokes
was close enough to be one of the "only two of Neville's friends
[who first] knew of his engagement" to Florence (Deane 2001: 107
n.39). And if Spokes was a "well-established barrister," how could
he have failed to know the basics of evidence law? Mayne and Jelf
were also members at the time. Keynes may have met them too.

Another real possibility is that Keynes could have simply
browsed the Inner Temple Library, possibly with someone pointing
him in the right direction. The Inner Temple Library Catalogue lists
the following works as held as of September 2013: John Pitt
Taylor, *A Treatise on the Law of Evidence as Administered in
England and Ireland, with Illustrations from Scotch, Indian,
American and other Legal Systems*, 9th ed. (1895); James Bradley
Thayer, *A Preliminary Treatise on Evidence at the Common Law*
(1895); Simon Greenleaf, *A Treatise on the Law of Evidence*, 15th
ed. (1892); 7th ed., vol. 1 (1854); 6th ed., vol. 2 (1856); and 3rd
ed., vol. 3(1856); Thomas Starkie, *A Practical Treatise of the Law
of Evidence and Digest of Proofs, in Criminal and Civil
Proceedings* 4th ed. (1853); Thomas Peake, *A Compendium of the
Law of Evidence*, 2nd ed. (1804); and Sir William Blackstone*,
Commentaries on the Laws of England in Four Books*, 23rd ed.
(1854) (Inner Temple 2013). But we cannot tell from these
holdings in 1913 what was available to Keynes in 1904. That is
because, as the online site of the Inner Temple Library says:

The accommodation for the Library has had a chequered
history. The old building used by Coke and Selden was
burned down in the Great Fire of 1666, and its
replacement was blown up in 1678 in an endeavour to
stop the spread of another fire. There was another
rebuilding, this time in gothic style, in 1835. The
Victorian building (1870), designed by Smirke in the
same perpendicular style as the hall, was remarkable for
its distinctive clock-tower surmounted by a pegasus
weather-vane. That building was destroyed in 1941, with
the loss of about 40,000 volumes, though the manuscripts and rarest books had been removed to the country
and saved. (Inner Temple 2013a)

James Conway Davies says, "In 1941 [the] Library ceased to be....
The records of the Library itself up to 1940 had been burnt"
(Davies 1972: 11). Thus whether its original holdings included any
of the treatises I listed, no one can say. There I will leave the matter
for other researchers. Even if we had, say, a 1904 card catalog
showing that Keynes signed out every treatise I listed, it would still
be only circumstantial evidence that he took the terminology of
logical relevance from one of them. Likewise for learning it from
one of his fellow Inner Temple members at dinner.

I shall not explore the possibility that Keynes learned of
logical relevance in evidence law from an attorney, friend, library,
or encyclopedia any further. That is a question for the Keynes
biographers. I discuss Edgeworth and Spokes only as examples of
the *sort* of personal connection one *ought* to be looking for. Keynes
could have just as easily learned of logical relevance from a book,
article, or court opinion. Certainly it would be very hard to prove
that his term "logical relevance" did *not* come from evidence law.
Where else could it have come from?

Conclusion: Keynes Most Likely Knew of
Logical Relevance in English Evidence Law

This concludes my examination of the topic of relevance in
modern evidence law, so as to document that it is by far the most
probable historical origin of Keynes' theory of probability as
degree of logical relevance. My conclusion is that it is far more
likely than not that Keynes did not invent the concept and
terminology of logical relevance himself, but took them from
evidence law, and then formalized and Platonized the relevance
relation in the manner of the early Russell.

Evidence law required evidence to be "relevant" as early as
the 1791 Gilbert. Thayer enthroned "logical relevancy" as the most
basic requirement of evidence law as early as 1880–81.[5] And we do
not find talk of probable evidence as relevant evidence in any other
field. At least, I have not. Legal terms that are equivalent to
"relevant" go back at least to 1628. I believe that further research
can only strengthen my case with additional material.

Keynes developed his basic theory of probability some six
years before Russell's *Problems of Philosophy*. Based on Russell's
acknowledgment of Keynes in that work, it seems far more likely
than not that the 1912 Russell knew of and adopted Keynes' theory
of probability, if not the term "relevant," and not the thesis that
every item of evidence must make a difference. These things are
not in *Problems*. But they are in Russell's review of Keynes
(Russell 1922: 153), and also in Russell's discussion of Keynes in

Human Knowledge (HK 374–75). No doubt Russell learned of
them by 1914, when he read the proofs of Keynes' book.

Three Objections

There are three main problems with my argument that legal
scholars are the origin of Keynes' theory of probability as degree of
logical relevance.

(1) All my evidence is purely circumstantial. I found no
direct evidence that Keynes was aware of legal talk of logical
relevance. In his *Treatise*, Keynes refers only to four legal cases
and one legal treatise (Keynes 1962 / 1921: 24–27). These are:
Sapwell v. Bass, 2 K.B. 486 (1910); Chaplin v Hicks, 2 K.B. 786
(1911); Watson v Ambergate, Nottingham, and Boston Railway
Company, 15 Jur. 448 (1851; "Ambergate" is misspelled as
"Ambergah" in my copy of Keynes); Simpson v. London and North
Western Railway Company, 1 Q.B.D. 274 (1876); and *Mayne's
Treatise on Damages* None of the legal cases mentions logical
relevance, or even relevance at all. But Mayne uses the terms
"relevant evidence" and "directly relevant" as early as 1872
(Mayne 1872: 112, 577). Keynes does not cite Mayne for any of
the cases; but Mayne (1894) lists both *Ambergate* and *Simpson* in
the Table of Cases. (*Sapwell* and *Chaplin* were decided 1910–11.)
Keynes' five legal citations only show that he was studying English
law on the question whether there are degrees of probability which
cannot be numerically measured. And Skidelsky says:

> On 16 July [1905] Neville had written in his diary, "We
> have not yet decided whether Maynard shall take Part II
> of the Moral Sciences Tripos or the Economics Tripos."
> Fearing the worst, he had also kept open the legal option,
> making his son a member of the Inner Temple in
> London. (Skidelsky 1986: 162)

Thus it seems that Neville Keynes had his son enrolled as a student
member merely as an emergency backup career option which was
never exercised.

(2) When legal scholars say that relevance is a logical
relation, their understanding is not the same as Keynes', in that
their understanding is not metaphysical. The American scholar
George F. James says, "Relevancy is [a] formal relation between
two propositions" (James 1992 / 1941: 384 n.15 / 696 n.15). James
observes that in an evidentiary argument at law, the premiss is an
evidentiary proposition describing the item of evidence, and the
conclusion is a material proposition describing the material fact

(James 1992 / 1941: 384 n.15 / 696 n.15). This much is the same in Keynes. But Keynes understands his degrees of logical relevance as intellectually intuited, Platonically real logical relations of premisses to conclusions. Again, I doubt that Anglo-American law is committed to such an extreme metaphysical realism.

(3) Skidelsky gives a far simpler and more elegant account which may be regarded as the principal account today. He holds that Keynes simply developed his theory that probability is degree of logical relevance on his own, then added the early Russell's formal approach and metaphysical Platonism.

Replies to the Objections

I admit all three problems as genuine, and reply as follows.

(1) Yes, my evidence is only circumstantial. But it is still a fantastic coincidence that so many English and American evidence law treatises discussed logical relevance some years before Keynes started working on probability in 1904, that Keynes studied English legal cases discussing degrees of probability which cannot be numerically measured, and that Keynes eventually advanced the theory that degrees of probability are degrees of logical relevance, even if they cannot be numerically measured, not even ordinally.

I have not found the term "logical relevance," or "logically relevant," used as referring to probable evidence, in any of the other main fields the early Keynes studied, including mathematics, economics, and philosophy. Among philosophers and logicians, I do not find the term or its grammatical variants so used, or used at all, in Kirwan (1807), Venn (1994 / 1889; 1973 / 1907), John Stuart Mill, Neville Keynes, Jevons, or the pre-Keynes William Ernest Johnson. It is only in evidence law that I find the term and its grammatical variants so used, and used abundantly, in the decades before Keynes wrote on probability.

(2) Yes, the legal scholars of and before Keynes' time were not particularly metaphysical in their legal studies of evidence. But I never said that Keynes' Platonic realism came from the legal scholars. I agree with Skidelsky's mainstream account that this aspect of Keynes came from Russell and Moore. That said, we saw that several legal scholars expressly say that relevance is a "logical relation": Chamberlayne's Taylor (1897: 2[6]); Thayer (1900: 308); Elliott 1904: 199). (George F. James, who also says that relevance is a logical relation, comes later.) This is not to mention grammatical variants, including "logically relevant to" and "logical relevancy to."

(3) On the mainstream account, Keynes developed his theory that probability is logical relevance out of his own head, like

a deus ex machina, or Athena springing out of the head of Zeus, or even creation ex nihilo, including even his specific term "logical relevance." On my account, we have a very specific explanation of where Keynes' theory came from, and his specific term. Namely, it came from evidence law. Probably, it came from a fellow member of the Inner Temple. Of course, even on my account, I cannot be perfectly specific by naming one single person or text as the origin.

This concludes the main argument of this book, which may be stated as a syllogism: (1) The circumstantial evidence is overwhelming that Anglo-American evidence law is the origin of Keynes' theory of probability as degree of logical relevance. (2) Keynes influenced the 1912 Russell into accepting Keynes' logical theory, and into making the principle of induction a logical principle, though weaker than deductive logic. Again, Russell thanks Keynes in the preface to *Problems*. And what would he be thanking him for, if not his theory of probability as *a priori* and as admitting logical degrees of strength? Therefore (3) the case is very strong indeed that evidence law is the origin of the 1912 Russell's logical theory of probability, indirectly through Keynes.

Other Possible Influences on Keynes

If I am wrong, then Skidelsky's theory that Keynes arrived at his theory of probability independently while criticizing Moore's probability arguments concerning ethics would be the best theory. Moore had no theory of probability in *Principia Ethica*, and it is quite a leap from *Principia Ethica* to the concept of probability as logical relevance. Thus Keynes scarcely found it in Moore's book, nor for that matter in Moore's *Ethics* (Moore 1912: ch. 5). But we cannot rest here with Skidelsky's view that Keynes simply made up his theory himself, if there are other possible origins of Keynes' theory yet to be explored.

If neither Skidelsky nor I am right, then the next best candidate for chief influence on Keynes' theory of probability as logical relevance might be Keynes' father's best friend, William Ernest Johnson. Howard E. Smokler says:

> Johnson was committed to an analysis of probability as a logical relation between propositions which is not in all cases numerically determinable or even quantitatively comparable. This analysis was, in fact, very close to the one that Keynes provided. (Smokler 1967: 293)

Keynes praises Johnson first and possibly foremost, even before he praises Moore and Russell, on the first page of the Preface to his *Treatise* (Keynes 1962 / 1921: 3). Keynes says later in the book:

> A further occasion of diffidence and apology in introducing this Part of my Treatise arises out of the extent of my debt to Mr. W. E. Johnson. I worked out the first scheme in complete independence of his work....But there was an intermediate stage, at which I submitted what I had done for his criticism....The result is that in its final form it is difficult to indicate the exact extent of my indebtedness to him. (Keynes 1962 / 1921: 116)

But there are two points to make about this eulogy. First, Keynes says he developed his "first scheme in complete independence of [Johnson's] work." Second, Keynes places this praise of Johnson at the beginning not of Part 1 of the *Treatise*, "Fundamental Ideas," but of Part 2, "Fundamental Theorems." Also, Johnson does not discuss probability in his major pre-Keynes published contribution to logic, a series of three papers in *Mind* (Johnson 1892)

After Johnson, the next best candidate for chief influence on Keynes might be Hugh MacColl. MacColl makes degree of probability part of logic, and makes logic basically propositional. And Keynes cites several works by MacColl in the bibliography of his *Treatise*, including MacColl's 1906 book, *Symbolic Logic*, as well as several papers before 1904. But Keynes says that he arrived at his theory independently before he read MacColl:

> The conception of probability as a relation between propositions underlies [MacColl's] symbolism, as it does mine.[1]
> 1. I did not come across [MacColl's writings] until my own method was considerably developed. Mr. M[a]cColl has been the first to use the fundamental symbol of Probability. (Keynes 1962 / 1921: 155, 155 n.1)

After MacColl, the next best candidate for chief influence on Keynes might be Bolzano. But Hailperin says:

> For Bolzano probability was a part of logic....Almost a century before Keynes (whose *1921* makes no mention of him), Bolzano takes probability to be a relation between propositions but, unlike Keynes for whom it was an undefined, informally described, primitive notion, Bolzano provides a definition. (Hailperin 1988: 148; Bolzano 1972: 238–45)

Thus Hailperin finds two problems with the thesis that Keynes' theory of probability originates from Bolzano. First, Bolzano defines probability, while Keynes says "'probability' is in the strict sense indefinable" (Skidelsky 1983: 184 quoting Keynes 1907: ch. 1). (I do not entirely agree that this problem exists, since I hold both that Keynes holds that probability is degree of logical relevance, and that this qualifies as a theoretical definition.) Second, Bolzano is not mentioned in Keynes' *Treatise*. Here I might add that as discussed in my (2015: ch. 8), Russell apparently did not read Bolzano's *Theory of Science*, so that there is no indirect link of Bolzano to Keynes via Russell.

Beyond that, there were plenty of early modern writers in the logical tradition of probability theory, such as Bernoulli and Leibniz, as we saw earlier.

I omit Dorothy Wrinch and Harold Jeffreys. Braithwaite says that "Keynes had not seen" "an article by Dorothy Wrinch and Harold Jeffreys in 1919" (Braithwaite 1973: xvi). The article also appeared twelve years after Keynes had basically developed his theory in his 1907 dissertation.

I also omit Thomas Bayes. Bayes' Theorem is provable from the axioms of the uninterpreted probability calculus, of which frequency theory, Keynes' theory, and Ramsey's theory are all rival interpretations. Thus Keynes is *interpreting* Bayes, not taking his interpretation or theory *from* Bayes. Keynes briefly discusses Bayes' Theorem, finding it "of great importance" (Keynes 1962 / 1921: 174ff., 379ff.) Of course, Keynes' theory must conform to Bayes' Theorem. But then Keynes' theory must conform to *every* axiom and *every* theorem of the probability calculus, and so must every other theory or interpretation of that calculus.

Keynes-Russell Logical Probability Theory as Philosophical Foundation of Evidence Law

I have argued it is more likely than not that Keynes takes both his conception and his terminology of logical relevance from modern evidence law. If I am right, then it seems clear that modern evidence law indirectly influenced Russell as well. And if all of that is right, then it is only natural to note that, in effect, Keynes and Russell can return the favor by providing their theories as a philosophical analysis, and thereby philosophical foundation, of the evidence law community's own most considered views. In fact, whether I am right or not about the legal origins of Keynes' theory of probability, Keynes' and Russell's being open to both mathematical and non-mathematical probabilities might be the best theoretical framework for resolving conflicts among legal theorists on whether and when mathematical probabilities ought to be allowed in judicial proceedings. By admitting three sorts of probability—cardinal, ordinal, and incommensurable—the Keynes-Russell framework provides an accommodating synthesis which can find a reasonable place for all the rival legal views. (Russell at least reports this threefold distinction as Keynes' in Russell 1922: 153; HK 373; MPD 143. But I am sure this is Russell's view as well; compare *Principles* on sorts of magnitudes.) The legal views range from the thesis that mathematical probabilities can be useful and ought to be admissible as legal evidence, to the antithesis that they ought never to be so used. The antithesis may seem extreme, but Lawrence Tribe has an important point when he says that someone should not, say, be ordered to pay restitution based on a purely mathematical argument that it is exactly 51% likely that she owes the money (the example is mine). For that is too much like justice by spinning a roulette wheel. For brief summaries of these conflicts, see Terence Anderson (2005: 250 discussing Michael Finkelstein and William Fairley, Tribe, Lempert); and Twining (1994: 119ff. citing and sometimes discussing Finkelstein and Fairley, Tribe, John Kaplan, Richard Eggleston and Glanville Williams, Alan Cullison, and Jonathan Cohen). Although Lempert does not focus on any of the great philosophers on probability, such as Keynes or Russell, he suggests a sophisticated, conciliatory approach for which Keynes or Russell could easily provide the philosophical foundation. Terence Anderson, David Schum, and William Twining say:

> An influential paper by Richard Lempert on relevance (1977) considers how the weight of evidence should be graded in probabilistic terms. In this work Lempert advised other legal scholars and practitioners not to ignore research on probabilistic reading regardless of what Professor Tribe said about the evils of [the use of] mathematics [in making legal decisions, as in "Trial by Mathematics"]. Lempert's essential argument was that probabilistic analyses of evidential issues could be very informative to jurors in a variety of ways. Lempert's work was very influential in arousing interest in probabilistic issues on the part of other evidence scholars in law. (T. Anderson 2005: 250 citing Lempert 1977)

I compliment Lempert on his judicious view. In effect, Lempert's human weighing and balancing approach to using merely statistical evidence completely admits the existence of Tribe's problem, and then goes on to solve it in, I think, the only way we can.

Probability in Russell's *Theory of Knowledge*

Chapter 1 discussed Keynes as the origin of Russell's early theory of probability in *The Problems of Philosophy*. But Russell had much more to say about probability in his later works from 1913 to 1959, and I would like to say at least a little about them, to sketch a complete picture of Keynes' influence on Russell on probability.

Problems was published in 1912. The next year, Russell wrote a much more technical book-length work called *Theory of Knowledge*. Elizabeth Ramsden Eames says "*The Problems of Philosophy* was a first sketch" of the 1913 work (Eames 1993: xxi). Perhaps the work is most noted for Russell's abandoning it due to Wittgenstein's brief criticism of its theory of judgment. Wittgenstein wrote in a June 1913 letter to Russell:

> I can now express my objection to your theory of judgment exactly: I believe it is obvious that, from the prop[osition] "A judges that (say) a is in the Rel[ation] R to b", if correctly analysed, the prop[osition] [Rab ∨ ¬Rab] must follow directly *without the use of any other premiss*. This condition is not fulfilled by your theory. (Eames 1993: xxvii quoting Wittgenstein)

But the condition *is* fulfilled by Russell's theory. It is fulfilled by *any* theory, true *or* false, since *Rab* ∨ *¬Rab* is a logical truth, and *any* true or false statement (a theory is a conjunctive statement) strictly implies any logical truth. And the "following from" *is* direct, on Wittgenstein's own theory of truth-tables in the *Tractatus*. It is direct in virtue of the direct truth-ground containment shown by the truth-table. Thus Wittgenstein's criticism is surprisingly poor. Of course, it is pre-Tractarian.

The last chapter of *Theory of Knowledge* is "Degrees of Certainty." Oddly, from the present perspective, Russell does not discuss Keynes, but mainly Meinong. For at about this time, Russell was "going through the proofs of Keynes' *Treatise on Probability* and discussing it with...Keynes" (Eames 1993: xxxvii n.79). Another oddity is that Russell distinguishes degrees of (objective) certainty from degrees of (objective) probability. (Russell 1993 / 1913: 168). No doubt the concepts differ, but the distinction is without a substantive difference. For the degrees can scarcely vary inversely, or in any way but exactly together. The main thing is that the 1913 Russell's theory is basically the same as in *Problems*, and therefore remains basically the same as Keynes'. However, one major difference is that Russell finds the sole difference between full certainty and degrees of certainty to be cognitive vagueness in the latter (Russell 1993 / 1913: 174–76).

This is nothing like partial entailment as in Keynes (1962: 52) or Wittgenstein (T 5.15), though it arguably might be a logically sufficient basis of Keynes' degrees of probability in indefinitely many cases. Instead, Russell's theory that degrees of certainty equate to degrees of cognitive vagueness seems much more like Aristotelian intellection, which I discuss at the end of this book.

Probability in Russell's *Outline*

Bas C. van Fraassen, in a paper called "Russell's Philosophical Account of Probability," finds "two main episodes in Russell's thought about probability and inductive inference," the first being around 1930, and the second beginning in 1944 (Fraassen 1979: 384). The first phase begins with the 1927 book *Philosophy*, later reprinted as *An Outline of Philosophy*. The second phase flowers into *Human Knowledge: Its Scope and Limits* (Fraassen 1979: 384–85). Thus Fraassen overlooks Russell's 1912 *Problems*, his 1913 *Theory of Knowledge*, and basically everything discussed in this book. I cannot discuss *Outline* or *Human Knowledge* in detail here, but I shall make brief remarks about each.

Fraassen thinks that in *Outline*, Russell takes a harsh view of Keynes. He says that "Russell explicitly notes his dissatisfaction" with Keynes' answers to several questions raised by Keynes' theory, and that "Russell is not satisfied with Keynes' interpretation of probability as a logical relation" (Fraassen 1979: 386). While this is strictly correct, I think Fraassen misreports the tone of Russell's discussion. Russell himself cautiously concludes:

> [T]he frequency theory, if it could be maintained, would be preferable to Mr. Keynes's, because [i] it would get rid of the necessity for treating probability as indefinable, and [ii] would bring probability into much closer touch with what actually occurs....Nevertheless, the difficulties of the frequency theory [many of which were raised by Keynes] are so considerable that I cannot venture to advocate it definitely. (OP 286)

Thus Russell basically leaves the Keynes-versus-frequency theory dispute undecided in *Outline*. Keynes himself states advantages (i) and (ii) of frequency theory (Keynes 1962 / 1921: 94–95). Thus Russell may well have taken them from Keynes.

Probability in Russell's *Human Knowledge*

In 1948 in *Human Knowledge*, Russell resolves the tension between frequency theory and Keynes' theory by adopting them both in what may be called a mixed theory of probability in which Keynes' theory plays the major role and frequency theory plays a minor role. Russell says that in his "examination of probability[,] the conclusion reached is, in the main, that advocated by Keynes" (HK xv). Thus Russell was basically a Keynesian in the end (1948 HK), just as he was in the beginning (1912 PP), despite some wavering in the middle (1927 OP).

Russell admits objectively rational intuited "degrees of credibility" in *Human Knowledge* (HK 342–44, 380–99). This is basically just Keynes' theory, since as we saw earlier, all Keynes means by "degree of logical relevance" is simply degree of intuited objective rational probability (Keynes 1962 / 1921: 4, 98).

Part 5 of *Human Knowledge* is entitled "Probability." In the introduction to part 5, Russell distinguishes "mathematical probability" from "degrees of credibility" and finds the two "quite different" (HK 335–37). He distinguishes the latter from Keynes' theory on the ground that "data and inferential premises may be uncertain" (HK 337), but it is hard for me to think that Keynes would not agree with this. If probabilities are incommensurable, how can they fail to be uncertain?

In part 5, chapter 1, Russell finds that mathematical probability, considered as pure mathematics, is unproblematic, and says that "the simplest course" is to hold that "any concept which satisfies [the] axioms [of probability theory] has an equal right, from the mathematician's point of view, to be called 'probability'" (HK 339). For example, we can interpret mathematical probability as the ratio or proportion of any two classes of occurrences. This sort of probability works for arbitrarily defined classes (HK 339–41). Mathematical probability applies to artificial situations such as coin tossing or drawing black or white balls out of a bag (HK 348–49). But it is useless in real life situations because:

> the proportion will vary according to our choice of class B; we shall thus obtain different probabilities, all equally valid from the mathematical standpoint. If probability is to be a guide in practice, we must have some way of selecting one probability as *the* probability. If we cannot do this, all the different probabilities will remain equally valid, and we shall be left without guidance. (HK 341, Russell's emphasis).

And we cannot even always choose classes whose memberships are definite and known (HK 341–42).

Russell says:

> But there is another sort [of probability], which I call
> "degree of credibility." This sort applies to single
> propositions, and takes account always of all *relevant*
> evidence....It is this sort, and not mathematical
> probability, that is *relevant* when it is said that all our
> knowledge is only probable, and that probability is the
> guide of life. (HK 343–44, my emphasis)

Here Russell uses the term "relevant" twice in the manner of
Keynes and the evidence law tradition. Degree of credibility: (a)
"applies to single propositions" (HK 344), (b) "is relative...to all
data" (HK 342) as opposed to selected arbitrary classes, and (c)
"applies even in certain cases where there is no known evidence"
(HK 344). But there are also cases where (d) degree of credibility
concerns "what may be called 'intrinsic doubtfulness'" (HK 342).
This improves on Keynes, since no prior body of evidence is
required.

Degree of credibility can only sometimes be analyzed into
mathematical probability. Nonetheless, "it is not...purely subject-
I've" (HK 342–43). There is a "subjective" sort of "degree of"
merely psychological "conviction," but that is not what Russell has
in mind (HK 343). There is also an objective sort of "degree of
conviction" which "is objective in the sense that it is the degree of
credence that a rational man will give;" and this is what Russell has
in mind (HK 343). It is rational because here an increase in
conviction "goes with an increase of evidence" (HK 343), and I
assume similarly for a decrease. This seems somewhat circular to
me. Russell is explaining degree of objective conviction or
credibility in terms of degree of objective evidence. Grice and
Strawson might call it a "family circle" of interdefinable terms
(Grice 1956). Yet I think Russell's it is intrinsically a very
plausible and natural explanation, and much the same as Keynes'.
For both Russell's and Keynes' explanations go in the right direction. It is better to define objective credibility (relevance) in terms
of objective evidence (probability) than the other way around. Note
that this implies that objective evidence must make a difference to
objective credibility.

Russell says that these two concepts of probability, the
mathematical concept and the degree of credibility concept, "have
an equal claim to be called 'probability'," and both merit study; but
only the latter is "the guide of life" in Butler's sense (HK 343).
This is Russell's mixed theory of probability, with the Keynesian
concept clearly predominating as the guide of life.

In *Human Knowledge*, part 5, chapter 2, Russell discusses
mathematical probability. He says, "Following [W. E.] Johnson and

Keynes, we will denote by 'p/h' the undefined notion, 'The probability of p given h'" (HK 345). He says the notion *is* defined by the axioms of mathematical probability theory, but only in the sense that Peano's axioms define the natural numbers, namely, that any interpretation that satisfies the axioms is as valid as any other (HK 345). And for Russell, this is a very limited sense. For Russell rejects Peano's definition of the natural numbers, since on it they cannot even be used to count things (HK 345; see my 2005–2007 paper on Peano, Russell, and Quine).

I shall omit *Human Knowledge*, part 5, chapters 3 and 4 as basically irrelevant to the topic of relevance. In chapter 3, Russell discusses what he calls the "finite-frequency" theory of probability, where at least one of two classes is finite, and we simply ask the probability that any randomly chosen member of the other class is also a member of the first class. In chapter 4, Russell discusses the Mises-Reichenbach frequency theory.

In part 5, chapter 5, Russell discusses Keynes' theory of probability. Among other things, he discusses Keynes' conception of irrelevance. He says, "Roughly speaking, an added premise is 'irrelevant' if it does not change the [existing] probability" (HK 374). This is just Keynes' conception.

Russell considers a typical empiricist objection to Keynes' theory. Namely, only "tautologies" can be known independently of experience, and Keynes' basic probability relations are not (even claimed by Keynes to be) tautologous; so how can they be known (HK 375)? Russell is sympathetic to the objection, but he does not find it "decisive," since on this sort of "strict" empiricism, "science is impossible" (HK 376). Indeed, the objection is even more general than Russell indicates. For it applies not just to science, but to any attempt to justify probable knowledge, including Russell's own principle of induction as a weak synthetic *a priori* principle in his 1912 *Problems*, and Russell's own five postulates of nondeductive inference in *Human Knowledge*. All of these are non-tautologous, and the five postulates are not even *a priori*.

The objection overlooks that synthetic *a priori* principles can be known independently of experience, and arguably can justify probable knowledge. This includes the 1912 Russell's principle of induction, at least on his own view, as well as my own neo-Chisholmian, neo-Carneadean synthetic *a priori* principle that if something *seems* to us to be the case, then we have reason to believe it. Indeed, the most natural line of defense for Keynes is to say that his theory that probability is degree of logical relevance, and that the probability relations we intuit between our statements of what the evidence is and our statements about what the evidence is for, are all synthetic *a priori*. Indeed, I do not see how else he could justify them, since he says they are rationally intuited, yet they are not analytic.

Appealing to synthetic *a priori* intuitions or principles is arguably the best way to justify the later Russell's five postulates of nondeductive inference as well. This cannot be done directly, since the postulates themselves are not even *a priori*. Perhaps it can be done on a higher or meta-level. For insofar as they objectively *seem* to be correct, *my* synthetic *a priori* principle of seeming entails that we have objective reason to believe them. That is, if, based on all our experience, Russell's five postulates objectively *seem* more likely than not to be true, my principle would justify them as rational. Likewise, the 1912 Russell's principle of induction might be used to justify them, if it is indeed *a priori*. Indeed, taking all our experience as our body of evidence, even Keynes might rationally intuit that Russell's five postulates have some probability of being true. This is ironic, since Russell is trying to rescue Keynes by means of these postulates, and it should be the other way around.

A deeper question arises. Assume I am right that either (1) my *a priori* principle of seeming, (2) the 1912 Russell's allegedly *a priori* principle of induction, or (3) Keynes' seemingly *a priori* intuitive judgments of probability can be used to justify the 1948 Russell's five non-*a priori* postulates of nondeductive inference as having some minimal objective reason for their acceptance, based on our experience. Then what about using any of (1), (2) or (3) to justify the other two in an *a priori* way? Or more simply, which of (1), (2), or (3), if any, is or ought to be the most basic within the *a priori* foundations of our epistemology?

I shall argue that my principle is a better candidate than the others for being taken as the most basic. The principle of induction does not seem to be *a priori* in the first place. Certainly Hume did not think so. Hume's problem of induction would not even exist if the principle were *a priori*. I am tempted to suggest that Russell is the only philosopher, or almost the only philosopher, who thought that it is *a priori*. If I and the vast majority of thinkers are right that it is not, then (1) can justify (2), but (2) cannot justify (1). I turn now to Keynes. My principle simply and directly applies to anything that seems to be the case, from single statements considered on their intrinsic merits to complex bodies of evidence. But Keynes' theory has a more complex structure. It involves a two-step approach. First, we intuit a basic probability relation between one set of propositions and another proposition, i.e., between the premises and conclusion of our probability argument. Second, we intuitively judge the (not necessarily exact or numerical) probability of the other proposition (the conclusion) on the basis of the probability relation we intuited in the first step. But my principle eliminates the first step as needless baggage. Thus it is simpler and more elegant. In fact, it is a deep objection to Keynes that we often cannot describe our evidence.

It might be objected that precisely because Keynes' theory involves two steps, it is deeper because it is more analytic. It finds two components where I find only one. One reply might be that in a sense, my principle has two steps too. First, we find that something seems to us to be correct. Second, we infer that we have reason to believe it. But these steps are different in kind from Keynes' steps. My steps do not require a probability relation among propositions, or even a plurality of propositions at all. I can consider a single proposition by itself, find that it intrinsically seems to me to be true, and infer from this that there is reason to believe that it is true. But Keynes cannot do that. On his theory, he can only find a proposition to be likely in relation to some set of other propositions. And even where we do appeal to a body of evidence, my theory does not need that body of evidence to be describable in a set of propositions.

The deeper reply to the objection is simply that my theory is simpler and more elegant. This is not a matter of Ockham's razor. It is a matter of best logical analysis of our justification of probability.

We can see the relationality of Keynes' theory in the very word "relevance." The relevance is always of a set of propositions to some other proposition. (If the propositions were the same, then we would have deductive containment relevance.) But the only relationality involved in my principle is a proposition's seeming true *to me*, and in *my* having reason to believe it. This is a different kind of relationality entirely. For as a general rule, I myself am not evidence for the proposition that I have reason to believe. The only exceptions would be arguments like "I exist as a private mind and cause my behavior to be purposive, therefore probably other minds animate the other human bodies around me which appear to be acting purposively." It is in the sense of not requiring any prior evidential premises, any already existing body of evidence, that my principle is simple and Keynes' is complex. My principle requires only a proposition being considered and a considerer of it.

Next in *Human Knowledge*, Russell discusses two objections to Keynes. He takes the second to be "more vital" than the first (HK 377).

The first objection is that one and the same proposition would have different probabilities at the same time for the same person if we consider different subsets of propositions already known to that person, so that we should make the proposition's probability relative to the totality of propositions already known to that person (HK 376–77). But Russell then says, "All this, however, Keynes no doubt would admit. The objection is, in fact, only to a certain looseness of statement, not to anything essential to the theory" (HK 377). As we saw earlier, the frequency theory has much the same problem. What is usually the case can vary relative to the class of cases we consider. Thus we should state the frequency theory with a qualification: "Relative to the totality of already known propositions, what is probable is what is usual." Recall that Russell does admit 'frequent' as one of the two main valid *senses* of "probable," and admits frequency theory as a valid but comparatively unimportant part of his own mixed theory.

Russell's second and "more vital" (HK 377) objection is based on a more complex argument. He starts by saying that he is "merely inquiring how we *can*" know Keynes' basic propositional relations of probability (HK 377, Russell's emphasis). So far, the objection is a very plausible and natural one, and not very different from Ramsey's. As we noted earlier, it was Ramsey who criticized Keynes for relying on logical intuitions which nobody could intuit. Ramsey could not discover such intuitions in himself, and found that other people's supposed intuitions of probabilities conflict with each other (Ramsey 1931: 161–63). But after that first sentence, Russell suddenly veers off into a rather different line of objection for the rest of the paragraph and beyond. He notes that all our logically clear systems have primitive terms and unproved axioms. He notes further that a primitive term cannot occur in a theorem proved from the axioms unless it already occurs in at least one of the axioms used in the proof. In short, every primitive term must occur in some axiom if it is to occur in any theorem at all. (Ironically, this is very close to the basic intuition of Anderson and Belnap (1992; 1975) on variable sharing, and far from Russell's own modern classical logic, in which we can prove theorem "*p* or *q*" from axiom "*p*".) In contrast, no *defined* term needs to occur in any axiom *or* theorem, since it can be replaced by the primitive terms that define it. Russell then poses the problem: if probability "cannot be defined, [then] there must, if we are to know anything about it, be propositions [about it] which we know without extraneous evidence" (HK 377). He then goes on to ask what Keynes thinks we "directly know" as axioms "in our knowledge of probability" (HK 377). He then argues in some detail that "what the principle of indifference really asserts is that probability is a relation between propositional functions, not between propositions" (HK 379). The principle of indifference is that "The probabilities of *a* and *b* relative to given evidence are equal if there is no *relevant* evidence relating to *a* without corresponding evidence relating to *b*; that is to say, the probabilities of *a* and *b* relative to the evidence are equal, if the evidence is symmetrical with respect to *a* and *b*" (HK 375, my emphasis). The term "relevant evidence" here is to be understood in terms of the basic definition that "an added premise is '*irrelevant*' if it does not change the probability" (HK 374, my emphasis). He says, "My conclusion is that the chief *formal* defect in Keynes' theory of probability consists in his regarding probability as a relation between propositions rather than between propositional functions" (HK 380, Russell's emphasis). The details of Russell's argument need not detain us because three of my comments concern the nature of his conclusion, and the fourth concerns how he sets up the objection in the first place.

My four comments follow.

First, Russell himself admits that his criticism is merely one of "*formal* defect" (HK 380, Russell's emphasis). This leaves it open that there is no substantive problem with Keynes, and what is more, leaves it open that there is no substantive difference between Russell and Keynes on degree of probability (or credibility). And on Russell's own view, there will be no difference between Russell and Keynes, if we apply Russell's theory of propositional functions so as to remove the formal defect Russell purports to find in Keynes, as least as far as this "more vital" objection is concerned.

Second, the specific formal defect Russell finds in Keynes is that Keynes conflates propositions and propositional functions. But the 1927 Russell abolishes the distinction between real variables and apparent variables, and finds that the propositional function "'Fx' is always true" is logically equivalent to and rewritable as the proposition "$(x)(Fx)$". Thus we can rewrite Keynes to avoid the objection—or rewrite Russell himself to face it. For, to quote Curt Ducasse, it is:

> perfectly arbitrary which one of such a pair of sentences we chose to describe as a "disguise" of the other, and which one therefore to describe as what the other "really" is.... (Ducasse 1941: 94–95)

Thus, just as we saw earlier that Russell and MacColl sink or swim together, so Russell and Keynes sink or swim together. And since Russell abolishes the distinction in his introduction to the 1927 second edition of *Principia*, Russell in effect destroys his 1948 criticism of Keynes twenty-one years before he makes it.

Just as with his objection to MacColl's theory of modality, Russell's objection of formal defect in Keynes loses all credibility in light of Russell's abolition of the distinction between real variables and apparent variables. This is not just an ad hominem or tu quoque against Russell. The distinction between real variables and apparent variables can be intelligibly stated as a merely formal distinction, and is easily understood and applied even by first-year logic students. Basically, all we need to know is the distinction between propositions and propositional functions. But it is really quite pointless, as Russell came to see. For, as Russell in effect admits when he abolishes the distinction between these two sorts of variables, "always true" and "not always true" are nothing more than crude early syntactical versions of his later universal and existential quantifiers. I say crude because they cannot distinguish multiple, not to say nested, variables. This is as opposed to "(x)", which we know right away concerns variable x and not variables y or z. To eliminate the crudity, we would have to use cumbersome expressions such as "is always true with respect to x", or "is not always false with respect to y". Whether or not Russell greatly changes his semantic *theory* of variables and quantification from *Principles* to *Principia* does not detract from this syntactical point. For a discussion of whether he changed his theory, and in particular, of whether his variables still range over all entities or now only over particulars, see Landini (2007: ch. 1–4).

That Russell's objections to MacColl and Keynes should be the same, and should lose all credibility for the same reason, is not surprising. For MacColl and Keynes are as one in regarding a universal statement as stating a probability of 100%, or a certainty, and in that sense a necessity. In that respect, their views coalesce.

Third, when we look for a substantive difference between Keynes and Russell, there seems to be none. The difference between degree of "probability" (Keynes) and degree of objective rational "credibility" (Russell) seems merely terminological. And it seems to me that Russell uses the very same family circle of terms to describe credibility that Keynes uses to describe probability: "rational," "objective," and "(rational objective) evidence." In this way, and indeed I think that in any event, credibility is exactly as definable (or indefinable) for Russell as probability is for Keynes.

Fourth, Russell sets up the problem as the question whether "probability" is definable, since if it is not, then it must occur in at least one axiom we must know directly, if we are to know what probability is at all. This was Russell's second and "more vital" (HK 377) objection to Keynes. But here Russell has forgotten his own philosophy of analysis. As shown in my (2015: ch. 9), Russell argues in several works that it is unimportant whether we can define everything at the present time, since there is no reason to expect either that analysis will end in simples or that analysis can go on forever because there are no simples (PLA 202; IMP 3–4; HK 252; MPD 164 quoting PLA 202; MPD 165 quoting HK 252). Now, this applies universally to all topics, including probability. This is not just an internal conflict in Russell's views. The issue of whether logical analysis involves a vicious infinite regress of analyses of analyses is a substantive issue that directly bears on

Russell's second and "more vital" objection to Keynes. Russell does not even see the problem, much less discuss it. The problem is just that if analysis goes on forever, then everything can be defined on indefinitely many levels of analysis, including probability. If so, then the term "probability" is not primitive, and need not occur in a directly known axiom if we are to know what probability is. Or, if definitions require an undefined term (definiendum) as an ultimate starting point, on pain of vicious infinite regress of definitions of defining terms (definientia), then we cannot define what anything is, if all series of definitions are in fact endless.

In the rest of the book, Russell presents his own theory of probability. He offers various technical criticisms of Keynes, but they are more in the nature of improvements to, than rejections of, Keynes' theory (HK 386–87, 408–10, 435–38, 439–43). They are all in the nature of pointing out correctable "formal defects" which Russell proceeds to correct. And Russell's concept of degrees of objective rational credibility is basically the same as Keynes' concept of degrees of probability. Russell also agrees with Keynes that induction is not axiomatic but derivative (HK part 6 ch. 2; MPD 144, 148, 149). Russell says that his own postulates of nondeductive inference "are designed only to confer that antecedent probability which Keynes needs to validate his inductions" (MPD 149). Thus the whole point of Russell's own postulates of nondeductive inference is to "validate" Keynes. (As we saw earlier, the validation ought to be the other way around.)

The deepest and most general similarity between Russell and Keynes is that for Russell, a mathematical probability is "the ratio of the numbers of two finite classes," i.e., a frequency relation between two propositional functions, while epistemic probability concerns individual propositions, i.e., the objective rational credibility of a proposition in light of "all *relevant* evidence" (HK 381, my emphasis; see 384–91). Thus in Russell's *Human Knowledge*, the two thinkers agree on Keynes' most basic view, with Russell using Keynes' own term "relevant evidence."

The major distinction I see between Russell and Keynes on probability is one I have already mentioned. Namely, Keynes has a complex two-step process for assigning probabilities to individual statements, while Russell accepts directly intuited likelihoods that some individual statements are true, which likelihoods are not based on the known truth or likelihood of any other statements, in major works from *Problems* to *Human Knowledge* (PP 135–40; IMT ch. 9–11; HK 381–84; 391–92). He calls such statements "self-evident truths" (PP 109, 114), "basic propositions" (IMT ch. 10), or "data" (HK 392). In the extreme case, for the early Russell, we have "knowledge by acquaintance" of their truth. But even the early Russell seems to find no datum absolutely certain, not even in logic (PM 12–13, 59–60).

The greatest difference between Russell and Keynes on probability is that Russell can and does admit epistemologically foundational data, including sense-data and the principle of induction itself, while Keynes, with his two-step process, cannot. One might even suspect Keynes' theory of implying a vicious epistemological regress for this reason: how does he come by his initial probabilities for his initial relational statements? My reply is that the difference between Russell and Keynes is not that great. For Keynes, we directly intuit the evidentiary *relations* among propositions, so that *these* are his self-evident or basic data. But I think there may be a vicious regress in Keynes after all, concerning not these intuited relations among propositions, but the first *relatum* of each such relation. I am referring to his bodies of evidence, i.e., his antecedent or background assessments of probability that such bodies of evidence are themselves veridical, or at least more likely veridical than not. These are what is really "initial" for Keynes. The dilemma is that either his two-step process applies to the statements describing his bodies of evidence or it does not. If it does, then we have a vicious regress of applications of the two-step process. If it does not, then the two-step process is a false analysis of probability. For there will always be a probability it never applies to, namely, the probability that the body of evidence is veridical. If I am right, then Russell and Keynes are very different indeed. For Russell prevents any such regress by admitting self-evident statements and statements about self-evident data. This is just the same as my earlier point that my principle of seeming is simpler and more basic than Keynes' theory. Some seemings are self-evident; and in a certain sense they all are, as when it just seems to me that a certain complex argument is sound.

Russell argues that vagueness is in many ways the basis of degrees of credibility (HK part 5, ch, 6, sect. c). I find this circular, since vagueness is by definition the absence of the very sort of determinacy that allows mathematical probability, as opposed to degrees of credibility, to apply. This is certainly so on Russell's definition of "vagueness" in his 1923 paper entitled "Vagueness." There Russell first defines precision as a one-one correspondence of terms and the relations among terms in a representing structure and a represented structure (Russell 1923: 89). Then he says:

> *Per contra*, a representation is *vague* when the relation
> of the representing system to the represented system is
> not one-one, but one-many. For example, a photograph

which is so smudged that it might equally represent
Brown or Jones is vague. (Russell 1923: 89)

Thus for Russell, vagueness is by definition a necessary condition
of the applicability of the concept of degrees of epistemic
credibility as opposed to the concept of mathematical probability.
But it is not a sufficient condition, since for the 1923 Russell
vagueness also occurs in logic and mathematics, and in general
whenever we cannot prove or disprove a universal statement. For
example, Goldbach's conjecture is the claim that every even
number is the sum of two primes. Since we cannot prove or
disprove it, we do not know if there is a one-one correspondence
between even numbers and sums of two primes. Thus it is vague in
Russell's sense, at least until we prove or disprove it. Yet the
concept of degrees of credibility seems inapplicable to it, or
minimally applicable at best, since the even numbers are infinitely
many, and we only know finitely many of them to be sums of two
primes. This is unlike rough or estimated arithmetic, where we
round the numbers or otherwise simplify the calculation so as to
approximate the correct result. In rough arithmetic, degree of
credibility does apply, and corresponds to degree of roughness.
One might object that the more even numbers we find to be sums of
two primes, the closer we approximate the conjecture as the result.
But that is only if the conjecture is *true*. In contrast, in rough
arithmetic we are approximating a result we *know* we can prove. In
fact, if we could not prove the actual determinate result, we would
not know if we were approximating it at all. Thus we cannot even
approximate Goldbach's conjecture by a tally of the even numbers
we have confirmed as sums of two primes so far. And perhaps that
is the best argument why the concept of degrees of credibility does
not apply to Goldbach's conjecture, and in general why vagueness
is not a sufficient condition of the applicability of that concept.
This is just an illustration of the general fact that many
philosophical issues have a way of becoming clearer in philosophy
of mathematics. This is also like my criticism of Ramsey that if we
do not already know an objective probability, then we cannot know
if our learning curve of bets approximates to it.

Probability in *My Philosophical Development*

In 1959 in *My Philosophical Development*, Russell briefly
summarizes his theory of knowledge in *Human Knowledge* as
follows. "There are two kinds of probability," (1) statistical and (2)
"degrees of credibility" (MPD 142–43). This is his mixed theory
again. Now, the frequency theory is that the *only* kind of proba-

bility is statistical (MPD 142). Thus for Russell, the frequency theory is strictly false, since it has only a limited scope of application. Considered as pure mathematics, the statistical theory of probability is perfectly acceptable, but it applies only to a narrow range of cases in the empirical world, namely, clear and definite cases, such as drawing cards out of a deck (MPD 142). Thus "wherever probability is definite, the frequency theory is applicable" (MPD 143). Russell says that Keynes holds a theory of kind (2) in his *Treatise on Probability*. For Keynes, the probability relation obtains between two propositions, "is indefinable[,] and capable of varying degrees" including truth, falsehood, and every degree in between (MPD 142–43). For Keynes, not all degrees of probability "are measurable or reducible, even in theory, to frequencies" (MPD 143). Russell's own theory of degrees of credibility is a "conception...to which something more like Keynes's theory is applicable" (MPD 143). Thus Russell holds a mixed theory that includes both kinds (1) and (2). He holds that (1) applies to a narrow range of definite cases, and he holds that (2) applies to everything else. He says that probability in the sense of degrees of credibility is "much more important" than probability in the sense of frequency of occurrence (MPD 143).

For Russell, probability can be justified only by principles which are "not logically demonstrative" (MPD 143). Based on his own study of non-demonstrative inference, he admits induction, but not as one of the basic or primitive principles (MPD 144). This is very different from his view in 1912. But one view remains the same: in modern science, causation is not a matter of simple laws of the form "If *A*, then *B*," but of complex laws that are multi-variable and often statistical (MPD 146–47).

Russell then briefly reiterates his five basic "postulates" of non-demonstrative inference. He says that they are neither *a priori* nor even necessary conditions of probable inference, but are sufficient to justify the ordinary and scientific probable inferences we normally accept. For us, the most important thing he says is that his five postulates "are designed *only* to confer that antecedent probability *which Keynes needs to validate his inductions*" (MPD 149, my emphasis). This shows that Russell intends his own theory not to destroy Keynes' theory, but to fulfill it.

On the whole, I think Russell gives a very fair summary of *Human Knowledge* in *My Philosophical Development*.

Induction and Intellection

Supposedly, Aristotle sharply separates deduction from induction. Supposedly, Aristotle takes an exclusively frequency approach to probability. But at bottom, Aristotle basically justifies probability just as Keynes and Russell do, namely, as an objective, rational, direct evidential presentation, either of a degree of logical relevance (Keynes), a degree of objective credibility (Russell), or a degree of intellectual intuition (Aristotle). The great Aristotle scholar W. D. Ross says, "Essentially, induction for [Aristotle] is a process not of reasoning but of direct insight, mediated psychologically by a review of particular instances" (Ross 1960: 44). Ross says:

> The root nature of induction seems to be, for [Aristotle], that it is the "leading on" of one person by another from particular knowledge to universal. Whether one instance or a few or many or all are needed depends on the relative *intelligibility* of the subject-matter....Where the form is easily separated in thought from the matter, as in mathematics, the mind passes from the perception of the truth in a single instance to grasping its applicability to all instances of a kind; where the form is less easily dissevered from the matter, an induction from several instances is necessary. But *in both cases the same activity of "intellection" is involved.* (Ross 1960: 43, my emphasis)

I see no real difference between Aristotle on degree of intelligibility and Russell on degree of vagueness. In fact, the two appear to be mirror inversions of each other. Ross concludes, "The passage from particulars to the universals implicit in them is described as induction; the grasping of the universals which become the first premisses of science must, we are told, be the work of a faculty higher than science, and this can only be intuitive reason" (Ross 1960: 58, 168, 211; see *Posterior Analytics (An. Post.)* 88a12–17, 100a5–b15 / Aristotle 1968a: 154–55, 185–86). For Aristotle, "'imperfect induction'...reaches a merely probable conclusion" (Ross 1960: 211). Clearly, this is not only consistent with Aristotle's frequency theory of probability, but can underwrite that theory as justified by intellectual intuition as probably true. Perhaps then the ultimate origin of Keynes' and Russell's theory, through the medium of millennia of inductive logic, is Aristotle.

While Keynes is well aware of Aristotelian induction, he does not base Aristotle's frequency sense of induction on Aristotle's abstractive intellective sense, and keeps Aristotle's two senses "quite distinct" (Keynes 1962 / 1921: 274). The honor of justifying the principle of induction as probably true based on a weak but direct *a priori* intellectual intuition may be due to Russell in *Problems*.

Thus it appears that both Russell and Aristotle hold a mixed theory of probability on which frequency theory and induction alike are justified by a deeper, more general theory of objectively intuited probability. This sophisticated and complex theory is very hard to argue for or against, I think the best argument in its favor is that it is hard to find a more plausible account. This may sound like an appeal to ignorance, but appeal to ignorance is a fallacy only in deductive logic. I prefer to think of it as more like a deductively valid proof by cases, since there are only a few major rival theories of probability. What major rival to this mixed theory are there, besides pure frequency theory, pure logical theory, and pure subjectivist theory? As in ontology (my 2003), the pace in epistemology is glacial.

The most serious problem facing Russell's extension of logical relevance to inductive logic is explaining partial containment of the conclusion in the premises. While probabilistic *syllogisms* are deductive, their deductive form is mere window dressing, as we saw. The problem is that neither the principle of induction, nor specific cases of induction, seems to involve, nor even seems able to involve, any such partial containment.

Perhaps we may appeal to Wittgenstein's logical theory of probability in the *Tractatus*. The theory extends his conception of extensional truth-ground containment to inductive logic (T 4.464, 5.15–5.156). If a conclusion is true on every row on which all the premises are true, we have a deductively valid, i.e., tautologous inference, which we may call 100% logical probability. If a conclusion is true on no row, we have a logically false inference, which we may call 0% logical probability. But in many truth-tables, a conclusion is true on some *proper subset* of the rows on which all the premises are true. We may call this "partial truth-ground containment." For example, $P \supset Q$ has a logical probability of 75%, since it is true on exactly three of the four rows of its truth-table. Now, this sort of logical probability applies to truth-tables for any finite number n of atomic statements, approaching infinity.

Georg Henrik von Wright notes that "equal possibilities," often called indifference, exchangeability, or equiprobability in the literature, are logically guaranteed in Wittgenstein's theory. Wright says:

> A purified and generalized form of the possibility view was suggested by Bolzano in his *Wissenschaftslehre* of the year 1837, and renewed by Wittgenstein in the *Tractatus Logico-Philosophicus* (1921–22). The Bolzano-Wittgenstein definition does not mention equal possibilities. Yet it can be shown that this definition is a sufficient basis for the deduction of the branch of

mathematics known as the ("classical") Calculus of Probability. " (Wright 1960: 168)

But this is not enough for probability as a guide to life, which rarely offers equal possibilities outside the gaming halls.

I propose the following further extension of Wittgenstein's extension. By applying the methods of the infinitesimal calculus to Wittgenstein's purely logical theory of probability, we can come infinitesimally close to tautology without reaching it. The notion of an infinitesimal can be analyzed using Karl Weierstrass's theory of limits, as Russell himself does. Or it can be logically defined as in Robinson arithmetic (A. Robinson 1996; 1979; 1979a / 1961). (This is Abraham Robinson's arithmetic, not to be confused with Richard Robinson's arithmetic.) Thus this application of the calculus can be interpreted as consistent with the logicist program of analyzing mathematics in terms of logic. For example, Robinson uses Skolem sets with infinite members. But I wonder why Frege could not have just as easily logically defined an infinitesimal, or one simple sort of infinitesimal, as the number one divided by Cantor's number aleph null. Frege defines aleph null as the number of positive integers; and the set of positive integers has infinitely many members. Since sets with infinitely many members are called nonstandard, Robinson arithmetic is called nonstandard, and so is the resulting calculus. Robinson's nonstandard arithmetic is not the only one today (they differ in logical foundations, but give the same mathematics), but it was the first. But a Fregean / Cantorian infinitesimal, e.g., 1/aleph null, would be in effect nonstandard too.

My proposed extension of Wittgenstein's logical theory of probability to truth-tables for any finite number of atomic statements approaching infinity gives us infinitely many infinitesimal gradations of degree of purely logical probability. However, it fails to give us indeterminate or incommensurable degrees of probability. And it is impracticable. There are only so many atomic statements we can write in a lifetime, or discover to be relevant to the statement with whose probability we are concerned, unless we use mathematical induction over atomic statements. I conclude that my proposed extension is too theoretical and too artificial to ground probability as a guide to life either, though it does give a better approximation in its way. In fact, it is not so much an extension of Wittgenstein's theory as it is a mere recognition that his truth-tables can have any finite number of rows and columns.

Wittgenstein's theory of logically relevant probability is a modern link between deductive and inductive logical relevance very different from the ancient link I find in Aristotle's conception of induction as a main kind of intellection. For Aristotelian intellection is intensional, while Wittgenstein's theory of probability is extensional, and might well be called logical bean-counting, since it is truth-table row counting. Thus ironically, Wittgensteinian logical probability is a special kind of frequency theory. But this purely extensional theory of probability is surely only the genus of which the sorts of probability we are interested in are species. If so, then this even more ironically makes frequency theory the genus of probability theory, and Keynes-Russell degrees of relevance or credibility merely a differentia. This may seem an unusual result for those of us who think of frequency theory as mainly useful only for large and definite populations of study, i.e., for epidemiology. But Wittgenstein's theory is a very special kind of frequency theory. It is very different from the ordinary sort of mathematical probability that is used by game players and other epidemiologists. The existence of this ordinary sort of mathematical probability is why I, too, hold a mixed theory of probability. Perhaps the best statement of my theory is my (2012a: 60–65), but my most recent statement is note 4 in the notes section of this book.

Summary of Main Argument of the Book

Again, the main argument of this book may be stated as a syllogism. (1) From 1912 *Problems of Philosophy* on, Russell's theory of probability originates from Keynes and is fundamentally that of Keynes. This is both accepted in the literature (Skidelsky 2005: 286; Monteiro 2001: 66) and fairly obvious from a "smoking gun" acknowledgment by Russell in the book's preface (PP vi), not to mention from the nature and later time of Russell's theory. (2) The circumstantial case is overwhelming that Keynes' theory of probability originates in turn from Anglo-American evidence law and is fundamentally that of Anglo-American evidence law. It took 132 pages (368–500) to show this. This is except for Keynes' Platonic realism, which originates from and is basically the same as that in Russell's *Principles*. (3) Therefore, the circumstantial case is basically overwhelming that except for its Platonic realism, Russell's theory of probability as logical relevance indirectly originates from Anglo-American evidence law through Keynes, and is fundamentally that of Anglo-American evidence law. Premiss (2) and conclusion (3) are what is new to the study of Russell on probability, and bring it to a new level of depth and understanding. But I have no evidence that Russell was ever aware of this indirect legal origin of his theory. In fact, I have no evidence that Keynes was aware of the full extent of the legal origin of his own theory, or was even aware of it to the limited but substantial extent to which I have described it. I am arguing only that Keynes was very likely aware *that* his theory that probability is degree of logical relevance *did* originate in evidence law, concerning premiss (2) of my argument. He may well have simply taken that theory as common knowledge, at least among legal scholars.

Summary of Purpose of the Book

This is the first full book-length treatment of the history of the concept of logical relevance in English evidence law. At least, I know of no other. There are many articles on the *concept*, but only brief discussions of its *history*. Thus I seem to be presenting the most comprehensive history of the concept ever written, not to say philosophically the deepest. But it is still only introductory. I can only hope to have placed the concept into a new historical light for further study.

Second, I seem to be the first even to suggest that the origin of the logicist probability theory of Keynes and Russell is English evidence law. The prevailing theory has been Skidelsky's view that Keynes thought up the theory all by himself, like Athena springing fully armored from the head of Zeus, or like a deus ex machina.

These were plums ripe for plucking. Many legal scholars knew the concept had a history and wrote something about it. In fact, I discuss the main scholars here. Any one of them could have written a whole book about it. And anyone familiar with the most basic ideas of both evidence law and Keynes' theory of probability could have come to wonder if there was a historical connection. For the most basic idea, that probability is logical relevance, is the same. If it is not relevant, it is not evidence. If it is not evidence, it is not relevant.

Thus it looks for all the world as though for the old evidence law writers, logical relevance is a logically essential feature, and is the *only* logically essential feature, of evidence. (What else would or could be a logically essential feature for them?) If so, then it takes only the slightest charity to gloss them as implicitly regarding evidence as *definable* as logical relevance, and turn, probability as definable as degree of logical relevance.

Even the old legal Latin maxims give the game away. "Frustrà probatur quod probatum non relevat" means, "It is useless (vain, idle) to prove (show, establish by evidence) that which, when proved, is not relevant." "Non potest probari quod probatum non relevat" means, "It is impossible (impermissible, unacceptable, incorrect) to prove that which is not relevant." "Allegari non debuit quod probatum non relevat" means, "Matters which are not relevant if proved ought not to be alleged." All this is use-relevance.

Notes

1. Arthur N. Prior credits John Neville Keynes with anticipating C. I. Lewis on the paradoxes of strict implication (Prior 1967: 551). Routley, Plumwood, Meyer, and Brady say "Lewis...rediscovered in 1913 the modal definition of strict implication known to modal logicians" (Routley 1982: 358). And as we saw earlier, Prior also credits Diodorus Cronus with discussing much the same paradoxes of strict implication that Lewis does (Prior 1955: 193–94).

William Ernest Johnson is the only person John Maynard Keynes cites in *A Treatise on Probability* regarding ("favourable") relevance (Keynes 1962 / 1921: 68). The context does not suggest that the notion of logical relevance is actually due to Johnson.

2. Lempert and Saltzburg principally mention Thayer, whom I shall discuss later (Lempert 2011: 224; 1983: 153).

It does not appear that Keynes was conversely an influence on legal discussions of logical relevance. One looks in vain for mention of Keynes in legal scholarship. In the Westlaw databases for American state and federal cases up to 1999, there are only thirteen cases which mention Keynes, and they do so only in connection with his economic or political views. When they mention his views on probability at all, they mention only his using risk analysis in economics. In the Westlaw database for combined legal journals and law reviews, Keynes' book *A Treatise on Probability* is cited in only four articles. Of the four, only one discusses his views on relevance in probability theory, but not in connection with Rule 401 or any similar rule of evidence (Kaye 1986). Nor does the official comment to Rule 401 mention or cite Keynes (West 1995).

3. The very term "relevant" suggests Keynes. But as we shall see, the term flourishes in the history of evidence law, and that is the origin of its use in Rule 401.

4. I myself advocate a mixed theory of probability. The idea of a mixed theory is not new (Braithwaite 1975: 239–40). For mass repetitive events, I adopt frequency theory. For unusual or nonrecurrent particular events, I reject both Keynes and Ramsey, and offer a rationalist cognitive interpretation of my own. This two-level or "mixed" theory is much like Russell's in *Human Knowledge*, but substitutes Continental-style phenomenological objects for his British empiricist sense-data or his (later) noticed events (see especially HK 392). For unique or nonrecurrent events, I interpret degrees of probability as being what cognitively seems more or less strongly to be the case. Simplifying Roderick M. Chisholm's fine work, which is based in turn on that of Carneades,

I admit a principle which I call the principle of seeming. The principle is that if it objectively seems to subject S that proposition P is true, then, regardless of whether S actually believes P, S has (some minimal objective) reason to believe that P. An even simpler statement of the principle would be: If it seems to S that P, then it is reasonable to S that P. See Chisholm (1966: 44–55); compare Snyder (1971: 204–5; see 208 for Snyder's list of epistemic theorems). (Probationes debent is if it is *clearly evidence*, it is *evidence*.)

The principle has a phenomenological antecedent and an epistemic consequent, and I therefore consider it to be synthetic *a priori*. It is what equates, in my theory, to Keynes' implicit principle that if we intuit a degree of logical relevance of body of evidence e to hypothesis h, then h is to that extent probable given e. I consider that principle to be intended to be synthetic *a priori*, not just because it follows from his theoretical definition that probability is degree of logical relevance, but also because of what its own nature would be if it were true. I simply replace Keynes' intellectual intuition of a logical relation between e and h with my relation that, based on e, it objectively seems to subject S that h is true. If e is itself simply the seeming that h seems to be true, then e itself seems to be h. For example, if we simply seem to see an apple, then the seeming apple seems itself to be the apple. Or if my principle simply seems to be true, or intrinsically plausible, or self-evident, then the seemingly true principle itself seems to be the true principle. In both cases, the relation is that the seeming seems to be F. Thus, where Keynes' theory is that probability is degree of logical relevance, my theory is that probability is degree of stronger or weaker reason for S to believe P, which is in turn degree of stronger or weaker objective seeming to S that P. Thus on my theory, degree of objective seeming grounds degree of rational strength for belief (though not *of* belief, since actual belief is not required); and degree of rational strength for belief grounds degree of probability in turn, all to subject S. By "ground" I mean explain or account for in virtue of being the metaphysical basis of, so as to result in an intuitive mutual entailment, or at least in an explanatory logical equivalence. Degree of rational strength in my theory equates to degree of logical relevance in Keynes; and as Keynes tells us, that is all he *means* by "logical relevance." Thus, as with Keynes, I ground probability as degree of logical relevance. But for me, degree of logical relevance is not directly intuited, and is not the ultimate explanation, but is instead grounded in turn as degree of objective seeming. Thus I ground probability more deeply as degree of objectively seeming to be the case. And *that* is our direct "intuition." Thus I see Keynes not so much as wrong, but shallow.

As with Keynes, the degrees of probability in my theory of seeming can be cardinal, ordinal, or incommensurable. Certainly they objectively seem that way! And in my opinion, the fact that degrees of probability are often a matter of one's best intuitive and experienced judgment is far better and more naturally explained in terms of objective phenomenological seemings, which come and go and change in this world, than in terms of intellectual intuitions of timelessly real relations among timelessly real propositions in a Platonic realm of changeless being. It is not only more elegant in not needing to postulate such a Platonic realm of being, but more natural in that its ontological *locus* is in the natural world of change. Of course, our logical seemings may well include logical seemings of logical intuitions of logical entities and their logical relationships to logician *L*. And there may well be reason to believe that such logical intuitions and logical entities exist. But our logical seemings belong to the world of change, just as the logicians who have them do.

All the main starting points (data) in epistemology, such as the data of common sense, or of science, ordinary language, or the intellectual light of reason, are grounded in what seems to be the case, but the reverse is not so. If these other starting points did not even seem to be the case, or better, if it did not even seem to be the case that they were good starting points, or that they were evidence or evidentiary data for anything, then we would not rely on them. But conversely, if the data of common sense, science, and so on do seem to be the case, then (and only then) would we, or could we rationally or justifiably, start from them.

The principle of seeming is grounded even more deeply than just in objective seemings. For in my theory of qualified objects, I ground objective seemings in turn as qualified objects. And if they are veridical or illusory (not: delusory) objective seemings, I ground that which they seem to be as unqualified objects, i.e., objects in themselves. A qualified object is an object which is an objectual way an object in itself can be (rightly or wrongly) conceived or regarded. If there is an object in itself, then the qualified object "is" the object in itself, in a certain special sense of the term "is." If there is no object in itself, then the qualified object is an objectual way an object in itself *would* or *could* be conceived or regarded, if there *were* an object in itself. The first disjunct covers both veridical ("true") and illusory ("false") perception. The second disjunct covers delusory ("there is no object in itself") perception. For example, the Morning Star and Evening Star are basically veridical qualified objects both of which "are," in a special sense of "are," the planet Venus, which is an object in itself.

The notion of a qualified substance or qualified thing may be traced from Aristotle through antiquity, the middle ages and beyond. But as far as I know, I am the only one who allows illusory or delusory qualified objects. That is because I have redefined the notion so as to allow it to play a basic role in explaining informative existence and informative identity statements on the level of generality of Frege's senses and Russell's descriptions. The *traditional* notion explains informative identity statements only for *veridical* situations, as in "Coriscus in the Lyceum is the musical person," and explain informative existence statements not at all. And my qualified objects are more natural and ordinary than Frege's obscure, abstract senses, and are not limited to linguistic situations the way Russell's descriptions are. Further, my qualified objects can be and often are epistemological seemings. They can be and often are what objects in themselves seem to be. But no ordinary object in itself can seem to be a sense or a description.

Qualified objects may be defined as objects that (1) essentially involve how an object in itself can be conceived or regarded, but such that (2) there may or may not be an object in itself, and such that (3) if there is an object in itself, the qualified object may or may not conceive or regard it veridically. So defined, they are logically prior to the dispute whether epistemological data are private ("first person" or Cartesian) or social ("third person" or scientific / holistic). We conceive or regard some things as private mental entities, and others as public or social; and we can conceive or regard some things either way, as when the idealist George Berkeley assays a house as a bundle of mental ideas across persons.

My theory of qualified objects is based on and is very much like Panayot Butchvarov's theory of objects (Butchvarov 1979). But I use publicly available ordinary "qualified objects" in place of Butchvarov's private, momentary objects, which cannot be singled out twice even by the same person. And I use (sometimes merely probable) real entities which are "out there" in place of Butchvarov's entities, which are mere conceptual constructions of his objects. Again, just as Butchvarov eliminatively replaces the subjunctive conditional notion of existence as identifiability indefinitely many times (i.e. we *would* single it out if we *were* there now) "with the idea that a thing exists if *there is* [indicative tense] an indefinite number of objects[,] each identical with it, whether or not we have encountered any of them" (Butchvarov 1994: 44), so I can do the same thing using an indefinite number of my qualified objects. And my qualified objects are ordinary (qualified) public things, while Butchvarov's objects, like Russell's sense-data, are creatures of analysis we are almost never presented with as such in ordinary life. Russell gives the game away when he says that to become acquainted with sense-data, we must learn to see things as the painter sees: "the painter has to unlearn the habit of thinking that things seem to have the colour which common sense says they 'really' have, and to learn the habit of seeing things as they appear"

(PP 9). These are difficult topics I cannot discuss here (see Dejnožka 2003: xxvi, 47, 61, 73, 123–35; Butchvarov 1979: 122–53, 212–38). Thus I am describing this deeper level of my theory only to set it aside; and I shall discuss only objective seemings and the principle of seeming in the present book.

Again, the principle of seeming does not require a realm of timeless being the way Keynes' theory does. But by no means does my theory *preclude* admitting such a realm, and one might have *other* reasons, having nothing to do with probability theory or with theory of knowledge, for admitting such a realm. For example, one might find it best to ground the timeless truths of logic and mathematics in a timeless realm of abstract entities in the manner of Frege and the early Russell; and that would include the uninterpreted probability calculus as a branch of mathematics. In fact, my principle of seeming allows us to admit both intellectual seemings of abstract entities and perceptual seemings of ordinary physical objects; and both would be kinds of objective seemings. For example, we can admit logical seemings (I mean objective seemings *about* logic) as *phenomenological* intellectual intuitions of logical entities in our phenomenology of logic. Logical seemings would be a species of the genus intellectual seemings, within the summum genus of objective seemings. And we would not be liable to Ramsey's criticisms, since our logical seemings are merely the objective seemings we obviously do have in this world. They are not obscure, occult Platonic intuitions, but are simply how logic seems to us. Some things certainly seem to us to be the case in logic. And surely what is true in logic objectively seems different to different people.

I do not claim that the frequency side of my mixed theory resolves David Hume's famous problem of induction. Indeed, I agree with Mises that frequency theory presupposes induction (Mises 1961: ix). At least it does insofar as we cannot observe a total empirical frequency across the whole of space and time. But it seems to me that my principle of seeming is our best hope of justifying *both* the frequency-inductive side of my theory *and* the nonrepetitive or unique event side. Namely, if it objectively seems to us that the frequency theory of probability is true for mass repetitive events, and that the principle of induction on which it is based is true, then we have reason to believe that they are true, even if we cannot describe the reason.

I believe that my principle, that if it objectively seems to *S* that *P*, then S has reason to believe that *P*, is *a priori*. I also believe that if it objectively seems to *S* that the principle of induction is true, then *S* has reason to believe that the principle of induction is true. But I believe that my principle does not and cannot explain or justify the principle of induction as being *itself* a weak synthetic *a priori* truth, as Russell claims. I believe with Hume against Russell that the principle of induction is not and cannot be *a priori*. More than that, I believe that the principle does not even *seem* to be *a priori*. The same point applies to the frequency theory of repetitive events. That theory is not itself *a priori*, nor does it even seem to be. Now, if the total frequency of events across space and time could be perceptually presented to an omnipresent observer, then for such an observer, the theory *might as well* be *a priori*, for all practical intents and purposes. But the empirical frequency of all events in space and time themselves would still be *a posteriori*, could not be otherwise, and would not even seem to be otherwise, even to such an omnipresent observer. The principle of induction would be *known to be true or false* by such an observer, but that would not make it *a priori*. Even an omniscient observer could only know the principle of induction to be true by empirical experience. And all my principle implies is that if it objectively seems to us that the principle of induction is true, then we have reason to believe that it is true, even if we agree with Hume that the principle is not *a priori*, and even if we agree with him that we are unable to state a noncircular argument for the principle, and are thus unable to describe the reason it seems to be true.

We need not be able to explain *why* it objectively seems to us that *P*, that is, describe the *reason* we have to believe that *P*. (Again, this is regardless of whether we *actually* believe that *P*.) That is not required by my principle about seeming. I believe, as many do, that we can have reason to believe something even if, for whatever reason, we cannot describe the reason or reasons we have, or cannot describe them well. Lord William Murray Mansfield goes even further than that. He notes that there are people who make good decisions based on their common sense or long experience, but who can only describe, perhaps because they can only find, *bad* reasons for their decisions. Such people are good intuitive judges of things, i.e., of what seems to be the case, but bad at describing the reasons for their judgments. Nor are they just lucky guessers. To the contrary, such people are often known to be both intuitively skilled and very experienced at weighing what seems to be the case in various practical matters, but to be very bad at verbally describing why they weigh, or should weigh, things the way they do. In fact, all or most of us are like this to some degree. But allow me to give Mansfield's extreme and thereby very clear example.

A general was appointed Governor of a West Indies island, and would therefore now also have to be a judge for the first time. Having no legal background, he asked his old friend Mansfield for advice. Mansfield famously replied, "[C]onsider what you think justice requires, and then decide accordingly. But never give your reasons;—your judgment will probably be right, but your reasons will certainly be wrong" (Campbell 1878: 481, quoting Mansfield). John Campbell says that things went very well for the new judge—until he came to have so high an opinion of himself as a jurist that he actually described his reasons for a decision, and they turned out to be very bad reasons indeed (Campbell 1878: 481). My principle about seeming is very much like that. Mansfield knew this particular friend of his well. But we all know, or ought to know, how hard it is to state good reasons for us to believe in, say, the existence of an external world, even though it objectively seems to us to exist. Of course, sometimes we *can* state the reasons we have, or at least state them to some degree; and we should state our reasons if we can. But that might be easier in practical life than in fundamental philosophy.

There is a major qualification to what I just said. Namely, we can in general *always* describe our reason to believe as follows: The minimal objective reason for *S* to believe that *P* is simply and precisely that it objectively seems to *S* that *P*. The qualification is that *other than* that always describable and always correct *general* reason, we need not be able to describe any more *specific* reason for *S* to believe that *P*, in order for the principle of seeming to be true.

I also must distinguish within phenomenology between a mere presentation as such, and an objective seeming. An objective seeming is a presentation that objectively seems to be veridical. I think the distinction was well-established by Plato in the form of his thesis that mere sensation is not knowledge or, for that matter, even evidence. We have many presentations that do not objectively seem to be the case, from mirages in the desert to optical illusions.

Again, my theory avoids Ramsey's criticism of Keynes that we simply do not have the Platonic "logical intuition[s]" (Keynes 1962 / 1921: 18) Keynes' theory is based on (Ramsey 1931: 161). For I have replaced logical intuitions with seemings. The existence of seemings is not in doubt. Certainly, and in a perfectly ordinary sense, it objectively seems to us that many things are the case. And even objective seemings about logic and mathematics are themselves neither timeless nor *a priori*. Their existence is always *a posteriori* and relative to at least a possible thinker. When it seems to me that two plus two equals four, the seeming is always at a certain time. Public seemings can occur across times and people.

My theory also avoids Ramsey's other main criticism, that any logical intuitions of probability would be unreliable, since we disagree so often on how probable a thing is. For my theory is relative to subject *S* to begin with. If it seems that *P* to *S1*, and if it seems that *not-P* to *S2*, then on my theory, *S1* has reason to believe that *P*, and *S2* has reason to believe that *not-P*. There is nothing self-contradictory about that. In fact, it happens all the time. I think the 1948 Russell avoids these criticisms too. My only advantage is that I have a more natural, ordinary, and plausible phenomenology. In fact, Ramsey's second criticism does not even apply well to Keynes. I see nothing wrong with conflicts among weak logical intuitions about degrees of logical relevance. Such conflicts are only to be expected. We are not ideal logicians with perfect logical intuitions. Still, on Keynes' theory, if people disagree in their intellectual intuitions about what is the case in the Platonic world, at most one of them can be right, the rest must be wrong, and we simply cannot tell who is right or wrong. There is nothing like that in my theory. Yes, if there are conflicting objective seemings, at most one can be veridical, the rest must be illusory or delusory, and we cannot tell what is really the case behind the veil of seemings. I mean that on my theory, there is more to it than just that. There are all sorts of degrees of objective seeming, and degrees of reason to believe, for us to weigh and assess as best we can. This is not at all the bang-bang, yes-no, right-wrong, binary, polarized sort of logical-intuition-or-no-logical-intuition theory Keynes has, or at least that Ramsey believes Keynes has.

To be sure, I may be unable to estimate a probability even roughly due to complicated conflicts in my own evidence, i.e., in what objectively seems to me to be the case. But my theory admits and explains that fact in terms of phenomenologically presented incommensurabilities among conflicting seemings, and does not even attempt to resolve what no theory of probability can resolve.

On a deeper and more general level, my theory *is* much like Keynes'. I do reject his view that logical intuitions play a role in probability theory. But both my theory of objective seemings and his theory of logical intuitions are species of his more general theory that degrees of probability are "degrees of rational belief" (Keynes 1962 / 1921: 20, Keynes' emphasis omitted). We disagree only on what rationality *consists of* in probability judgments. For Keynes, it consists of timeless Platonic logical intuitions of degrees of reason to believe. For me, that rationality consists of phenomenological objective seemings, including seemings about logic, in the world of change.

I shall now discuss six objections to my principle of seeming. The first three concern seeming counterexamples.

First, it might be objected that it may objectively seem to S that P, where P is *not* reasonable to S. I have two replies . First, this is not a reason to reject my principle, but a mere, flat, bald denial of its truth. Second, I wholly grant that it is both categorially possible and analytically possible that my principle is false. For its denial is neither ill-formed nor self-contradictory. But my principle is still a necessary truth, since it is a synthetic *a priori* truth.

Second, it might be objected that it may be reasonable to S

that *P*, even though it objectively seems to *S* that *not-P*. I have two replies. First, my principle says only that if it objectively seems to *S* that *P*, then it is reasonable to *S* that *P*. It does not say or imply the converse. That is, it does not say or imply that if it is reasonable to *S* that *P*, then it objectively seems to *S* that *P*. That is not part of my principle. My principle is not a biconditional, i.e., not an "if and only if" statement. I come now to a fine point. Insofar as I hold that there is no way to have reason to believe other than by an objective seeming, I am committed to the converse of my principle, even if my principle itself does not imply its converse. That is, insofar as that is what I hold, then I am committed to two different principles, my principle of seeming and its converse. And the objection would apply to the converse principle. But it begs the question against the converse principle. It is a mere, flat, bald denial that the converse principle is true. And both my principle of seeming and its converse objectively seem to be synthetic *a priori* truths, at least to me. And if I am right, then there are not going to be any counterexamples of this sort. My second reply is that if this type of situation is possible, then it can only be a misjudged conflict in our evidence. We often choose among reasonable alternative beliefs in subtle, complex situations. Obviously, if it objectively seems to us that *P*, then we know that it seems to us that *P*, since even an objective seeming is a presented seeming; and as Descartes says, at least we know what seems to us to be the case. And on my theory, we would *have* reason to believe that *P*. But we may not know what would be *most* reasonable for us to believe, since we may not have done the *best* reasoning about the situation. Here I think we can and must distinguish between the best reason we actually have, or even could have actually come up with under the circumstances, and the best reason we could have found under ideal circumstances, or perhaps in retrospect. This reply also addresses cases where it seems that it is more reasonable to *S* that *P* than not, but objectively seems to *S* that *not-P* more than not.

A third objection to my principle of seeming is this. It may the case that: (1) it seems to *S* that *P*, (2) *P* is reasonable to *S*, and (3) *P* is more reasonable to *S* than not-*P*, yet (4) *S* may (and logically can) believe not-*P*, even though not-*P* is *absurd* to *S*, perhaps out of pure and simple faith. Tertullian says he believes that God exists *because* it is absurd, perhaps meaning that he must believe in God by faith alone, since reason goes against it. In my discussion, I shall flip *P* and not-*P* around for convenience in writing. One reply is that if *S* truly finds *P* absurd, or sufficiently absurd, then it does *not* seem to *S* that *P*, and *S* does not and cannot believe *P*. Of course, this begs the question against the possibility of belief through faith. A second reply is that *P* might be reasonable *enough* to *S* for *S* to believe *P*, even though *S also* finds absurd *aspects* to *P*. This would be just a case of conflict in one's own evidence. The second reply subsumes the first insofar as *S* finds believing out of pure and simple faith to be reasonable enough. The problem with this reply is that the specified counterexample does not logically require or entail any such conflict of evidence. A third reply is that when we believe on faith, we usually have some minimal reason to believe, such as apostolic or other testimonial evidence. The problem with this reply is that the counterexample logically allows pure and simple nonrational belief based on pure and simple nonrational faith. And it is quite true that there is nothing in my principle of seeming which logically prohibits belief for no reason, or even for a bad reason. It implies only that *if* it objectively seems to *S* that *P*, and *if S* believes that *P*, *then S* has reason for *S*'s belief that *P*. But the fourth and best reply is that the principle of seeming has nothing to do with actual belief in the first place. The principle concerns not the mere fact of belief as such, but the rationality of any belief there may be.

The principle of seeming has nothing to say on the question whether people can choose their beliefs. We often say that people believe what they want, or even what they choose. But we also admit that if several ordinary people are looking at an apple in a basket under ordinary conditions, then they have no choice but to believe there is an apple in the basket. The only thing my principle implies is that *if* it objectively seems to us that we have a (or no) choice to believe that *P*, then we have *reason* to believe that we have a (or no) choice to believe that *P*. And I think that if there is no objective seeming that there is any evidence at all, then we cannot *rationally* believe, much less *rationally* choose to believe. This includes not only metaphysical statements about what is in the real world behind the curtain of seemings, but also statements known to be randomly selected. I myself hold that we *do* have objective seemings giving us minimal reason to believe that there is at least a real physical world, but that we have no objective seemings giving us even minimal reason to believe statements known to be randomly selected, or even statements deterministically selected by a computer algorithm known to have nothing to do with any relevant evidence.

The principle of seeming has nothing to do with irrational, subjective, or merely psychological beliefs. Not all beliefs are rational. Far from it. The principle may be spelled out more fully as, "If it *objectively* seems to *S* that *P*, then *S* has *objective* reason to believe *objectively* that *P*." So spelled out, the principle is not even indirectly about merely psychological beliefs, or what might be called subjective seemings. And degree of psychological strength of belief is not the same as degree of objective likelihood of belief. That it might be hard or sometimes even impossible to tell in practice whether our belief is objective or subjective, the difference in the concepts is clear enough. This is shown by the fact that it is quite intelligible that we can and often do later judge a belief as either more subjective or more objective than we had thought at first. Compare Kant's view that in practice we cannot always tell whether our motives are moral or selfish, though the distinction is clear in theory.

Next, I consider two dialectical objections to my principle.

Fourth, the contrapositive of my principle is that if we have no reason to believe that *P*, then *P* does not seem to us to be the case to us to be the case. And this implies that if we have no reason to believe either *P* or not *P*, then neither *P* nor not-*P* seems to us to be the case. And trivially, if we have no reason to believe either P or not-P, then we cannot rationally believe anything about whether *P* is true. We may call this the "doxastic equivalent," or perhaps better, the doxastic instance, of the problem of Buridan's ass. Jean Buridan questions the principle of sufficient reason, i.e., the principle that everything has a reason, or more fully stated, that if anything exists, then there is *some* kind of reason or explanation that suffices to explain why it exists. (For an Aristotelian, any one of Aristotle's four kinds of cause would do.) Buridan asks us to consider an ass standing equidistant from two equally good piles of hay. The ass would starve to death if the principle of sufficient reason were true, since there is no reason for it to choose one pile over the other. Likewise, one might urge, for the principle of doxastic sufficient reason, i.e., the principle that every belief has a reason. Suppose we humans are rationally equidistant from all the indefinitely many logically possible metaphysically real worlds that could exist hidden behind the curtain of empirical appearances. Then we could never believe anything about the real world, if the principle of doxastic reason were true. For, setting up the issues in this way, we could have no more reason to believe that God, physical objects, and other minds exist than to believe they do not. But people do have in fact all kinds of beliefs about the real world, therefore my principle is false by contraposition. Here I am waiving nonrational causes of beliefs.

My reply would be to note that the principle of doxastic sufficient reason is an instance of the far more general principle of sufficient reason. For if everything has a reason, then all our beliefs have reasons. Therefore, any *solution* of a problem with the general principle also applies to the doxastic principle by instantiation. (Again, I am waiving the distinction between reasons for believing and other sorts of causes of why our beliefs exist, such as efficient causes.) Now, the problem of Buridan's ass is commonly held to be solved by admitting higher level reasons. Namely, the ass will choose a pile at random precisely to avoid starving to death; and that is a higher level reason. In similar situations, we often toss a coin, simply to make an arbitrary choice. We may even say the ass does a mental equivalent of tossing a coin. Pascal's Wager is arguably a higher level reason for believing in God, if not a spiritually very admirable one. Inference to the best explanation, and Quinean considerations of simplicity and conservatism, are arguably higher level reasons for believing in, say, physical objects. Compare my (2006) on Quine's view that simplicity and conservatism of theory are literally kinds of scientific evidence. Quine admits a robust realism of physical objects behind the curtain of observations; and simplicity and conservatism are his reasons for doing so. Thus Quine conforms to the principle of sufficient reason by having higher level reasons; and this is arguably so even if he is wrong to think that simplicity and conservatism are literally kinds of evidence. By parity of reason, or by instantiation, the first dialectical objection to the principle of doxastic sufficient reason can be resolved by using higher level reasons as well. In fact, Quine's beliefs are a case in point. And if Quine, then why not us?

The fifth (and second dialectical) objection to my principle is this. It may be very well for Keynes, Russell, and Broad to hold that our empirical evidence for the principle of induction is always getting stronger, since as time goes on, we are always continuing to see further examples of the future's resembling the past. But when Frege says that "once given the possibility [that other people exist], the probability [based on my perceptual evidence] is very great, so great that it cannot be distinguished from certainty" (Frege 1968: 530), this is totally different. For, at least waiving our "higher reason" resolution of the first dialectical objection, no confirmation of *any* sort is possible even in principle of what, if anything, lies behind the curtain of appearances. This leads to a philosophical standoff. On the one hand, if my principle is right, then it allows us to go behind the curtain, in the sense of having reason to believe that there is an external world, since it objectively seems to us that there is, even if we cannot describe what the reason is, beyond merely saying that it objectively seems to us to be the case. On the other hand, if the problem of whether there is an external world behind the curtain of appearances is an instance of the problem of Buridan's ass, then my principle must be false. As in so many other topics, one philosopher's modus ponens is another philosopher's modus tollens. My solution is, of course, that my principle is the very sort of higher level reason that can resolve Buridan's problem. But that is only because it does objectively seem to us that there is an external physical world. The solution would not help the ass, if the piles of hay objectively seem equally good to it. The ass needs to choose on the basis of a very different sort of higher level reason, if it rationally chooses at all.

Russell describes several versions of Buridan's ass for the real world behind the curtain of appearances. Famously, he asks us to disprove that "the world sprang into existence five minutes ago, exactly as it then was, with a population that 'remembered' a wholly unreal past" (AMI 159; see 160), and "complete with fossils" (OP 7 indirectly citing Gosse 1857). But he also says more fully:

> The hypothesis that the heavenly bodies are permanent "things" is not logically necessary....This may be called the hypothesis of "complete realism." At the other end is the hypothesis of "complete phenomenalism," according to which bright [heavenly phenomenal] dots exist [only] when observed. Between these two are an infinite number of other hypotheses, e.g., that Venus is "real" but Mars is not, or that Venus is "real" on Mondays, Wednesdays, and Fridays, but not on Tuesdays, Thursdays, and Saturdays. Both extremes and all intermediate hypotheses are consistent with the observed facts; if we choose between them, our choice cannot have any basis in observation alone. (HK 481)

Here, observed facts are the curtain of appearances, and theories like Keynes', Russell's, and mine try to provide a rational basis for belief in a real world that goes beyond empirical observation alone. Again, my solution is simply an application of my principle of seeming. It objectively seems to us that Venus exists every day of the week; therefore we have reason to believe that it does.

The sixth and final objection is this. A few paragraphs ago, I waived the difference between a reason for believing a statement and a reason for the mere existence of the belief, such as an efficient cause. The concepts are different. Of course, my reason for believing may *happen* to be the reason for the existence of the belief. I may even happen *never* to believe without reason. But it would seem logically possible that I might sometimes believe without having any reason to do so, and that the cause of my belief be nonrational, or even irrational, or in a word, a *mere* efficient cause.

My reply echoes my reply to the third objection. Namely, the principle of seeming is not even about belief in the first place. I mean it does not say that if it objectively seems to S that P, then S *believes* that P. The principle says only that if it objectively seems to S that P, then S has *reason* to believe that P, regardless of whether S actually believes that P or not. And the principle of seeming does not imply that all beliefs are rational. That is the very different principle, "If B is a belief, then B is rational." We may also state it as, "If *S* believes that *P*, then *S* has reason to believe that *P*." We may call that the principle of belief. The principle of belief seems obviously false to me. However, it can be restated to make it true: "If *B* is an objective belief held by *S*, then *B* is rational to *S*."

My second reply is this. For our purposes here, we need not even try to answer such questions. To defeat radical skepticism about the external world, and to justify the principle of induction, it is enough if my principle of seeming is true, and if we have the objective seemings in question. We need not have a principle of belief and objective beliefs as well.

My concluding discussion is mostly but not entirely review.

The principle of seeming is best understood in light of Hume's skepticism about induction, which in turn is best seen as skepticism about probability in general. Hume argues that there is no reason whatsoever to believe that the principle of induction is true, that the future will resemble the past, or that the sun will rise tomorrow. In sharp contrast, I am arguing that if it objectively seems to us that the sun will rise tomorrow, then we have some minimal objective reason to believe that it will, even if we cannot describe the reason other than to say that it objectively seems to us to be the case, and even if the reason might not be sufficient reason to justify our belief, if any, even as more likely than not. Likewise for the principle of induction itself, the thesis that the future will resemble the past. the thesis that every physical event has a cause, and for the principle of sufficient reason, which is that there is a reason for every thing. On the principle of seeming, we have reason to believe that all of those principles are true, if they objectively seem to us to be true. This is so regardless of whether they are *a priori*. On my principle of seeming, if they seem to be *a priori*, then we have reason to believe that they are *a priori*. But they do not even seem to be *a priori*. The only principle that seems *a priori* is the principle of seeming itself. It seems synthetic *a priori*.

My principle of seeming may be understood as a case of containment entailment as follows. If something objectively seems to us to be the case, then we have some minimal objective reason to believe it; and this minimal objective reason is simply and precisely that it objectively seems to us to be the case. However, although that *is* what the reason is, the concepts of seeming and of reason are clearly different. Seeming belongs to phenomenology, and reason belongs to logic. Thus the principle of seeming is not analytic, and it is not a tautological containment entailment. Rather, it is a synthetic *a priori* entailment. It is a containment entailment much like that in "If anything is red, then it has color." Just as red contains color, so objective seeming includes objective reason to believe. And this explains why people cannot ever have irrational objective seemings. We cannot have irrational objective seemings for the same reason that there cannot be colorless red apples.

As is often noted, we would accept the explanation that the weather near the Great Lakes is unpredictable because its causes are complex and poorly understood; but we would never accept the explanation that it is unpredictable because it has no cause. And that might be taken as evidence that, or even as showing that, the principle of sufficient reason is true *a priori*. But I think it shows nothing of the kind. For the point is not about the weather, but about what we would accept as an explanation. Thus the point is about us, not the weather. It would be about the weather only on a Kantian theory that we impose causation on our experience. Thus the point is not evidence that the principle that every physical event has a cause is *a priori*, nor even that it is true, and likewise for the principle of sufficient reason. Thus, such principles stand in need of justification themselves, much as Hume would say. My principle of seeming will justify them, but only if they objectively seem to be true or likely to be true. If it objectively seems to *S* that *P*, and does not objectively seem to *S* that not-*P*, then *S* has some minimal reason to believe that *P*, and no reason to believe that not-*P*, and it follows further that to *S*, it is more likely than not that *P*.

The principle of seeming is consistent with, and can help us understand, conflicts in our evidence. Cases of conflicting evidence are cases of conflicting objective seemings. It may objectively seem to me that I just saw Smith shoot Brown in a dark alley. But because the alley was dark, I may not be sure of this. If it seems to me, upon reflection, that the alley was really too dark for me to identify the shooter, then it will no longer even seem to me that I saw Smith. It will then seem only that I had thought I saw Smith.

The principle of seeming is that if it objectively seems to subject *S* that proposition *P* is true, then *S* has objective reason to believe that *P*. The principle does not say or imply that if it objectively seems to *S* that *P*, then *S* *does* believe *P*, or that *S* has *sufficient* reason to believe that *P*, or even that *S* *ought* to believe *P*. The principle implies only that if it objectively seems to *S* that *P*, then *if* S *does* believe that *P*, then *S* has reason to believe that *P*.

The principle of doxastic sufficient reason is that if subject *S* believes that *P*, then there is a reason of *some* kind that suffices to explain why *S* believes that *P*. (Again, this principle is an instance of the principle of sufficient reason.) The reason may be rational, i.e., evidentiary, or it may be a mere efficient cause that is not rationally related to the belief. I never said or implied that we have rational or evidentiary reason to believe every belief we have. The principle of seeming implies only that *if* we have a belief, then *if* what we believe objectively seems to us to be the case, then we have some minimal objective reason for our belief. This implies further that *if* we have a belief, then if we have *no* reason for our belief, then our belief does *not* objectively seem to us to be true. This simply contraposits the conditional consequent of the first conditional statement.

Let us call the following principle the principle of belief: "If subject *S* believes proposition *P*, then it objectively seems to *S* that *P*." Some philosophers seem to think that this principle is true, and true *a priori*. But I think that it is quite false. And I think the reason is a familiar one. Namely, people have nonrational and even irrational beliefs all the time. As Keynes says, "the actual beliefs of particular individuals...may or may not be rational" (Keynes 1962 / 1921: 4). Thus the principle of belief is not true synthetic *a priori*. If it were true, it would be a logically contingent truth. But as Keynes points out in effect, the principle of belief is simply false. In contrast, the principle of seeming is true synthetic *a priori*. That is because for conceptual reasons, there simply cannot be nonrational or irrational objective seemings.

Thus I disagree with Chisholm, who advances principles that base having reason to believe on believing (Chisholm 1966: 45 principle B, 47 principle C). In my opinion, Chisholm would have done better to stick to Carneades' phenomenological principle. To be fair, Chisholm does require the beliefs to be about perceived states. But this by itself does not entail that the beliefs are rational. In this connection, there is a well-known ambiguity in the word "perceive." In normal circumstances, "I perceive a rat" implies that there is a real rat there to be perceived. But "Last night in a dream, I perceived a rat" implies no such thing. I am not saying that this ambiguity applies to Chisholm's principles. But I am saying that his talk of perception in his principles cannot be taken to imply that the beliefs are veridical, or even to give any reason to believe that the beliefs are veridical, without begging the question of the truth of his principles. Believing and objective seeming are not the same. But an objective seeming is rational in virtue of its very objectivity.

We might rescue Chisholm by distinguishing objective beliefs from subjective beliefs, and placing objective beliefs on a par with objective seemings. And if we mean by "objective," rational, this begs the question for either seemings or beliefs. But the fundamental thing is the seeming that gives rise to the belief. Also, an objective seeming can give some minimal reason to believe without our actually being led to believe. Thus my theory is on the proper level of generality, but Chisholm's theory is too narrow. For we do not always actually believe when we have some minimal reason to believe based on an objective seeming. Far from it. Thus I think that my theory, which is far more like that of

Carneades than like that of Chisholm, is better than Chisholm's.

There can be higher levels of objective seemings. If I objectively seem to see a pink rat, then I have reason to believe there is one. But what if it occurs to me that I am drunk? Or what if I find out later that someone gave me a drug? This invites talk of higher levels of objective seeming, based on taking in more epistemically relevant context. I think that our epistemic thinking often does have this sort of subtle complexity. There may be no easy answer to such questions. But my principle of seeming was never intended to remove every difficulty or vagueness about objective seemings, much less remove every difficulty or vagueness in phenomenology or epistemology.

The deeper questions are, What are objective seemings? Do we ever have them? How can we know that a seeming is objective? Can we define them by genus and difference as seemings that are objective? But how helpful is that? Is that not circular? This may be rock bottom. There may be no deeper or more illuminating answers to be had, and either we accept that the principle of seeming is true and that we have objective seemings, or we do not. To *define* objectivity in terms of rationality would be for my principle of seeming to become analytic, which might seem better; but such a definition would only beg the question. Or we can try to explicate objectivity in negative terms, such as 'not influenced by our thoughts, beliefs, feelings, and so on'. But we should not understand a term negatively unless the term is a negative one. And it is not clear that "objective" is essentially a negative term. On the face of it, it seems positive. And the "and so on" seems lame. But the positive analogy, "Objective seeming implies reason to believe as red implies color," seems to apply straightforwardly. And this analogy seems enough for my principle to be noncircularly understood. After all, if a thing is red, it must have color; but its being red is normally not taken to be a begging of the question as to its having color.

Finally, we now have four ontological *loci* for probability, depending on which theory we accept. On frequency theory, the *locus* of a natural (empirical) probability is in the natural world, or in classes of things in the natural world. On Keynes' theory, the *locus* is his Platonic realm of timeless relations among what can only be timeless propositions. On Ramsey's theory, the *locus* is in ourselves: our disposition (willingness) to bet, and our learning curve as created by rewards of winning and punishments of losing. On my theory, the locus is phenomenological seemings, or more deeply, qualified objects which are mind-independent, but whose logical possibility depends on the logical possibility of minds.

5. Dov M. Gabbay and John Woods write as if today there are still "two notions of relevance. One is probabilistic (or what legal

theorists call logical) relevance. The other is called legal (i.e. worth-hearing or practical) relevance. It is a useful distinction" (Gabbay 2010: 242). They cite Thayer as "[w]riting to the same effect" (Gabbay 2010: 243), as if Thayer embraced the very distinction he rejects. Their own quote of Thayer, and their own highlighting of that quote, suggest the opposite: "To discuss such questions...even if we introduced *the poor notion of legal relevancy, as contrasted with logical relevancy*—tends to obscure the nature of the inquiry" (Gabbay 2010: 243 quoting Thayer 1927 / 1898: 5108, Gabbay's and Woods' emphasis).

The legal theorist George F. James had it right when he said in his famous essay, "Relevancy, Probability, and the Law" that by replacing the concept of legal relevance with a set of exclusionary rules which operate to restrict logically relevant evidence for a wide variety of largely unrelated policy reasons, "[t]he largely unrelated principles making up the concept of 'legal relevancy' [might] be disentangled, and that ambiguous phrase returned to the grave wherein the great Professor Thayer laid it almost fifty years ago" (James 1992 / 1941: 392 / 705).

Gabbay and Woods even think that *I* accept the concept of legal relevance. They say:

> Some legal writers make the point that historically the gap between a logician's and a lawyer's appreciation is not all that wide, as witness (Dejnoska [sic], 2004):
>
>> My conclusion is that it is both possible and likely that [the logician] Keynes was inspired by English law. English law required evidence to be "relevant" as early as 1783, and *articulated relevance as "logical relevance"* as early as 1897.... [Gabbay's and Woods' square brackets in their quote of me]
>
> *In fact, however*, it is easy to show that there is a considerable *difficulty* in associating *legal* probability with the concept analyzed by the probability calculus (Gabbay 2010: 250 quoting my 2004 /1996, my emphasis)

Just as with Thayer, their own quotation of me shows the opposite. As I hope my italicized emphases make clear, I was writing about logical relevance, not legal relevance. The paper of mine that they cite does not even mention legal relevance. Besides logical relevance, the only types of relevance I mention are relevance in analogical arguments, and causal-statistical-scientific-explanatory relevance; and I mention them only to set them aside.

I follow Thayer, James, and almost every legal writer in the Anglo-American tradition today in accepting only logical relevance, and in replacing the confused concept of legal relevance with a set of exclusionary rules. The concept of an exclusionary rule is not the concept of a kind of relevance at all. It is the concept of a rule for excluding evidence that *is* relevant for policy reasons. Thayer's point is that there is no such thing as legal relevance, no such concept, but only a grab bag of policy rules for excluding logically relevant evidence.

Douglas Walton is another logician who makes this mistake. Walton says, "Rule 403 shows most dramatically the distinction between logical relevance and legal relevance, as defined by the FRE" (Walton 2004: 21). Rule 403 shows no such thing. There is no such distinction anywhere in the *Federal Rules of Evidence*. The *Federal Rules* do not even mention legal relevance, much less admit a distinction between legal relevance and logical relevance. The *Federal Rules* follow Thayer in abolishing the concept of legal relevance and replacing it with the concept of admissibility. As far the *Federal Rules* are concerned, Thayer consigned legal relevance to the dust bin of history.

Rule 403 says:

> **Rule 403. Exclusion of Relevant Evidence on Grounds of Prejudice, Confusion, or Waste of Time.** Although relevant, evidence may be excluded if its probative value is substantially outweighed by the danger of unfair prejudice, confusion of the issues, or misleading the jury, or by considerations of undue delay, waste of time, or needless presentation of cumulative evidence. (West 1995: Rule 403)

The term "relevant" occurs only once, and it is used in the sense of logical relevance. Note that implicitly, the rule would permit even a scintilla of evidence to be admissible, if its probative value is not substantially outweighed by the dangers and considerations listed, including *needless* presentation of cumulative evidence. As I noted concerning Rule 401 and elsewhere in this book, items of evidence often must work together, since often the true probative weight (or even relevance at all) of each item is apparent only in the context of the group or collection taken as a whole. This includes *needful* presentations of cumulative evidence as having *collective* weight, and to think otherwise is to commit the fallacies of composition and division. I classify Rule 403 as a meta-rule of admissibility which weighs probative value against certain policy reasons for excluding relevant evidence as inadmissible.

References

These are abbreviations for selected works with dates of original publication. Citations are below.

Russell:
AMA   *The Analysis of Matter* (1927)
AMI   *The Analysis of Mind* (1921)
HK   *Human Knowledge: Its Scope and Limits* (1948)
IMP   *Introduction to Mathematical Philosophy* (1919)
IMT   *An Inquiry Into Meaning and Truth* (1940)
MPD   *My Philosophical Development* (1959)
OP   *An Outline of Philosophy* (1927)
PL   *A Critical Exposition of the Philosophy of Leibniz* (1900)
PLA   "The Philosophy of Logical Atomism" (1918)
POM   *The Principles of Mathematics* (1903, 2d ed. 1938)
PP   *The Problems of Philosophy* (1912)

Wittgenstein:
T   *Tractatus Logico-Philosophicus* (German 1921)

Anderson, Alan Ross, Nuel D. Belnap, Jr., and Jon Michael Dunn. 1992. *Entailment: The Logic of Relevance and Necessity.* vol. 2. Princeton, N.J.: Princeton University Press.
——, and Belnap, Jr., Nuel D. 1975. *Entailment: The Logic of Relevance and Necessity.* vol. 1. Princeton, N.J.: Princeton University Press.
Anderson, Terence, David Schum, and William Twining. 2005. *Analysis of Evidence.* 2d ed. Cambridge, England: Cambridge University Press.
Anonymous. 1911. Review of Chamberlayne (1911). *Oklahoma Law Journal.* 9 Okla. L. J. 468.
Aristotle. 1968. *The Basic Works of Aristotle.* Ed. by Richard McKeon. New York: Random House.
——. 1968a. *Posterior Analytics.* Trans. by G. R. G. Mure. In (1968).
——. 1968b. *Prior Analytics.* Trans. by A. J. Jenkinson. In (1968).
——. 1968c. *Rhetoric.* Trans. by W. Rhys Roberts. In (1968).
——. 1960. *Topica.* Trans. by E. S. Forster. In *Posterior Analytics / Topica.* Cambridge, Mass.: Harvard University Press. The Loeb Classical Library.
Baker, John. 2003. *The Oxford History of the Laws of England: 1483–1558.* vol. 6. Oxford: Oxford University Press.
Barbé, Lluís. 2010. *Francis Ysidro Edgeworth: A Portrait with*

Family and Friends. Trans. by Mary C. Black. Cheltenham, England: Edward Elgar Publishing Limited. Substantially revised from the Catalan 1st ed., 2006.

Barnett, Vincent. 2013. *John Maynard Keynes.* London: Routledge. Routledge Historical Biographies Series.

Bateman, Bradley W., and John B. Davis, eds. 1991. Introduction to (1991a).

——, and John B. Davis, eds. 1991a. *Keynes and Philosophy: Essays on the Origins of Keynes's Thought.* Aldershot, England: Edward Elgar Publishing Limited.

Bayes, Thomas. 1963. *Facsimiles of Two Papers by Bayes.* New York: Harper.

Beccaria, Cesare. 1963. *On Crimes and Punishments.* Trans. by Henry Paolucci. Indianapolis, Ind.: Bobbs-Merrill. The Library of Liberal Arts. 1764 Italian.

Bentham, Jeremy. 1827. *Rationale of Judicial Evidence, Specially Applied to English Practice.* "From the Manuscripts of Jeremy Bentham, Esq.[,] Bencher of Lincoln's Inn." vols. 1, 3, 4. London: Hunt and Clarke.

——. 1825. *A Treatise on Judicial Evidence.* Extracted from the manuscripts of Jeremy Bentham by M. Dumont. Trans. into English from Dumont's French translation. London: Messrs. Baldwin, Cradock, and Joy.

Berkowitz, David S., and Samuel E. Thorne, Selectors. 1979. *Classics of English History in the Modern Era.* New York: Garland Publishing. Inc. A Garland Series.

Best, William Mawdesley. 1883. *The Principles of the Law of Evidence with Elementary Rules for Conducting the Examination and Cross-Examination of Witnesses.* American ed. from 7th English ed. Ed. by Charles F. Chamberlayne. Boston: Soule and Bugbee.

——. 1854. *A Treatise on the Principles of Evidence and Practice as to Proofs in Courts of Common Law.* 2d ed. London: S. Sweet.

Black, Henry Campbell, Joseph R. Nolan, and Jacqueline M. Nolan-Haley. 1991. *Black's Law Dictionary.* Abridged 6th ed. Centennial Edition (1891–1991). St. Paul, Minn.: West Publishing Co.

Black, Max. 1970. *A Companion to Wittgenstein's Tractatus.* Ithaca, N.Y.: Cornell University Press.

Blackstone, William. 1854. *Commentaries on the Laws of England.* 21st ed., collated with the edition of 1783, together with notes adapting the work to the American Student by John L. Wendell. New York: Harper and Brothers.

——. 1768. *Commentaries on the Laws of England.* Book 3. Oxford: Clarendon Press. Facsimile of the first edition.

Special Edition privately printed for the members of the Legal Classics Library. New York: The Legal Classics Library, 1983.

Blount, Thomas. 1717. *Law-Dictionary and Glossary, Interpreting such Difficult and Obscure Words and Terms, as are found either in Our Common or Statute, Ancient or Modern, Laws.* 3d ed. London: Browne, Walthoe, Nicholson, Tooke, Midwinter, Cowse, Wellington, Gosling, Mears, Browne, Hooke, Clay, and Nutt.

de Bracton, Henry. 1968. *Bracton on the Laws and Customs of England.* Ed. by George E. Woodbine, trans. and rev. by Samuel E. Thorne. Cambridge, Mass.: Belknap Press of Harvard University Press. Completed in 1256 A.D.

Braithwaite, Richard B. 1975. "Keynes as a Philosopher." In M. Keynes (1975).

——. 1973. Editorial Foreword to John Maynard Keynes, *A Treatise on Probability.* New York: St. Martin's Press for the Royal Economic Society. *The Collected Writings of John Maynard Keynes*, vol. 8.

Broad, C. D. 1968. Critical notice of *A Treatise on Probability.* In *Induction, Probability, and Causation: Selected Papers by C. D. Broad.* Ed. by Donald Davidson, Jaakko Hintikka, Gabriël Nuchelmans, and Wesley C. Salmon. Dordrecht: D. Reidel.

——. 1922. Critical notice of *A Treatise on Probability. Mind* n.s. 31/121. Reprinted in Broad (1968).

Brunner, Heinrich. 1887. *Deutsche Rechtgeschichte.* vol. 1. Leipzig: Verlag von Dunckler & Humblot.

Buller, Francis. 1817. *An Introduction to the Law Relative to Trials at Nisi Prius.* 7th ed. Ed. by Richard Whalley Bridgman. London: R. Pheney and S. Sweet.

——. 1785. *An Introduction to the Law Relative to Trials at Nisi Prius.* 4th ed. London: W. Straham and W. Woodfall.

——. 1772. *An Introduction to the Law Relative to Trials at Nisi Prius.* 1st ed. London: W. Straham and W. Woodfall.

Burke, Edmund. 1955. *Reflections on the Revolution in France.* Ed. by Thomas H. D. Mahoney. Indianapolis, Ind.: Bobbs-Merrill. The Library of Liberal Arts. 1790.

——. 1852. "Report, made on the 30th April, 1794, from the Committee of the House of Commons, Appointed to Inspect the Lords' Journals, in Relation to their Proceeding on the Trial of Warren Hastings, Esquire." In *The Works and Correspondence of the Right Honourable Edmund Burke.* New ed. vol. 8. London: Francis & John Rivington. 1794.

Butchvarov, Panayot. 1994. "The Truth and the Untruth of Skepti-
    cism." *Proceedings and Addresses of the American Philo-
    sophical Association* 67/4.
——. 1979. *Being Qua Being: A Theory of Identity, Existence, and
    Predication*. Bloomington: Indiana University Press.
——. 1970. *The Concept of Knowledge*. Evanston, Ill.: North-
    western University Press.
Caine, Barbara. 2005. *Bombay to Bloomsbury: A Biography of the
    Strachey Family*. Oxford: Oxford University Press.
Campbell, Baron John Campbell, and Sir Joseph Arnould. 1878.
    The Lives of the Chief Justices of England. 7th ed. vol. 3.
    New York: Cockcroft & Company.
Carabelli, Anna. 1992. "Organic Interdependence and Keynes's
    Choice of Units in the *General Theory*." In Gerrard (1992).
——. 1991. "The Methodology of the Critique of the Classical
    Theory: Keynes on Organic Interdependence." In Bateman
    (1991a).
Chamberlayne, Charles Frederic. 1911. *A Treatise on the Modern
    Law of Evidence*. Albany, N.Y.: M. Bender. London: Sweet
    & Maxwell.
——. Preface to Taylor (1897).
——. Preface and notes to Best (1883).
Chisholm, Roderick M. 1966. *Theory of Knowledge*. Englewood
    Cliffs, N.J.: Prentice-Hall.
Coke, Edward. 1703. *The First Part of the Institutes of the Laws of
    England. Or, a Commentary Upon Littleton*. 10th ed.
    "Carefully corrected." London: Printed by William Rawl-
    ins and Samuel Roycroft, Assigns of Richard Atkins and
    Edward Atkins.
Copi, Irving M. 1978. *Introduction to Logic*. 5th ed. New York:
    Macmillan.
——. 1970. *Symbolic Logic*. 3d ed. New York: Macmillan.
Cross, Rupert, and Colin Tapper. 1985. *Cross on Evidence*. 6th ed.
    London: Butterworths.
Damaška, Mirjan R. 1997. *Evidence Law Adrift*. New Haven: Yale
    University Press.
Davies, James Conway. 1972. Introduction to ed., *Catalogue of
    Manuscripts in the Library of the Honourable Society of
    the Inner Temple*. vol. 1. Oxford: Oxford University Press.
Davis, John B. 1991. "Keynes's View of Economics as a Moral
    Science." In Bateman (1991a).
Deane, Phyllis. 2001. *The Life and Times of J. Neville Keynes*.
    Cheltenham, England: Edward Elgar Publishing, Inc.
Dejnožka, Jan. 2015. *Bertrand Russell on Modality and Logical
    Relevance*. 2d ed. Ann Arbor, MI: CreateSpace, December

2015. Reprinted with minor corrections 2016, 2017, 2018. 1st ed. published by Ashgate Publishing Ltd., Aldershot, England, February 1999, Avedale Series in Philosophy. 1st ed. republished by Routledge, London, August 2018, Routledge Revivals Series edition.

——. 2012. *The Concept of Relevance and the Logic Diagram Tradition*. Ann Arbor, MI: CreateSpace.

——. 2012a. *The Growth of a Thinker: A Chapbook of Poems*. Ann Arbor, MI: CreateSpace.

——. 2010. "The Concept of Relevance and the Logic Diagram Tradition." *Logica Universalis* 4/1.

——. 2006. "Observational Ecumenicism, Holist Sectarianism: The Quine-Carnap Conflict on Metaphysical Realism." *Philo* 9/2.

——. 2005–2007. "Are the Natural Numbers Just Any Progression? Peano, Russell, and Quine." *The Review of Modern Logic* vol. 10, nos. 3–4 (issue 32).

——. 2004. "Logical Relevance." http://www.members.tripod.-com/~Jan_Dejnozka/logical relevance.pdf. Edited for the Web. 1996.

——. 2003. *The Ontology of the Analytic Tradition and Its Origins: Realism and Identity in Frege, Russell, Wittgenstein, and Quine*. Lanham, MD: Littlefield Adams. Reprinted with further corrections, 2003. Reprinted with corrections, 2002. Original printing, 1996.

Dickson, William Gillespie. 1864. *A Treatise on the Law of Evidence in Scotland*. 2d ed. Ed. by John Skelton. Edinburgh: Bell & Bradfute.

Ducasse, Curt John. 1941. *Philosophy as a Science, Its Matter and Its Method*. New York: Oskar-Piest.

Duncombe, Giles. 1739. *Trials per Pais: Or, The Law of England Concerning Juries by Nisi Prius, &c...With a Compleat Treatise of The Law of Evidence....* 7th ed. "with large additions." "[B]y Giles Duncombe late of the *Inner-Temple*." London: E. and R. Nutt and R. Gosling.

——. 1702. *Tryals Per Pais: Or, The Law of England Concerning Juries by Nisi Prius, &c.,...To which is now Added, a farther Treatise of Evidence*. 4th ed. "with Large Additions." "By G. D. of the *Inner-Temple*." London: Printed by the Assigns of Richard and Edward Atkins for John Walthoe in the Middle-Temple Cloysters.

Eames, Elizabeth Ramsden. 1993. Introduction to Russell (1993).

Edgeworth, Francis Ysidro. 2003. "Probability and Calculus of Probabilities." In *Mathematical Psychics and Further Papers on Political Economy*, ed. by Peter Newman.

Oxford: Oxford University Press. Originally in Palgrave's *The Dictionary of Political Economy*, vol. 3, 1899.

——. 1996. *F. Y. Edgeworth: Writings in Probability, Statistics, and Economics*. Ed. by Charles Robert McCann, Jr. vols. 1–3. Cheltenham, England: Edward Elgar Publishing Limited. 1922.

Elliott, Byron K. and William F. Elliott. 1904. *A Treatise on the Law of Evidence*. vol. 1. Indianapolis, Ind.: Bobbs-Merrill.

Eure, Samson. 1666. *Tryals per Pais, or the Law, Concerning Juries by Nisi Prius, &c. Methodically Composed for the Publick Good, in the 16th Year of the Reign of our Soveraign Lord CHARLES the Second, King of England, Scotland, France and Ireland, &c*. London: Printed for George Dawes over against Lincoln's-Lane Gate in Chancery Lane. Reproduction of the original in the Lincoln's Inn Library in London, England. Early English Books Online (EEBO). ProQuest. Print digitization undated.

Fact-Index.com. 2015. "Alexander Cockburn (Lord Chief Justice)." http://www.fact-index.com/a/al/alexander_cockburn_lord_ chief_justice.html.

Fagin, Ronald, Joseph Y. Halpern, Yoram Moses, and Moshe Y. Vardi. 1995. *Reasoning about Knowledge*. Cambridge, Mass: The M.I.T. Press.

Fitzgibbons, Athol. 1991. "The Significance of Keynes's Idealism." In Bateman (1991a).

Føllesdal, Dagfinn. 1971. "Quantification into Causal Contexts." In L. Linsky (1971a).

van Fraassen, Bas C. 1979. "Russell's Philosophical Account of Probability." In G. Roberts (1979).

Franklin, James. 1991. "The Ancient Legal Sources of Seventeenth-Century Probability." In Gaukroger (1991).

Frege, Friedrich Ludwig Gottlob. 1974. *The Foundations of Arithmetic*. Trans. J. L. Austin. Evanston, Ill.: Northwestern University Press. German 1884.

——. 1968. "The Thought." In Klemke (1968). Trans. by A. M. and Marcelle Quinton. German 1918.

Friedman, Richard D. 1991. *The Elements of Evidence*. St. Paul, Minn.: West Publishing Company.

Gabbay, Dov M. and John Woods. 2010. "Relevance and the Law." Ch. 12 in Dov M. Gabbay, Patrice Canivez, Shahid Rahman, and Alexandre Thiercelin, eds., *Approaches to Legal Rationality*. Dordrecht: Springer. Logic, Epistemology, and the Unity of Science Series, vol. 20.

Gaukroger, Stephen, ed. 1991. *The Uses of Antiquity: The Scientific Revolution and the Classical Tradition.* Dordrecht: Kluwer.

Gerrard, Bill and John Hillard, eds. 1992. *The Philosophy and Economics of J. M. Keynes.* Aldershot, England: Edward Elgar Publishing Limited.

Gilbert, Lord Chief Baron Geoffrey. 1754. *The Law of Evidence: With all the Original References, Carefully Compared, To which is Added, A Great Number of New References, from the Best Authorities.* "And now first publish'd from an Exact Copy taken from the Original Manuscript." 1st ed. Dublin: Printed for Sarah Cotter under Dick's Coffee-House in Skinner-Row. Facsimile reprint in Berkowitz (1979).

——. 1805. *The Law of Evidence.* 7th ed. vol. 1. Philadelphia: Joseph Crukshank.

——. 1791. *The Law of Evidence.* Considerably enlarged by Capel Lofft. No ed. number. vol. 2. London: A. Straham and W. Woodfall.

——. 1760. *The Law of Evidence by a Late Learned Judge.* 2d ed. vol. 2. London: W. Owen.

Gillett, John Henry. 1897. *A Treatise on the Law of Indirect and Collateral Evidence.* Indianapolis. Ind.: The Bowen-Merrill Company.

Gillies, Donald. 2003. "Probability and Uncertainty in Keynes's *The General Theory.*" In Jochen Runde and Sohei Mizuhara, eds., *The Philosophy of Keynes's Economics: Probability, Uncertainty, and Convention.* London: Routledge.

Gosse, Philip Henry. 1857. *Omphalos: An Attempt to Untie the Geological Knot.* London: John van Voorst.

Graydon, Katharine Merrill, ed. 1927. *The Butler Alumnal Quarterly* 16/2. Greenfield, Ind.: The Butler University Alumni Association. Digitized by Internet Archive.

Greenleaf, Simon. 1997. *A Treatise on the Law of Evidence.* Holmes Beach, Florida: Gaunt, Inc. Reprint of Boston: Charles C. Little & James Brown, and London: A. Maxwell. 1842.

——. 1899. *A Treatise on the Law of Evidence.* 16th ed. vol. 1. Ed. by John Henry Wigmore. Boston: Little, Brown, and Company.

——. 1846. *A Treatise on the Law of Evidence.* 3rd ed. vol. 1. Boston: Charles C. Little and James Brown. London: A. Maxwell & Son.

Gresley, Richard Newcombe. 1847. *A Treatise on the Law of Evidence in the Courts of Equity.* 2d ed. Ed. by Christopher Alderson Calvert. London: William Benning & Co.

Grice, H. Paul and Peter F. Strawson. 1956. "In Defense of a Dogma." *The Philosophical Review* 65/2.

Hacking, Ian. 1978. *The Emergence of Probability: A Philosophical Study of Early Ideas about Probability, Induction and Statistical Inference.* London: Cambridge University Press.

Hailperin, Theodore. 1988. "The Development of Probability Logic from Leibniz to MacColl." *History and Philosophy of Logic* 9.

Hald, Anders. 2003. *History of Probability and Statistics and Their Applications before 1750.* Hoboken, N.J.: John Wiley & Sons, Inc. Wiley Series in Probability and Statistics.

Harrod, Roy F. 1951. *The Life of John Maynard Keynes.* London: Macmillan.

Halsted, Jacob R. 1859. *Halsted's Digest of the Law of Evidence, Embracing the Rules Established by Writers of Acknowledged Authority, and Affirmed by the Decisions of the Federal Courts, and the Courts of All the States, Down to the Present Time, with Copious References to English Adjudications.* 2d ed. vol. 1. New York: John S. Voorhies.

Hostettler, John. 2013. *Twenty Famous Lawyers.* Sherfield on Lodden: Waterside Press.

Hunt, Ted Robert. 2012. "Reconstructing Relevance in Missouri Evidence Law." *Journal of the Missouri Bar* 68.

Ilbert, Courtenay Peregrine. 1902. "Evidence, Law of." In *The New Volumes of the Encyclopaedia Britannica, Constituting[,] in Combination with the Existing Volumes of the Ninth Edition[,] the Tenth Edition of that Work.* vol. 28 (the fourth new vol.). Ed. by Sir Donald MacKenzie Wallace, Arthur T. Hadley, and Hugh Chisholm. Edinburgh & London: Adam and Charles Black.

Inner Temple Library. 2013. http://www.innertemple-library.org/.

——. 2013a. http://www.innertemplelibrary.org.uk/templehistory/-inner-temple-history-the-library.htm.

James, George F. 1941. "Relevancy, Probability and the Law." *California Law Review* 29/689–705. Reprinted in Twining (1992).

Johnson, William Ernest. 1921. *Logic.* Part 1. Cambridge, England: Cambridge University Press.

——. 1892. "The Logical Calculus." Published in three parts. "The Logical Calculus. I. General Principles." *Mind* n.s. 1/1. "The Logical Calculus. II." *Mind* n.s. ½. "The Logical Calculus. (III.)." *Mind* n.s. 1/3.

Kaye, David H. 1986. "Symposium: Probability and Inference in the Law of Evidence." 6 *Boston University Law Review* 657.

Keynes, John Maynard. 1962. *A Treatise on Probability.* New York: Harper and Row. Also published as vol. 8, *The Collected Writings of John Maynard Keynes*, New York: St. Martin's Press for the Royal Economic Society, in 1973. 1921.

———. 1908. *The Principles of Probability.* Keynes Papers, King's College Library. Revision of 1907 paper of the same name.

———. 1904. "Ethics in Relation to Conduct." Keynes Papers, King's College Library.

Keynes, John Neville. 1887. *Studies and Exercises in Logic, Including a General Application of Logical Processes in their Application to Complex Inferences.* 2d ed. revised and enlarged. London: Macmillan and Co.

Keynes, Milo, ed. 1975. *Essays on John Maynard Keynes.* London: Cambridge University Press.

Kirwan, Christopher. 1807. *Logick.; Or, An Essay on the Elements, Principles, and Different Modes of Reasoning.* London: Payne and MacKinley.

Landsman, Stephan. 1990. "From Gilbert to Bentham: The Reconceptualization of Evidence Theory." *Wayne Law Review*, vol. 36.

Landini, Gregory. 2007. *Wittgenstein's Apprenticeship with Russell.* Cambridge, England: Cambridge University Press.

Langbein, John H. 1996. "The Historical Foundations of the Law of Evidence: A View from the Ryder Sources." Yale Law School Legal Scholarship Repository. Faculty Scholarship Series. Paper 551. http://digitalcommons.law.yale.edu/fss_papers/551.

von Leibniz, Gottfried Wilhelm. 1966. *New Essays on Human Understanding.* Trans. and ed. by Peter Remnant and Jonathan Bennett. Cambridge, England: Cambridge University Press. Cambridge Texts in the History of Philosophy. First published 1765. First draft 1704.

Lely, J. M. 1883. Preface to Best (1883).

Lempert, Richard O., Samuel R. Gross, James S. Liebman, John H. Blume, Stephan Landsman, and Fredric I. Lederer, eds. 2011. *A Modern Approach to Evidence: Text, Problems, Transcripts and Cases.* 4th ed. St. Paul, Minn.: West Publishing Company. American Casebook Series.

———, Samuel R. Gross, and James S. Liebman. 2000. *A Modern Approach to Evidence: Text, Problems, Transcripts and Cases.* 3rd ed. St. Paul, Minn.: West Publishing Company. American Casebook Series.

——, and Stephen A. Saltzburg. 1983. *A Modern Approach to Evidence: Text, Problems, Transcripts and Cases.* 2d ed. St. Paul, Minn.: West Publishing Company. American Casebook Series.

——. 1977. "Modeling Relevance." 75 *Michigan Law Review* 1021 –1057.

Locke, John. 1959. *An Essay Concerning Human Understanding.* Collation of 1st ed. of 1690 by Alexander Campbell Fraser in 1894. New York: Dover.

MacColl, Hugh. 1906. *Symbolic Logic and Its Applications.* London: Longmans, Green, and Co.

——. 1905. "The Existential Import of Propositions." *Mind* n.s. 14.

——. 1905a. "Symbolic Reasoning (6)." *Mind* n.s. 14.

——. 1905b. "Symbolic Reasoning (7)." *Mind* n.s. 14.

——. 1903. "Symbolic Reasoning (5)." *Mind* n.s. 12.

——. 1902. "Symbolic Reasoning (4)." *Mind* n.s. 11.

——. 1900. "Symbolic Reasoning (3)." *Mind* n.s. 9.

——. 1897. "Symbolic Reasoning (2)." *Mind* n.s. 6.

——. 1880. "Symbolic Reasoning (1)." *Mind* n.s. 5.

Macnair, Michael Richard Trench. 1999. *The Law of Proof in Early Modern Equity.* Berlin: Duncker and Humblot.

Mahoney, Thomas H. D. 1955. Introduction to Burke (1955).

Mares, Edwin. 1997. Electronic correspondence to Jan Dejnožka dated June 12, 13, 18 (six messages), 22, and 23.

Mayne, John Dawson. 1909. *Mayne's Treatise on Damages.* Ed. by Lumley Smith. 8th ed. London: Stevens and Haynes.

——, and Lumley Smith. 1894. *Mayne's Treatise on Damages.* 5th ed. London: Stevens and Haynes.

——. 1872. *A Treatise on the Law of Damages: Comprising Their Measure, The Mode in Which They are Assessed and Reviewed, the Practice of Granting New Trials, and the Law of Set-Off.* 2d ed. by Lumley Smith. London: Stevens and Haynes.

McCann, Charles R. Jr. 1996. "Introduction: Edgeworth's Contributions to Probability and Statistics." In Edgeworth (1996 / 1922), vol. 1.

Mill, John Stuart. 1872. *A System of Logic: Ratiocinative and Inductive, Being a Connected View of the Principles of Evidence and the Methods of Scientific Investigation.* 8th ed. London: Longmans, Green, Reader, and Dyer. 1st ed. 1843.

Mini, Piero V. 1994. *John Maynard Keynes: A Study in the Psychology of Original Work.* New York: St. Martin's Press.

von Mises, Richard Edler. 1957. *Probability, Statistics and Truth.* 2d English rev. ed. and based on 3d German rev. ed. by author in 1951. Trans. based on 1939 trans. of J. Neyman, D. Scholl, and E. Rabinowitsch. London: George Allen and Unwin. 1st German ed. 1928.

Moggridge, D. E. 1992. *Maynard Keynes: An Economist's Biography*. London: Routledge.

Monteiro, João Paulo. 2001. "Russell and Humean Inferences." *Principia* 51/2.

Montrose, James Louis. 1954. "Basic Concepts of the Law of Evidence." *The Law Quarterly Review* 70/527–55. Reprinted in Twining (1992).

Moore, George Edward. 1912. *Ethics*. London: Williams & Norgate.

Morgan, John. 1789. *Essays Upon 1. The Law of Evidence. 2. New Trials. 3. Special Verdicts. 4. Trials at Bar. and 5. Repleaders*. vol. 1. Dublin: Messrs. E. Lynch, H. Chamberlaine, L. White, P. Byrne, A. Gruebier, C. Lewis, J. Jones, and J. Moore.

Nissan, Ephraim. 2012. *Computer Applications for Handling Legal Evidence, Police Investigation and Case Argumentation*. vol. 1. Dordrecht: Springer. Law, Governance and Technology Series 5.

Murphy, Peter. 2008. *Murphy on Evidence*. 10th ed. Oxford: Oxford University Press.

Peake, Thomas. 1824. *A Compendium of the Law of Evidence*. The American edition from the London 5th ed. Philadelphia, Penn.: Abraham Small.

——. 1804. *A Compendium of the Law of Evidence*. 2d ed. London: Brooke and Clarke.

——. 1801. *A Compendium of the Law of Evidence*. 1st ed. London: E. & R. Brooke & J. Rider. Facsimile reprint in Berkowitz (1979).

Peloubet, S. S. 1880. *A Collection of Legal Maxims in Law and Equity, with English Translations*. New York: George S. Diossy.

Phillipps, Samuel March, and Thomas James Arnold. 1868. *A Treatise on the Law of Evidence*. 10th English ed., 5th American ed. vol. 1. New York: Banks & Brothers.

——, and Thomas James Arnold. 1859. *A Treatise on the Law of Evidence*. 10th English ed., 4th American ed. vol. 1. New York: Banks & Brothers. The title pages of Phillipps (1868) and (1859) both say "Tenth English Edition," but (1868) says "Fifth American Edition," while (1859) says "Fourth American Edition."

——. 1849. *A Treatise on the Law of Evidence*. "Sixth American, from the ninth London edition." Lower on the same title page: "Vol. I. Third Edition." New York: Banks, Gould, & Co.

——, and Andrew Amos. 1838. *A Treatise on the Law of Evidence.* 8th ed. "with considerable additions." London: Saunders and Benning.

——. 1822. *A Treatise on the Law of Evidence.* 5th ed. vol. 1. London: Joseph Butterworth and Son.

——. 1820. *A Treatise on the Law of Evidence.* 2d American ed. from the 3rd London ed. vol. 1. New York: Gould and Banks.

——. 1816. *A Treatise on the Law of Evidence.* 1st American ed., from 2d London ed. vol. 1. Albany, N.Y.: Gould, Banks, & Gould.

Pollock, Sir Frederick, and Frederic William Maitland. 2010. *The History of English Law Before the Time of Edward I.* 2d ed. Indianapolis, Ind.: Liberty Fund. 2d ed. 1898. 1st ed. 1895.

Powell, Edmund. 1904. *The Principles and Practice of the Laws of Evidence.* 8th ed. Ed. by John Cutler and Charles F. Cagney. London: Butterworth & Co.

——. 1859. *The Principles and Practice of the Laws of Evidence.* 2d ed. London: Butterworths.

Prior, Arthur N. 1967. "Keynes[, John Neville]." In "Logic, History of," in Edwards (1967), vol. 4.

——. 1955. *Formal Logic.* London: Clarendon Press.

Ramsey, Frank Plumpton. 1931. *The Foundations of Mathematics and Other Logical Essays.* Ed. by R. B. Braithwaite. London: Kegan Paul, Trench, Trubner & Co.

Rice, Frank Sumner. 1892. *The General Principles of the Law of Evidence.* Rochester, N.Y.: The Lawyers' Co-Operative Publishing Co.

Robinson, Abraham. 1996. *Non-Standard Analysis.* Rev. ed. Princeton, N.J.: Princeton University Press. 1st ed. 1974.

——. 1979. "Formalism." In (1979b).

——. 1979a. Non-Standard Analysis." In 1979b. First published in 1961 in *Koninklijke Nederlandse Akademie van Wetenschappen* Proceedings, ser. A, Mathematical Sciences, vol. 64.

——. 1979b. *Selected Papers of Abraham Robinson.* vol. 2, *Non-Standard Analysis and Philosophy.* Ed. by W. Luxemburg and S. Körner. New Haven: Yale University Press.

Roscoe, Henry. 1840. *A Digest of the Law of Evidence in Criminal Cases.* 2d ed. "with considerable additions...by T. C. Granger." Philadelphia: T. & J. W. Johnson.

———. 1831. *Digest of the Law of Evidence on the Trial of Actions at Nisi Prius*. 2d ed. London: Saunders & Benning.

Ross, William David. 1960. *Aristotle*. 5th ed. New York: Meridian.

Routley, Richard, with Val Plumwood, Robert K. Meyer, and Ross T. Brady. 1982. *Relevant Logics and Their Rivals: Part 1. The Basic Philosophical and Semantical Theory*. Atascadero, Calif.: Ridgewood.

Russell, Bertrand. 1993. *Theory of Knowledge: The 1913 Manuscript*. Ed. by Elizabeth Ramsden Eames in collaboration with Kenneth Blackwell. London: George Allen & Unwin. *The Collected Papers of Bertrand Russell*, vol. 7. 1984.

———. 1987. *Autobiography*. One volume edition. London: Unwin. vol. 1, 1967; vol. 2, 1968; vol. 3, 1969.

———. 1985. *An Inquiry into Meaning and Truth*. London: Unwin. 1940.

———. 1985a. *My Philosophical Development*. London: Unwin. 1959.

———. 1976. *Human Knowledge: Its Scope and Limits*. New York: Simon and Schuster. 1948.

———. 1974. *An Outline of Philosophy*. New York: Meridian. 1927.

———. 1974a. *The Problems of Philosophy*. London: Oxford University Press. 1912.

———. 1971f. "The Philosophy of Logical Atomism." In (1971) 1918.

———. 1964. *Principles of Mathematics*. 2d ed. New York: W. W. Norton. 2d ed. 1938; 1st ed. 1903.

———. 1954. *The Analysis of Matter*. New York: Dover. 1927.

———. 1937. *A Critical Exposition of the Philosophy of Leibniz*. 2d ed. London: George Allen & Unwin Ltd. 1st ed. 1900.

———. 1933. *The Analysis of Mind*. London: George Allen and Unwin. 1921.

———. 1923. "Vagueness." *Australasian Journal of Philosophy* 1.

———. 1922. Review of *A Treatise on Probability*. *The Mathematical Gazette* 32/300.

———. 1919. *Introduction to Mathematical Philosophy*. London: Allen and Unwin.

———. 1896. *German Social Democracy*. London: Longman, Green & Company. *Studies in Economics and Political Science*, vol. 7.

Shapiro, Barbara J. 1991. *"Beyond Reasonable Doubt" and "Probable Cause": Historical Perspectives on the Anglo-American Law of Evidence*. Berkeley: University of California Press.

——. 1983. *Probability and Certainty in Seventeenth-Century England: A Study of the Relationships between Natural Science, Religion, History, Law, and Literature.* Princeton, N.J.: Princeton University Press.

Skidelsky, Robert. 2005. *John Maynard Keynes 1883–1946: Economist, Philosopher, Statesman.* London: Macmillan. Rev. and abridged combined ed. of (2001), (1994), and (1986).

——. 2001. *John Maynard Keynes: Volume Three: Fighting for Freedom, 1937–1947.* 1st American ed. New York: Viking Penguin. 2000.

——. 1996. *Keynes.* Oxford: Oxford University Press.

——. 1994. *John Maynard Keynes: Volume Two: The Economist as Savior, 1920–1937.* 1st American ed. New York: Viking Penguin. 1992.

——. 1986. *John Maynard Keynes: Volume One: Hopes Betrayed, 1883–1920.* 1st American ed. New York: Viking Penguin. 1983.

Slomkowski, Paul. 1997. *Aristotle's Topics.* Leiden: Brill.

Sorabji, Richard. 1980. *Necessity, Cause, and Blame: Perspectives on Aristotle's Theory.* Ithaca, N.Y.: Cornell University Press.

Smokler, Howard E. 1967. "Johnson, William Ernest." In Edwards (1967), vol. 4.

Starkie, Thomas. 1876. *A Practical Treatise of the Law of Evidence.* 10th American ed. from the 4th London ed. Philadelphia, Penn.: T. & J. W. Johnson & Co.

——. 1830. *A Practical Treatise on the Law of Evidence, and Digest of Proofs, in Civil and Criminal Proceedings.* 3d American ed. Philadelphia, Penn.: P. H. Nicklin & T. Johnson.

Stephen, James Fitzjames, with Harry Lushington Stephen and Lewis Frederick Sturge. 1936. *A Digest of the Law of Evidence.* 12th ed. London: Macmillan.

——. 1903. *A Digest of the Law of Evidence.* From the 5th ed. of 1899, with American notes. Hartford, Conn.: Dissell.

——. 1876. *A Digest of the Law of Evidence.* 2d ed. London: Macmillan and Co.

——. 1872. *The Indian Evidence Act (I of 1872), with an Introduction on the Principles of Judicial Evidence.* London: Macmillan & Co.

Stephen, Leslie. 1895. *The Life of Sir James Fitzjames Stephen: BART., K.C.S.I.: A Judge of the High Court of Justice.* London: Smith, Elder, & Co.

Stigler, Stephen M. 1986. *The History of Statistics: The Measurement of Uncertainty before 1900.* Cambridge, Mass.: The Belknap Press of Harvard University Press.

Strachey, Giles Lytton. 1918. *Eminent Victorians.* New York: Random House. The Modern Library.

Straker, D. Augustus. 1899. *A Compendium of Evidence.* Detroit, Mich.: The Richmond and Backus Co.

Swinburne, Richard, ed. 2002. *Bayes's Theorem.* Oxford: Oxford University Press. Proceedings of the British Academy 113.

Taylor, John Pitt. 1897. *A Treatise on the Law of Evidence as administered in England and Ireland.* Ed. by Charles Frederic Chamberlayne. American ed. of the 9th English ed. vol. 1. "In part re-written by G. Pitt-Lewis....With notes as to American law by Charles F. Chamberlayne." Boston: The Boston Book Company. London: Sweet and Maxwell.

——. 1878. *A Treatise on the Law of Evidence as Administered in England and Ireland.* 7th ed. vols. 1, 2. London: William Maxwell & Son.

——. 1848. *A Treatise of the Law of Evidence, as Administered in England and Ireland.* 1st ed. vol. 1. London: A. Maxwell & Son.

Thayer, James Bradley. 1908. *Legal Essays.* Ed. by his son, Ezra Ripley Thayer. Boston: The Boston Book Company.

——. 1900. "Law and Logic." In Thayer (1908). First published in the *Harvard Law Review*: 14 Harv. Law Rev. 139.

——. 1898. *A Preliminary Treatise on Evidence at the Common Law.* Boston, Mass.: Little, Brown, and Company.

——. 1880–81. "Bedingfield's Case—Declarations as a Part of the Res Gesta." In Thayer (1908). First published in *The American Law Review* in three parts: 14 Am. Law Rev. 817; 15 Am. Law Rev. 1, 71.

The Annual Register. 1918. Ed. by Edmund Burke. vol. 160. June obituary section. London: Longmans, Green, and Co.

Twining, William. 1994. *Rethinking Evidence: Exploratory Essays.* Evanston, Ill.: Northwestern University Press. 1990.

——, and Alex Stein, eds. 1992. *Evidence and Proof.* New York: New York University Press.

——. 1985. *Theories of Evidence: Bentham and Wigmore.* London: Weidenfeld and Nicolson.

Venn, John. 1994. *The Principles of Empirical or Inductive Logic.* 1st ed. Bristol: Thoemmes Press. Reprint of 1st ed. of 1889. 2d ed. 1907.

——. 1964. "The Subjective Side of Probability." In Kyburg (1964). Reprinted from *The Logic of Chance*, 3d ed. 1888.

Walford, Edward. 1888. "Legal Obituary." In *The Law Times: The Journal and Record of the Law and the Lawyers*. From May to October 1988. vol. 85. July 28 issue. London: The Office of the Law Times.

Wallenmeier, Thomas E. 1967. *The Broad-Keynes-Russell Theory for the Explanation and Justification of Induction*. In Marquette University: *Master's Theses 1922–2009*. Paper 139. Milwaukee, Wisc.: Marquette University.

Walton, Douglas. 2005. *Argumentation Methods for Artificial Intelligence in Law*. Berlin: Springer.

——. 2004. *Relevance in Argumentation*. Mahwah, N.J.: Lawrence Erlbaum Associates.

West Publishing Company: 1995, *Evidence Rules: Federal Rules of Evidence and California Evidence Code*. St. Paul, Minn.: West Publishing Company.

Wigmore. 1913. *Select Cases on the Law of Evidence*. 2d ed. Boston: Little, Brown, and Company.

——. 1904–1905. *A Treatise on the System of Evidence in Trials at Common Law: Including the Statutes and Judicial Decisions of all Jurisdictions of the United States*. 4 vols. Boston: Little, Brown, and Co. The title soon changed, and eventually the work included ten volumes. My former law school advanced evidence professor, Richard D. Friedman, has been general editor of *The New Wigmore*.

——. 1899. Preface to Greenleaf (1899).

Wittgenstein, Ludwig. 1961. *Tractatus Logico-Philosophicus*. Trans. by D. F. Pears and B. F. McGuinness. London: Routledge and Kegan Paul. English 1922; German 1921.

von Wright, Georg Henrik. 1960. *A Treatise on Induction and Probability*. Paterson, N.J.: Littlefield, Adams, & Co. The International Library of Psychology, Philosophy and Scientific Method. 1951.

Zabell, S. L. 2005. *Symmetry and its Discontents: Essays on the History of Inductive Probability*. Cambridge, England: Cambridge University Press.

Index of Names

Index of Subjects

a priori evidence, degrees of inductive / weak (fallible), 1–3, 13, 26, 187, 195, 205, 212, 215–16, 218

admissibility, 21–22, 41, 49, 51, 57, 72–73, 74, 83, 84–86, 89–94, 97, 100, 102, 104, 110–11, 116, 124, 126–36, 140–42, 145–53, 157–60, 162, 190, 229

admission of prior verdict, 57

Allegari non debuit, 209

allegations, 58, 75, 84–85, 87–88, 90–91, 95–96, 100–4, 148, 154– 55, 156, 209

analysis, logical, 70, 117, 197, 200; informative, 117, 170

Apostles, Cambridge, 3, 12, 48, 68, 84, 136, 138, 168, 178

Bayes' Theorem, 15, 20, 22, 24–25, 56, 69, 189

best evidence rule, 52–55, 57–58, 60–62, 66, 69–70, 74–75, 78, 86–87, 91, 92–94, 96, 101, 104, 115, 117, 128, 134, 137, 147

Bloomsbury Group, 173, 177

Bristow v Wright, 65, 102

burden of proof, 90, 95

Buridan's ass, 33, 221–23

cause (legal), immediate, 106–11, 113; obvious, 106, 109, 111–112; proximate, 105–6, 108–9, 111, 113, 120, 130, 151; remote, 105, 109, 113, 120

cause (physical), 1–3, 105–8, 118–20, 145

collateral facts / issues / matters, 52, 77, 85, 88, 91, 96, 112, 155

conceptualization, 121–23; vs. description, 123

confinement rule, 63, 72

confinement to points in issue, 63, 71–73, 76–78, 85–88, 90–91, 93–96, 100, 102–4, 112, 116–117, 132, 134, 148–49, 154–55, 156

contracts, 53, 58, 63, 67, 110, 113, 168

damages, 99, 105–14; special, 85

definition, analytic / compositional, 18–19; circular, 44–45, 194, 202, 227; disjunctive, 108, 119–20, 124; formal, 18; (by) genus and difference, 19–20, 115, 137–38, 151, 227; informative, 17, 19, 117, 170; legal, 97, 106; logicist, 3, 21; theoretical, 3, 19, 157–58, 170, 189, 212; vicious infinite regress of, 201

descriptions, 3, 69, 73, 120–23, 214; accidental vs. essential, 120–22; knowledge by, 3; vs. conceptualization, 123

diagrams, see logic diagrams

Dutch book, 28, 30–34

entailment, 224; diagrams of, 14–15; probability as partial, 5, 192, see implication

epistemology / epistemic, 1, 4, 7–8, 11, 26, 121, 125, 167, 196, 201–3, 206, 212–14, 227

error, 74, 78, 89, 100, 139

ethics, 7, 10, 13, 169, 177, 187

evidence, as what seems to be the case, 121, 196, 213, 216, 217; circumstantial, 81, 103, 142; concept of, 39, 69–70, 92, 100, 131, 152, 159–60; definable or not, 69–70, legal standards of, 78–79; natural, 92–95,